Healing Sex Addiction

The Christian's Journey of Overcoming

Pastor Benno J. Bauer Jr.

Published by SuburbanBuzz.com LLC

ISBN: 978-1-959446-40-8

DEDICATION

In posthumous honor of my son Chad Eric Bauer

Dr. H. D. McCarty

Dr. Jim DeLoach (Posthumously)

Dr. Earl Banning (Posthumously)

Rev. John Franklin and Ella Franklin (Posthumously)

Dr. Patrick Carnes

Dr. Stephanie Carnes

Tami VerHelst

Anna Valenti-Anderson

Melinda Havard

Battle Lines Leaders and the Men of Battle Lines

Sister Bonnie Jean VanBerg & Husband Charles VanBerg, Jr.

Jan N. Bauer, my wife

Emily Grace Bauer, my daughter

Son, Colby Scott Bauer

CONTENTS

ACKNOWLEDGMENTS

I am grateful to God Himself and His Son, Jesus Christ, for giving me the knowledge and the words to help men heal from sexual compulsion and addiction.

I thank Melanie Saxton, editor, and Holly Chervnsik, publisher, for their time, wisdom, and assistance in making this book a reality.

INTRODUCTION

As of January 1, 2024, approximately 8.5 billion people live in the world. Since the inception of time, researchers estimate that 109 billion people have been born. Note here that God desires each person to know they are fearfully, wonderfully made, and meant to be!

According to God's Word, the Bible, Psalm 139:13–16 states:

> *13 Certainly you made my mind and heart; you wove me together in my mother's womb. 14 I will give you thanks because your deeds are awesome and amazing. You knew me thoroughly; 15 My bones were not hidden from you, when I was made in secret and sewed together in the depths of the earth. 16 Your eyes saw me when I was inside the womb. All the days ordained for me were recorded in your scroll before one of them came into existence.*

As we embark on the journey of understanding the issue of sex addiction, we must proactively educate ourselves as much as possible on how we were made and shaped, how the topic of sex addiction came about, and how authentic freedom and transformation can occur.

This book is filled with God's Holy Word. Please read and embrace every Scripture, even if you feel like your eyes will glaze over. Soak up the Divine message and allow it to seep into your core. If only we used our Bibles like we do our cell phones, we'd be connected to God in the most powerful ways. The more we read, the more our relationship with the Lord becomes full, powerful, and foundational. No addiction can bind us. Jesus truly sets men free through the Word…but it takes an enormous amount of work.

The Lord God made you unique; there has been no one like

you, and there will be no one like you in the future! You are fearfully and wonderfully made, and YOU were meant to be! This will be a repeat, repeat, repeat in this book. If you are a Christian, unfortunately, many live below their blessings and privileges while others have joy and victory in life. This book sheds light on having a proper relationship with the Lord and walking into the true blessing of freedom from addiction.

The great General George S. Patton Jr. was a well-read student of war. He lectured his subordinates on the history of the battlefields, Napoleon's lessons, and the experiences of earlier leaders who came this way. He had a classical quotation for every occasion.

"You son of a bitch," he gloated after outsmarting German field marshal Rommel of the German Army and defeating him in a North African battle. "I read your book!"

Patton sought to understand his enemies; he understood their previous warfare tactics. He sought to think ahead and outmaneuver. If he had been given free rein in World War II, the war, in my opinion, would have ended much sooner. However, he had to play politics with those above him and Great Britain. He was much admired and greatly feared in the same breath. Why am I sharing this with you? *If you do not become a student of the issues of sex addiction, then you will never walk into freedom!* You can become a victor if you work hard. Nothing will come easy for you, as this enemy of sex addiction does not want to lose its grip on you!

This book is not all comprehensive, as no literature can be about this issue called sex addiction. Understanding how your brain is positively or negatively influenced from childhood to the present is crucial, so a significant portion of the book discusses the brain. My purpose is to help you understand yourself, the problems, and the solutions. **You'll see recommended reading in the back of the book so that you can continue to learn and grow.**

I share my journey as a pastor/counselor who has worked over the last twenty-six-plus years with sexually addicted men and couples with husbands who have betrayed their wives. Thus, this book is part memoir and part mission. The mission was to fulfill a calling that God introduced by routing letters to my desk from desperate men whose lives were ensnared in sexual addiction. I was made aware of a great need in the Houston, Texas, area for support and healing, considering the pervasiveness of the disease.

I began Battle Lines, a men's sexual addiction group, in May 2004, with 28,432 men having attended on Tuesday nights and also, at times, an additional class on Saturday mornings through 2019. The topic of sex addiction (porn, prostitutes, affairs, massage parlors, etc.) dives deep and is often influenced by childhood trauma, but it is possible to overcome it. You are not alone. It takes incredible work and dedication, but men and marriages can heal. I've seen it firsthand.

General Patton made another statement: "In case of doubt, attack." **This issue of sex addiction will defeat you if you do not attack the issues, first in education, then in determination.** If you approach the subject of seeking freedom passively, plan on defeat. *Be a King David who approached Goliath with the attitude of success!*

In this society of quick fixes, going to a hamburger place where you can order from your car and go through the drive-through, you place an order from the speaker with the attendant inside. When you get up to the drive-through, you get impatient or angry if your order is not ready; that is society today! You cannot quickly solve sex addiction that has been in your life for a long time. You walk into freedom after investing in a recovery.

Plan for a long journey; however, if you are steady, watch what happens — change, healing, being set free from captivity, and then transformation. It's there and waiting FOR YOU! You must be prepared to seek *competent counseling* from someone who understands the issues of sex addiction and is an expert in this field. You have to attend a quality sexual addiction group, and I will explain what this should look like later in the book. All this will come forth.

One last thing — many topics in this book overlap. There is repetition, and purposefully so, because repetition impacts the neuropathways in our brains. You'll read raw and unvarnished truths over and over again to relearn how to live your best life.

Yes, we can be rewired. Much more on that later.

CHAPTER 1
Wishin' and Hopin'

This book is different, as it is founded upon the *Truth of God's Word*. In Luke 4:18, Jesus says, "The Spirit of the Lord is upon Me because He appointed Me to preach the gospel to the poor. He has sent Me to proclaim release to the captives, recovery of sight to the blind, and set free those who are oppressed."

God is not about "recovery" but about **"setting the captives free!"** Free means free! Free does not mean freedom from temptations; we all have and will face them, whether it be a new home, women dressing sexually, jealousy of a friend's new car, etc. What you do with temptations depends on you and me, and that is called *CHOICE!* God tests us; Satan tempts us. What are YOU and I going to do? That is YOUR *CHOICE* and MINE.

Only God sets the captive free, and only through a genuine relationship with HIM can that occur. Being baptized does not automatically classify you as a Christian. Simply having a belief in God and Jesus Christ does not qualify you as a Christian. After all, Satan and his demons believe, and they are not saved. Just because you attend church and teach the Bible does not save you. Men, you can sit in your garage all your life, and you will never become a car, and you can sit in church all your life and never become a Christian!

God cannot work in your life unless you have a genuine relationship with HIM. That requires many things, but you can go to John 15:1—8, which reads:

> *1 I am the true vine, and my Father is the gardener. 2 He cuts off every branch in me that bears no fruit, while every branch that does bear fruit he prunes so that it will be even more fruitful. 3 You are already clean because of the word I have spoken to you. 4 Remain in me, as I also remain in you. No branch can bear fruit by itself; it must remain in*

the vine. Neither can you bear fruit unless you remain in me? 5 I am the vine; you are the branches. If you remain in me and I in you, you will bear much fruit; apart from me, you can do nothing. 6 If you do not remain in me, you are like a branch that is thrown away and withers; such branches are picked up, thrown into the fire, and burned. 7 If you remain in me and my words remain in you, ask whatever you wish, and it will be done for you. 8 This is to my Father's glory, that you bear much fruit, showing yourselves to be my disciples.

To me, this is the secret of the Christian life!

God wants to change you from within, not just your behavior and actions, but your heart. In this book, I write about your having a body and a soul when you are born. That's it! Another plan is to receive HIS HOLY SPIRIT within you as you become a ***True Believer.*** That is where the indwelling spirit of the Lord can do HIS work within and through you as you do the work necessary to become healed and changed. Many will not agree with the two paragraphs preceding. Nevertheless, it is the bedrock foundation of TRUTH. Do you want to have a "fix," that is, BEHAVIORAL CHANGE, or do you want a ***TRANSFORMATION?*** It's YOUR CHOICE!

YOU HAVE TO DO IT FOR YOURSELF

Some of you might remember that old Dusty Springfield song from 1964, "Wishin' and Hopin'." Well, my rendition goes like this:

There is HOPING
There is WISHING
There is WANTING
There is RATHERING
And there is GOING TO ANY LENGTH

No matter what it takes and how long, the person who commits remains dedicated to CHANGE. Life brings about the "sooner or later" core issue about oneself that "I am worthy of fighting for." In the journey of transformation, the DECISION is to be healed. You have to be willing to come to your own assistance. *You have to ACT on your behalf. No one can do it for you.* Let me repeat *that no one can do it for you.* You cannot do it for your wife, job, parents, children, counselor, etc. You have to do it for yourself.

Most men who come to counseling or groups want to change, but most want a quick solution. Suppose they decide to go to a group. In that case, there are times they return to their homes and say to their wives, "If you think I have issues, you ought to hear what I heard tonight in the group." They compare their issues to others and think, *They are much worse than I am, and I can do this myself.* If married, they share this story with their wives, and they go right back into their addiction, unbeknownst to their wives, for a short time, as all buried secrets resurrect. They conned their wives into not going back to the group. I have seen this time and time again.

There are a lot of reasons we do not intercede on our own behalf:

- You seek comfort in your dreams rather than take great satisfaction in your accomplishments.

- Your fear paralyzes you — so the worst comes to pass.

- Within your PERFECTIONISM, you fear to change

- You ignore the obvious and live in the improbable.

- Life is demanding without adding the UNFINISHED.

Some or many of you are focusing on THE BEHAVIOR, AND YOU, AT BEST, will get to a temporary modest change. When YOU truly decide, down to the tip of your toes and the depth of your being, to begin the pathway for healing, there can be significant change within your inner man and the journey of change can be considerable in time!

The author Tony Robbins made this statement, and it's true, *"Change happens when the pain of staying the same is greater than the pain of change."* This is true in my counseling men and the Battle Lines group. Sadly, most men are lazy and give an effort, but not an all-out effort. However, the unbelievable happens when they do and put God at the forefront of their lives.

I will add a "Benno" here. You can pray until hell freezes over to take this addiction and other issues from you, but until you put your feet (action) to it, you will stay where you are. Bank on it! I have shared this so often in Battle Lines (my men's sexual addiction group) and counseling, seeking to bring about tough love. Some got it, and others refused to accept it.

Run the race to win the prize and beat your body to do so! Be inspired by 1 Corinthians 9:24, which states, "Do you not know that in a race all the runners run, but only one receives the prize? So run that you may obtain it."

Consider the following about change and if you want to begin the journey:

- The journey of change "someday" is where most men are at, and certainly with addictive issues.

- Our lives do not change until we make a "decision" to adopt a mindset that will create change.

- Decision-making is a "core transformation skill."

- The next step after deciding is committing to the tasks that must occur.

- If you are not engaged in the solution, you are still part of the problem!

- There has to be a commitment to reality at "all costs!" You are the only one who can decide that

- The word "decision" comes from the Latin word "to cut"

(which those in counseling and Battle Lines have heard from me for a very long time).

- Postponing "decision-making" creates more harm and hurt.

- Once you decide to walk in the transformation journey, the next step is to have a road map.

- It takes courage to stay on this journey.

Audie Murphy was the most decorated hero of WWII. He did not know the way when he began his journey in the infantry and on the battlefield. The Hobbit did not know the way in the *Lord of the Rings*. As you decide, the decision requires another decision.

I would add that if you are unwilling to go to any lengths for change and surrender your life to the Lord, then get a refund on this book.

Before you move on in this book, you must sit in a tranquil setting with a pen and paper — not a computer, only a pen and writing tablet — and get serious as a heart attack about WHY you want to change and what it will take.

1. Why do you want to be set free from your addiction and heal from internal issues?

2. What are you willing to do to be set free?

3. Do you want some relief, or do you want to stop your addictive behavior altogether?

4. Are you willing to cut out all negative relationships and places of familiarity and put yourself into a positive environment?

5. What do you think a positive environment must look like?

6. When are you willing to begin?

7. Will you go to regular counseling with an expert on sex addiction? You must have weekly appointments.

8. Are you ready to read book after book so you can become in tune with the issues?

9. Will you attend a men's addiction group no less than once a week?

10. Are you willing to have a minimum of two solid Christian accountability partners to hold your feet to the fire (a man of strong moral character can also be there for you if he is not a Christian)?

11. Are you willing to get involved in a Bible-believing church and Bible study at that church?

12. Will you seek the Lord in prayer and possibly surrender your life to HIM at some point?

13. Are you willing to give HIM your all in all? And in doing so, giving up your rights! You have no rights; no, you do not. Not to your next breath, you do not!

14. Are you an "impatient person?" Do you expect results in anything you do right then there?

15. Are you a "patient person?" And you realize that it takes time to get set free from old habits (sex addiction) and build new patterns and behaviors?

16. Are you willing to ask, "What will prevent me from succeeding?"

17. Are you willing to ask, "How can I overcome those obstacles?"

18. Do you really want to get well?

When you're answering these questions, be as specific as possible. When you know precisely what you want to do, why you want to do it, and when and how you will get started, you can make an informed decision about moving forward.

In addition, one book cannot cover all the issues of sexual compulsivity/addiction. Thus, this book is far from perfect.

What I have tried to do is for it to have a flow from birth onward, and the appropriate chapters advance from there.

I might also add, in all the years of my counseling others and with Battle Lines, I told the men, if you do not read and do the work, then I will not work with you. Be an active participant and don't expect to be spoon-fed. So, either get honest about your desire to change and/or continue in this rut where you have found yourself.

GOD HAS A PLAN FOR YOU

Jeremiah 29:11–14

11 For I know the plans I have for you, declares the LORD, plans for welfare[a] and not for evil, to give you a future and a hope. 12 Then you will call upon ME and come and pray to ME, and I will hear you. 13 You will seek ME and find ME when you seek ME with all your heart. 14 "I will be found by you," declares the LORD. "I will restore your fortunes and gather you from all the nations and all the places where I have driven you, declares the LORD. I will bring you back to the place from which I sent you into exile [captivity — my insert]."

(Benno, your author, brought forth capitalization. Why is that? I know GOD is HOLY, and we need to honor HIM in that way!)

DO NOT GO TO THE NEXT CHAPTER UNLESS YOU ARE SERIOUS ABOUT HEALING, CHANGE, BEING SET FREE, AND TRANSFORMATION.

SERIOUS IS AS SERIOUS IS.

UNLESS YOU ARE SERIOUS, YOU ARE WASTING YOUR OWN TIME AND, MORE THAN LIKELY, THE TIME OF OTHERS.

CHAPTER 2
Your Development from Inception to Birth

Children need their parents' positive influence to become independent and lead healthy lives. Nurturing care is crucial for a child's healthy brain development, as it involves growing up in a safe environment where parents protect them from neglect and extreme or chronic stress, and provide many opportunities for play and growth.

For now, I WANT YOU to imagine yourself in your mother's womb. Go to a patio, study, or bedroom, sit, and relax. Seek to see as best you can what you believe your atmosphere was with your family of origin while you were in your mother's womb. What do you feel you might have heard? How do you think you might have been affected?

Let's look at maternal stress and the emotional environment, of **negativity** outside of the womb, stress hormones (like cortisol) cross the placenta, and high, prolonged stress can affect fetal brain development. It may increase the risk of preterm birth or low birth weight. Children later may show higher rates of anxiety, attention problems, or emotional regulation issues.

Exposure to harmful substances, such as smoking, alcohol, or drugs, can cause congenital disabilities, growth restriction, and Fetal Alcohol Spectrum Disorders (FASD). In addition, environmental toxins like lead, mercury, pesticides, or pollution can interfere with brain and organ development and link to long-term problems with learning and behavior.

Now, as you process this, this is not about blaming your parent or parents. Still, it is important to understand that some issues later in life begin in the womb from negative experiences as you were being developed in the womb.

Violence or abuse during pregnancy can bring physical harm directly to the baby, and the emotional stress (trauma) increases maternal stress, which can program the fetus's stress response system.

Research suggests that children exposed to highly adverse environments in the womb may have an increased risk of the following:

- Behavioral difficulties (impulsivity, hyperactivity).

- Mental health challenges (depression, anxiety).

- Chronic health conditions (heart disease, diabetes, obesity) later in life - this is sometimes called the "fetal programming" effect.

Bottom line, a mother's physical health, emotional well-being, and living environment all strongly influence her baby's growth and future health. Supportive, safe, and healthy conditions during pregnancy are critical for giving the child the very best start in life.

A negative environment during pregnancy can affect a developing baby both physically and psychologically. The womb is very sensitive to the mother's health, emotions, and surroundings.

Conversely, in a **positive environment** for the baby in the womb with healthy maternal emotions and low stress, the mother's stress hormones stay balanced, and protect the baby's developing brain. In the womb, babies have healthier heart rates and movement patterns, which might help the child to handle stress, learn, and regulate emotions in the long term.

With good nutrition, a diet rich in vitamins, minerals, protein, and healthy fats supports organ and brain development, and folic acid helps prevent neural tube defects. Omega-3 fatty acids boost brain and vision development, and well-nourished mothers usually have babies with healthy birth weights and stronger immune systems.

Talking, singing, or playing gentle music may help with early bonding. Babies can hear sounds in the womb and may respond, and this can support emotional connection and possibly even early language recognition.

A big takeaway is that a positive environment for the mother – emotionally, physically, and socially - helps the baby grow stronger, healthier, and better prepared for life outside the womb.

Children born in positive prenatal environments are more likely to have:

- A strong immune system.

- Healthy weights at birth

- Better cognitive and language development

- Lower risk of anxiety, depression, or chronic illness later in life

Take note here – we are talking about YOU and your felt environment while in your mother's womb, which you must consider to free yourself from your issues, which include your addictive behavior.

Here's a story that weaves together the journey of a child growing in the womb under negative influences, and how those early experiences echo throughout their life:

The Story of Daniel

When Daniel's life first began, he was cradled inside his mother's womb. But the world outside was not peaceful. His mother often sat with her hands on her belly, tears streaming down her face as she argued with Daniel's father. Shouts rattled the small apartment. Doors slammed. Nights were filled with tension, not calm.

Her stress hormones—cortisol and adrenaline—flooded her body, seeping into Daniel's developing system. Instead of steady rhythms of peace, his tiny heartbeat often sped up, echoing the storm outside. His mother sometimes struggled to eat properly, and her sleep was broken. These small things, unnoticed by the world, were shaping Daniel's earliest foundation.

Childhood

When Daniel was born, he was smaller than most babies. He startled easily at loud sounds and cried often, struggling to be soothed. His mother loved him dearly, but her own pain and exhaustion sometimes made her distant.

As he grew, Daniel was sensitive. In preschool, he clung to his teacher's leg when other children played freely. His nervous system, tuned in the womb to constant stress, left him always watching, always waiting for something bad to happen.

At home, the arguing between his parents never entirely stopped. Eventually, they divorced. Daniel, still young, learned to read the mood of the surrounding adults—measuring voices, watching eyes—because safety depended on it.

Teen Years

By adolescence, Daniel carried invisible scars. He had trouble focusing in school, especially when tension was high. He often felt anxious, but he didn't have the words to explain it. Sometimes he acted out with anger; other times he withdrew, feeling unworthy.

Still, Daniel was resilient. He found comfort in music, where he could pour out the emotions he didn't know how to express. A caring mentor—a high school counselor—noticed his talent and his quiet pain. For the first time, Daniel felt seen.

Adulthood

As an adult, Daniel struggled with relationships. The early chaos in his nervous system made it difficult for him to trust.

When arguments arose, his heart would pound as if he were still in the womb, surrounded by shouts.

But Daniel also carried strength. Because he had endured so much, he had empathy for others' struggles. He volunteered with children, wanting to give them the steady encouragement he once longed for.

With therapy and support, Daniel understood how the stress his mother faced during pregnancy shaped him—but also how healing was possible. The same sensitivity that once felt like a curse became a gift: he could notice when others were hurting and offer them kindness.

Closing

Daniel's story illustrates how the womb retains memories. The environment before birth sets the initial stages of life, possibly with arduous experiences. Yet those early marks don't decide the complete picture. With love, support, and resilience, even a child shaped by negative influences can grow into an adult who finds meaning, healing, and strength.

The following is a story of Samuel growing up with positive influences in the womb:

The Story of Samuel

Samuel's world had peace from the very beginning. His mother often placed her hands gently on her belly, humming soft tunes. His father spoke to him, telling him stories even before he was born. Their home was not without its challenges, but it was filled with warmth, laughter, and care.

When Samuel's mother laughed, her body released endorphins that also reached him. When she rested, her heartbeat stayed steady, giving him a rhythm of calm to grow to. She nourished her body well, and Samuel received everything he needed—food, oxygen, and safety. His first environment taught him trust.

Childhood

When Samuel was born, he was strong and healthy. He cried, but the sound of his mother's heartbeat and the comfort of her arms quickly soothed his cries. He recognized his father's voice, already familiar from months before.

In preschool, Samuel explored freely. He was curious and eager to learn, secure knowing that someone would always be there for him. The calm he had known in the womb carried into his nervous system, helping him handle stress without becoming overwhelmed.

At home, Samuel's parents created routines—bedtime stories, shared meals, laughter after minor mistakes. Even when conflicts arose, they modeled calm and problem-solving rather than shouting. Samuel learned that mistakes were part of life, not something to fear.

Teen Years

As he grew, Samuel blossomed. He wasn't without struggles—he faced exams, peer pressure, and the normal turbulence of teenage years—but he carried resilience. When stress came, he remembered how to breathe through it. He trusted that help was always available.

Friends saw him as someone they could lean on. His secure beginnings gave him the confidence to stand up for himself without putting others down. He poured his energy into sports and music, encouraged by his family's steady support.

Adulthood

In adulthood, Samuel carried forward the calm foundation laid before birth. He pursued higher education with focus, not perfectionism. He was patient and communicative in relationships, capable of trusting and earning trust.

When Samuel became a father himself, he carried with him the quiet lessons of his own beginnings: that peace in the womb and stability in the home create ripples that last a lifetime. His children, too, grew up surrounded by warmth, laughter, and reassurance.

Closing

Samuel's story illustrates how a positive environment in the womb can be the first gift a parent gives their child. The rhythms of peace, love, and safety echo long after birth, shaping resilience, confidence, and the ability to form healthy bonds.

Can you relate to the above as a negative influence or a positive influence while being in the womb and afterwards?

Can you see how your world around you helps shape you, even in the womb?

ASSIGNMENT

1. What environment do you believe surrounded you as you were in your mother's womb?

2. What insights did you uncover about yourself in relation to what has been shared in this chapter?

3. What do you think you heard going on in this environment regarding your mother?

4. What do you think you heard going on in this environment regarding your father?

5. Do you know if you were an anxious child later in life, or do you feel you were a secure child?

6. Do you believe you were meant to be?

7. Do you believe you are fearfully and wonderfully made?

8. Do you believe that God created you in the womb?

9. Do you love you?

10. Do you want to get well?

CHAPTER 3
You Are Out of the Womb!

Many of you will want to skip certain parts of this book. Did you skip the introduction? Or did you skip a chapter or two above? If so, go back and start all over! Skipping creates gaps in your understanding of your person. Suppose you do not understand how your brain develops. Suppose you lack knowledge of the establishment of relationships from early childhood on. In that case, you cannot walk into healing, change, and transformation. Bank on it, men! The problem with most men is that they want instant change and do not want to do the work required for that change.

Proverbs 18:2 notes: "A fool takes no pleasure in understanding, but only in expressing his opinion."

Romans 1:22 notes: "Claiming to be wise, they became fools."

Did I just step on your toes? Good!

THE "GOLDEN HOUR"

Labor produced mechanical and physiological changes that helped prepare you for that first gulp of air. You received oxygen from your mother's placenta. But once you emerged, your umbilical cord was clamped, and the placenta lost its ability to function. This caused your lungs to take over, drying up the fluid in your lungs, which expanded and filled with air after birth.

Your lungs also began receiving more blood after birth. In the womb, the blood bypasses these organs because of pressure. During delivery, the pressure in the baby's lungs drops, and blood flows through them normally. Once you were ushered into the world, you arrived with neuropathways in place — neuropathways that would ultimately continue to grow (and change) throughout your life.

Now you are out of the womb! Imagine the nurse is holding you up after cleaning you after you were born. Close your eyes and think about YOU during your first moments. What do you think it was like?

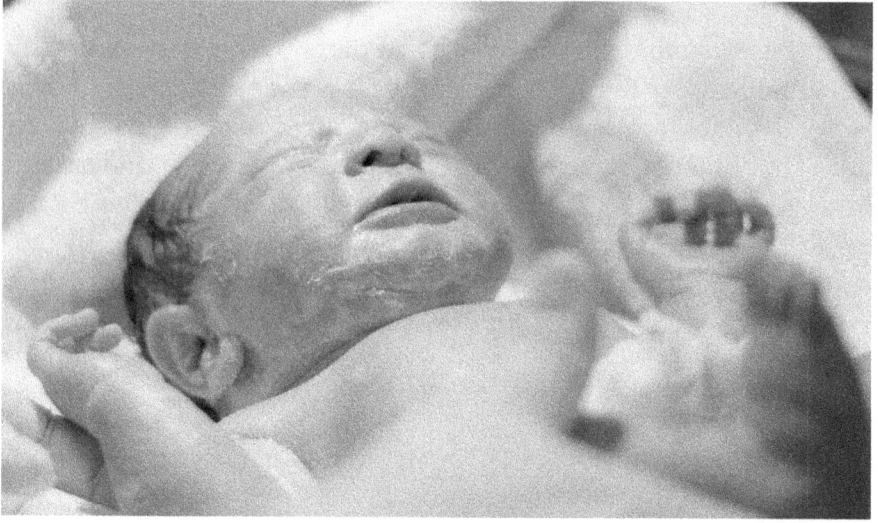

Just as there's no way to tell what kind of sensation a baby feels when they travel through the birth canal, doctors are also unsure about how much a baby sees or hears during labor. However, researchers have established that a baby possesses some auditory abilities before entering the world.

Doctors say that hearing a parent talk and sing while in the womb allows a baby to recognize the sound of their voices after birth and is a part of parent-child bonding.

Your eyesight before birth is more complex to gauge. But after you were born, we know your vision was blurry at first. You couldn't focus well. When held to fifteen inches from your parent's face (it's no coincidence that this is about the distance between your mother's face, cradled in her arms), you could detect her facial features — another element of initial bonding.

The first few minutes after birth are a magical time. What happened during the first sixty minutes of your life — the "golden hour" — helped with mother-baby bonding. Stay focused on the importance of this and keep your imagination engaged. Your first moments in this world.

Your External World

The environment you were born into is a huge factor — at home, school, with relatives, and while experiencing positive and negative events, etc. Your neuropathways continued to adapt to external forces, shaping how you think, respond, interact, etc., then and today. Traumatic experiences in adverse backgrounds affected you, but perfect homes that demanded perfection could also lead to trauma. Just as a fire can traumatize you, environments that are not positive can traumatize your brain (by events and by people). Thus, you developed a performance-based acceptance of living life.

Even before birth, you had a built-in expectation that adults would be available and care for your needs. During the first stage of development outside the womb, your initial attention focused on forming and strengthening secure connections. Your mother, father, and caregivers played a vital role in developing your attachments and your desire to move toward these pivotal figures. Rather than passively receiving care, you actively sought it out. You came into the world with physical and social skills that prepared you to take a role in your development. These human relationships shaped your young brain and the well-being of your mind.

Research has shown that attachment-seeking is part of our emotional wiring — the dominant activity during the first two years of brain development. It serves as the base for future emotional and social interactions, as well as language and intellectual advances. You noticed and developed perceptions using messages from your caregivers. They were your initial working model for engaging with others. Thus, the care you received early on directly affected the quality of attachment you formed with your caregivers and influenced your emotional interactions with others.

Your parents were your first "role models." You were wired with natural curiosity and the ability to learn, and you imitated them. Their emotional availability activated your brain's growth, influenced your physical and verbal actions, and enabled you to regulate your emotions and impulses. You, as a vulnerable child, depended on your parents for survival, emotional security, and a base for learning. Your ability to connect to others, i.e., grandparents, aunts, uncles, and others, depended largely on your sense of well-being derived from a safe environment provided by your parents and caregivers.

Eventually, you developed an awareness of your separateness from your caregivers and peers and a sense of individuality. You exhibited self-conscious emotions, were sensitive to other's judgments, and quickly felt shame and embarrassment when others critiqued your behaviors and appearance. You developed a conscience. During this stage, there was an explosion of brain growth in several areas of development, apart from earlier dominant emotional development. Intellectually, children hold ideas in their minds briefly, engage in pretend play, and become increasingly able to focus their attention on topics, people, and objects introduced by others. Their use of spoken language, new words, and complex sentences increases. Children develop perceptual and motor skills that allow them to run fast, climb high, and hit hard — making the development of self-control significant.

Fortunately, this self-definition stage also brings the early emergence of executive function skills, including developing working memory, mental flexibility, and self-control that influence all areas of development, increasing children's capacity to explore and learn about their social environment — and to navigate conflicts with others. As children understand independent interests, they realize they have choices, which is quite liberating. However, with choices — particularly those involving caregivers and peers — comes a dawning awareness of responsibility. This choice — responsibility tension is central to the drama of this stage.

How adults react during this tension-filled period of life greatly affects how young children come to see their rights and other's rights. Children's interactions with their caregivers, peers, and others shape their brains' social and emotional future. These experiences provide lessons for developing moral and ethical codes, gaining control of impulses and emotions, and learning and adapting to the rules of their family, culture, and society. However, they still need adult guidance, often through caring relationships.

Many experts consider parental care in early childhood to be one of the most important factors that help develop children's cognitive and non-cognitive abilities. The information gathered in these early relationships is at the heart of a rich and complex brain-building process. When children primarily have positive experiences, they perceive the behaviors and messages of others in positive ways and feel motivated to explore more of the world, including people and things.

But what if your early interactions were not ideal? What if you didn't receive the "tender loving care" you needed? When babies have repeated adverse early experiences, they come to expect the behaviors and messages of others to be negative, and they perceive new experiences with others negatively.

After repeated negative exchanges and interactions with their caregivers, infants start to build a primitive sense of self. They come to expect: "I am not listened to" or "What I choose to do isn't valued" or "How I choose to express my emotions isn't accepted" or "I am not allowed to explore" or "My needs are not met."

Thus, your early relationships, whether positive or negative, significantly affected your brain development and your ability to manage and buffer stress. As you experienced responses from your caregivers, your brain formed expectations for how you would be treated and how you should respond. If you experienced negative interactions, your emotional and social development, as well as your intellectual and language development, likely suffered.

YOUR PAST HELPED DEVELOP YOUR PRESENT

In counseling and my Battle Lines group, I ensured that family of origin was always an in-depth topic of discussion. It does not mean that all sex addicts come from adverse backgrounds regarding their family, nor does it mean that males who come from overall healthy families do not develop sexual addiction. *However, with that said, the family of origin and other relationships can undoubtedly affect sex addiction.*

I also want to add here that God created us in such a unique way that our brains have plasticity, which means we can be "rewired." We can change our brains! Also, with a relationship with the Lord, He can renew our minds!

Dr. Dan Siegel is one of my favorite researchers on the brain. He explains plasticity (neuroplasticity) in his book *MINDSIGHT* (among my favorites):

> *Our experiences sculpt synaptic connections in the brain itself. But here is the key: when neurons fire, you can get them to rewire, which that experience stimulates neurons, the basic cells of the brain, to fire patterns.*
>
> *One form of experience that we now know shapes neuronal firing and synaptic growth — changes in the development of the connections among the neurons — is how we focus our attention. And amazingly, when you learn to focus your attention on the mind itself, you actually can rewire essential parts of the brain that help regulate how your entire nervous system functions — so, for example, how your body regulates itself, how you balance your emotions — and also how you engage in relationships with other people. It also changes the*

way you relate to someone remarkably close to you and how you relate to yourself.

I call this reflective ability "Mindsight," and it's how you can learn to focus your attention on the mind itself to transform the connections in the brain, moving the brain to a more integrated, harmonious way of functioning. That is the promise of Mindsight. In the Mindsight approach, we see the brain as limited to what is in the skull and an extended nervous system that is the mechanism of energy and information flow. So, when we look at this connection between mind, brain, and relationships, we become empowered to move our lives from unhealthy to healthy.

Children are vulnerable to traumatic head injuries, infections, or toxins, such as lead; when I was a child, it was in most of the paint sold. Childhood vaccines, like the measles vaccine, can protect children from dangerous complexions such as brain swelling. The Polio vaccine was not available to me until my later teens, in the 1950s. The polio issue overshadowed the lead issues. In the 1960s, there was a debate on lead (which had its industry lobbyist, much as the tobacco industry had later, denying that lead was an issue). In the 1970s and 1980s, researchers discovered that America's lead problem was much larger than previously thought. Low-income households and homes where they had eliminated the most obvious lead sources, such as chipped paint and window sashes, were also affected. Lead in gasoline, as well as in houses, was a national problem. "Affluent Kids Also Harmed by Toxic Lead," announced a *Wall Street Journal* headline from 1981.

Just as recently as 2016, the *Journal of Urban History* by David Rosner stated, "The cost of detoxifying the entire nation of lead hovers around $1 trillion. Any federal effort to systematically identify and remove lead from infested households would be complex, decades-long, and require ongoing policy reform."

Imagine you have different colors of wires in your brain, and each experience is a wire. In that case, you might see how your brain is being developed. Over years of growth, the frontal lobe is the last part of the brain to develop, which completes itself around twenty-four years of age. These connections develop at a breakneck pace because, in the "outside world" of the womb, the exposure to so much is happening around the child constantly.

NURTURING

Your ability to learn a language, solve problems, do well in school, and develop in adulthood and beyond is determined by how your brain develops in the environment in which you grew up, including your parents. In addition, how you relate to people healthily or unhealthy way.

Constant toxicity negatively affects a child's brain. The parent's ability to know their child unknowingly gives the child healthy brain growth. Hugs and soft words are key to a child's healthiness, with "positive words" being shown in love and encouragement.

Affective touch is so essential that it speaks of how close relationships develop and is crucial in developing the "self (YOU)." Human touch can go a long, long way in showing love. I did not receive that, and I was unfamiliar with the human touch. It was so on both sides of my family, where Daddy had nine brothers and sisters, and Mother had five brothers and one sister.

Children and other caregivers can support healthy brain growth or deter it from developing unhealthily. Nurturing a child is understanding that child's particular needs and responding sensitively to help keep the child's brain from stress. Exposure to stories, songs, and reading books helps strengthen their language and communication, which puts them on a healthy path to learning and success in school.

Parents are responsible for the child's health by protecting them, as best as they can, from diseases that start in pregnancy, with a healthy diet for the mom. Vaccinations can protect the birth mom from infections that can harm the unborn child's brain.

During pregnancy, many types of risks, such as the Zika virus of the not-too-distant past, smoking or alcohol, toxins, cytomegalovirus, and again stress, trauma, or issues of depression, can affect the brain. It is a must for the birth mom to seek regular health care during her pregnancy.

I believe it is essential to know where personal emotional makeup may come from to help in the present. Again, this is not about blame but about creating understanding. For example, I was born during WWII. My father was away at war, and I was a firstborn. I was always fearful as a child. My mother was always afraid, insecure, and risk-averse. I became risk-averse and insecure. My father never said, "I love you." And he never gave hugs, kisses, and affirmations. There was silence around the dinner table, so sharing feelings was not there, and I kept things inside as they did. Because my parents had limited education and were working during the Great Depression, they did not emphasize the importance of education. All these created neuropathways that I (you) operate from unknowingly. My self-worth was non-existent. I was shy and lived in fear of failure.

Another example of this insecurity later in life was when my sister, who was four years younger, would visit her cousins in West Texas (Odessa) for two weeks each summer. We drove from Kerrville to San Angelo and met my uncle, aunt, and cousins there. I could have gone, but my fear and insecurity left me behind to return to Kerrville with my parents. I missed out on growth, unknowingly. This pattern continued into college, where I would get homesick, seek to leave, and fight with every ounce of my being not to return home and stay there. In fact, I did that twice with two different colleges and tried one more time at another, and I became a victor over that "power." My insecurity led me to believe I was not intelligent, yet I fought for my grades and was on the Dean's List throughout my college years to graduation.

I am trying to help you understand how our caregivers can influence the development of patterns and the formation of security or insecurity. Again, not to blame, but to seek understanding.

How can that help us in the NOW?

PLASTICITY AND NEUROPATHWAYS — YOUR BRAIN CAN CHANGE!

I believe we can **build new neuropathways** if we can understand cause and effect much more easily.

Later in life, I learned to practice hugging, and to stay in that touch, to stay in that hug that was extended to me, and me also giving. Just like being in a church where there is quiet praise and worship, you never get your hands off the pew because it was, and probably still is, incredibly uncomfortable to raise your hands in praise. When you go against that awkward feeling, raising hands at certain times becomes comfortable, and you flow into the love of praise to our Lord. The same holds true for giving and receiving hugs and touches.

The plasticity of the brain is constantly changing in the child's development. Reflect on your childhood, and think about your seeking to ride a bicycle, either with the support of parents or friends or only by yourself. You may have crashed a few times, but eventually, you got the hang of it. Neuropathways in your brain were being developed, and in due season, you did not even think about riding the bike; you got on and went. Your brain underwent changes, in effect.

Some self-taught guys who like to play golf have a score in the 90s. It's always the same when you come off the course, just a few scores varying each time, but overall, you are consistent. Then, you decide to seek a golf pro out to be better at this fine game, and he watches you. He moves your feet to be repositioned, your knees flexed more, you're moving away from the ball a couple of inches back, and works with your elbows and shoulders, hip movement, upper swing, etc.

At first, it is a tedious process, and then there may be a decent ball strike in that first session. It is like ONE you have never hit before. Wham, it goes out there! The golf pro tells you how to practice and wants to work with you twice a week. Over time, in your steady discipline of practice and working with the pro, the old swing disappears, and this new swing becomes more of a norm. Your brain is being changed, and you are building new neuropathways, and they can become dominant. There will always be the old in the brain, but in a way, the new swing becomes dominant.

Tiger Woods occasionally had a bad slice; he overcame it via the previous description of practice and working with a pro. However, sometimes, that old swing came up. That is the same with us; that old pattern jumps out, but we can now know or "should" that we must refocus on who we have become on our journey of being changed. There will be more on this later; however, you know that *YOUR brain can CHANGE!*

Your new experiences reshape you! You do not want to be a man that Mohammad Ali once said, *"A man who views the world at 50 the same way he did at 20 has wasted 30 years of his life."*

I would encourage you to purchase and slowly read Louis Cozzolino's *The Neuroscience of Human Relationships.* You'll glimpse the different parts and functions of that beautiful brain within you from birth into adulthood. In fact, become that man willing to go to any lengths to be healed and understand as much about your person as possible, which extensive appropriate reading provides.

We also learn by *"mirroring"* what is before us. In simple terms, we repeat what we experience and see. We bridge the networks by observing perception and movement. We pick up these experiences and reflect on dad, mom, teacher, or others who have influenced us. Jan, my wife, says it is laughable to watch me see a movie because I unknowingly act out what is on the screen with the characters. She sees it in my mouth, facial, eye movements, etc. This is called *mirroring*, and we build neuropathways from all these experiences. This is why, sometimes, you may have someone say to you, "You are just like your dad!" This provides us with a visceral emotional experience of what the other is experiencing, allowing us to know others from the inside out. We actively construct some neuropathways, while others are subliminally formed (our environment shapes us).

Researchers are learning new things about our brains daily, with modern technology ever-changing before us, giving a more in-depth insight into this gift that God has given us. It is beyond my comprehension how they know when someone touches your skin lightly, which part of the brain is affected, and the exact location of that part of the brain. They are learning more about the specific functions of the brain and where they are. For example, the social engagement system of automatic and emotional control is in the right cortex, the right central nucleus of the amygdala, and the right-sided nuclei of the hypothalamus. The right brain serves as the infrastructure for many primitive components of social brain functioning grounded in bodily and emotional experiences. The right hemisphere organizes the knowledge of a personal emotional self instead of the social person.

Scientists found that it was significant to note that the right brain responds to negative emotional stimuli before conscious awareness. Thus, unconscious emotional processing based on "experiences" invisibly guides our moment-to-moment thoughts, feelings, and behaviors. I might add, perhaps, that this is called our sixth sense, as you have more than likely heard it spoken of before. The right hemisphere of the brain develops first. Its dominance over bodily and emotional functioning and its ability to process this information reflexively and unconsciously. It organizes and stores many social and emotional experiences that can reemerge later, especially under stress. That has freed the brain's left hemisphere to attend more to the environment and engage in logical and abstract reasoning.

The brain's highly interconnected nature allows it to operate our bodies as a system. There is still so much about the brain that scientists and researchers do not understand. How can a thought be defined? Where does a thought come from, and by what mechanism does it stick around in our brains? Scientists haven't quite figured this out yet. It is a mystery that is, however, to be discovered. The only ONE who knows all the secrets of our body is the *creator — God Himself.* Deuteronomy 29:29 states, **"The secret things belong to the LORD our God, but the things revealed belong to us and to our sons forever, so that we may follow all the words of this Law."**

The absence of fathers during World War II had differing effects on the development of identity in boys and girls. Articles and research of the era discussed boys' separation from their fathers but failed to address daughters' loss of paternal influence. Evidence suggests that for both boys and girls, the problem was not primarily the separation of children from their fathers but the manner in which the mother dealt with the absence and the father's return. Recent research shows that girls derive their basic sense of identity from experiencing themselves as being like their mothers. They emulate their mothers' behaviors and continue to identify with their mothers through childhood.

ASSIGNMENT

1. In layperson's terms, please explain the shaping of your brain from the above, ensuring you grasp the physical brain development.

2. Imagine yourself coming out of your mother's womb. What world do you perceive you came into with your mom and dad?

3. What world do you perceive you came into with your father?

4. What world do you perceive you experienced with your father and mother's relationship, and what did you hear about what was going on between them?

5. Do you understand the term "mirroring?"

6. Can you share some positive memories of the early years in your family? Write this down as you connect with these positive memories.

7. Can you share and get in touch with any hostile environment you grew up in? Take time to get in touch with the wounds and write those down.

8. Do you want to get well?

CHAPTER 4
A Dysfunctional Environment

Someone once quoted trauma "as anything less than nurturing," and I agree. They define trauma and abuse in a dysfunctional family *as anything less than nurturing* on the caregiver's part. A dysfunctional family defines trauma and abuse as anything less than nurturing on the part of the caregiver, which is created within a child's relationship with their caregivers when either the parent or caregiver is too close and intrusive (enmeshment) or too far away (abandonment or neglect). Caregivers can be parents, grandparents, childcare workers, teachers, scout leaders, clergy, coaches, etc. Below are some examples of these relationship dynamics:

ENMESHMENT

Physical

- Use implements, face slapping, shaking, hair pulling, head-banging, and tickling a child into hysteria

- Having a child physically nurturing a parent

- Intrusive procedures (i.e., enemas)

Sexual

- Intercourse, oral sex, masturbation, sexual touching known as fondling, sexual kissing, and hugging

- Voyeurism, exhibitionism, verbal sexual trauma

- Failure to have sexual boundaries in the presence of a child

- Having a child witness sexual trauma

Emotional/Sexual

- Enmeshment by the parent or primary caregiver.

Intellectual

- Attacking, shaming, or over-control of the child's expression of thought.

Emotional

- Shaming a child's expression of emotion.

- Refusal to let the child express feelings.

- Improper expression of emotions by the parent or primary caregiver.

Spiritual

The Diagnostic Systems Manual for Mental Disorders (DSMV) does not designate enmeshment as a mental or religious disorder. Still, the criteria for addiction listed in the DSM guide how an addiction functions and takes over a person's mental life. Faith, religious activities, thoughts, and rituals can become a habit and a harmful compulsion. Religion is an integral part of life, even for millions of people, and is normal and beneficial. Since millions of people practice various religions with varying degrees of faith and intensity, *it's difficult to tell when practice becomes a harmful obsession by the parent or caregiver* (highlighted by Benno).

- Trauma at the hands of a religious caregiver.

- Parents act like they are the God or goddess of the family.

- Indulgence or false empowerment of the child.

- Perfection is demanded of or expected from the child.

ABANDONMENT / NEGLECT

Failure to provide:

- Food
- Clothing
- Shelter

Failure to provide adequate:

- Physical nurturing
- Emotional nurturing
- Sexual information (age-appropriate)
- Medical and dental care
- Financial assistance and information (age-appropriate)
- Education
- Spiritual nurturing
- Being dismissive or shaming of a child's wants

OTHER TRAUMA OR CHILD ABUSE

- Overt versus covert abuse
- Disempowering versus falsely empowering abuse

ARE YOU ANY OF THE ABOVE? FROM WHERE DID YOU RECEIVE INFLUENCE OF THE ABOVE?

Most adults are unaware of what lack of love and nurturing from their parents or caregivers does to them. So many want to say, *"My parents were wonderful parents; they worked hard and provided. They did the best they could. Their parents were the same."* And something along the lines. Again, this information is not to blame. Still, I seek to help you to understand what the effects your family of origin may have had on you. Many men in counseling or Battle Lines had difficulty looking into their past; they wanted to get "fixed!" Also, they want to be "fixed" now. Unless one processes all in counseling and groups, is ready to be educated, and does the work required in every area, which includes physical, emotional, and spiritual, **complete healing cannot take place and set the captive free.** And my brother, this is a fact!

Every home has its difficulties in family relationships. There can be disagreements, arguing, and perhaps even yelling at times. Still, in the overall scheme of things, the love, the hugs, and affirmations far override the typical negatives as children grow and experience their different periods of social and physical changes. Hopefully, both parents were actively involved in early attachment relationships to teach responses and challenging interpersonal relationships at home and school.

When our primary caregivers show positive facial expressions, actions, social communication, and give and take in ongoing behaviors, positive parenting contributes to building a healthy brain. This supports a positive self-image and the ability to engage in, sustain, and mutually regulate social interactions.

When a child grows up in a dysfunctional home, let us say, an alcoholic father and a violent mother, more than likely, no, let us say highly probable the child will have anger issues, amongst many other problems. A child can become combat ready as he grows to protect himself. And this brings about the shaping of neuropathways again as they mirror their environment. The young adult may say, "My mother was not the mothering type! She must not have wanted me!" Or something of the sort.

The therapy for this person will be a long process, as there are rejection issues and self-esteem issues, and when tied to sexual addiction, when they may have been involved for years, expect the healing process to take much longer. A therapist and YOU cannot deal with all the issues simultaneously. So, **patience** as a counselee must be a part of your **mindset** if you want to heal. **YOU cannot be in short-term therapy** and attend group occasionally or none! ***Do not even try to get well if you are unwilling to do the work required.*** You are wasting your time and the counselor's time. If your attendance in the group is hindering the progress and dynamics of the group, please have the kindness to depart, as it is affecting the possible healing of others.

Any counselor who says short-term counseling can work is not able and/or unwilling to inform appropriately or refuses to acknowledge an addiction's truth, healing from trauma, and other involved issues; **you must depart from that counselor** and seek a competent counselor who understands these issues in depth! *Remember, the brain has created neuropathways over a long period, which do not reverse overnight!*

Parents of child addicts who seek help often underestimate the information a child receives in the environment to which we expose them. Most are unaware of what modern technology has done to negatively shape a child's brain. Many studies are taking place today regarding technology's positive and negative effects on the brain. *However, when I point out negativity, I speak of violence, cussing, nudity, and morality issues in movies. On the internet, I am speaking of porn, social networking, gaming, side-chat rooms, etc. In words you have heard before, "JUNK IN, JUNK OUT. Negative in, NEGATIVE OUT!"* If you are a parent, seek appropriate boundaries for your children in this world of technology.

The same could be said for adult addicts who come in for individual therapy at a counselor's office. While this may be invisible to us, the receiver is almost always unaware of the unconscious process. It is certainly visible to others living with appropriate boundaries and lifestyles. Parents with unresolved trauma or conflicts will communicate their inner-emotional world to their children, and it is not a conscious effort of many parents, nor aware of how it affects their child. This early learning shapes the brain to determine behavior, thoughts, personality, belief systems, and social interaction without awareness. Most parents never seek a parenting book for that first child coming into their home, and in the years following, they seem to function in raising their children as their parents raised them. So, the parents pass on family behaviors, not because of genetics but because of their upbringing.

Sometimes, adults bring about self-harm to themselves repeatedly and "almost always" describe their childhoods as having included abuse, neglect, or deep and sustained shame. Endorphins regulate this, and as with heroin, the endogenous endorphins secreted because of self-harm become addictive and reinforce the continued use of self-harm injuries for emotional regulation or to seek recognition, which they feel they have never had in their lives.

Wolfram Schultz, a German professor of Neuroscience at the University of Cambridge, states, "The brain not only detects and analyzes past events but also constructs and dynamically modifies predictions about future events based on the previous experience." *The past often serves the present, but in many ways, it determines it.* Experience creates self-fulling prophecies by triggering behavior patterns and thought processes to react to a present situation. *Please note this: early social learning requires motivation, time, and discipline.* Therefore, I have found that in counseling and Battle Lines, most men are so resistant to any change.

Think upon this: if you have set neuropathways you function under, then to make a conscious change, even trying it just once, makes for sometimes extreme uncomfortableness. For example, you seek to heal your marriage. Your wife loves hugs and kisses and seeks to walk hand in hand in many places. You attempt to hug her when you get home, but it is so uncomfortable. As a child, I can almost predict that you were never hugged; it is something you have never done much of, maybe even in dating your wife. However, now you seek to heal your marriage, you must, and I say *"MUST,"* make a *disciplined effort* in the morning before going to work, when you come home, and maybe at bedtime to hug and kiss your wife. *You practice, practice, and practice some more, and over time, you are building new neuropathways, and it becomes comfortable. It truly becomes a part of you. Men, practice makes perfect!* Change is possible if you want to change, but that is a **CHOICE** only you can make. How badly do you want to change, inside and out?

What is implicit memory? The implicit social memory may begin in the womb, listening to the rhythms of our mothers' bodies and tones of voice. When a child comes out into the world, the child recognizes the mother by her voice, body smell, breast milk, or special touch. Implicit memory will later connect us to our father by seeking to connect to the child's raised arms, smiling, and a sense of safety and warmth. Deep associations in early childhood, such as intimacy, anxiety, love, and shame, are set in early implicit memory. People cannot consciously think about implicit memories because they are unconscious. Still, they show up in our behavior, attitudes, and beliefs.

I have often heard in counseling and Battle Lines that many men recall little about their childhood. This usually comes from their unhappy childhoods. It suggests high levels of anxiety in youth, and this goes against long-term memory. This shows that it sets dissociative defenses in place to protect oneself from uncomfortable situations that came about earlier. For example, I do not remember many details about my childhood, although my sister, who is four years younger, does. She even remembers much of what I experienced. She once told me, "Do you remember almost drowning on a youth outing in high school in the public pool in Fredericksburg (Texas)?"

I had no recollection of that event, and it caught me entirely off guard. As a child, I was afraid of the dark, I was shy, and, as stated earlier, insecure. That bonding with my father never took place, even though he was a hard worker and did extra jobs to bring income into the home. There was not much conversation between us or activity with each other. As previously mentioned, I did not see hugs, kisses, or communication between my parents in my house. My parents did not engage in social activities. I did not know how to be social and comfortable with that. I never felt secure or confident in myself in those early years and in my twenties. In effect, I was mirroring my parents and developing neuropathways I was unaware of.

Another example of our being unaware (implicit):

How can you tap into your unawareness? One way is to look for cues in certain behaviors and attitudes that may mean you're out of touch with how you're feeling. Some examples include:

1. Having a rigid opinion about almost anything: religion, politics, someone's character, etc.

2. Being told you're stubborn or "not listening"

3. Interrupting someone to offer an opinion before you've heard theirs in total

4. Being "right"

5. Consistently thinking about something besides what you're doing

6. Thinking you're wiser than your children

7. If a person seems to respond to you in an unpleasant way, what was your energy around what you just said or did?

8. Acting on impulse

9. Feeling anxious or angry. This is the most basic. Something in the present is connected to something in the past that was perceived as dangerous. By definition, you are there and not here. Awareness is impossible while you are in one of these powerful states. What is really ironic is that when you are angry, you feel like you have a perfect understanding of the issues. The term for this is "negative transference." You actually disconnect completely because you only focus on yourself

10. Judging yourself or others negatively or positively — being persistently critical of your spouse, partner, and/or

children, giving unasked-for advice, or gossiping.

We are all programmed from birth to act and be in specific ways by our parents, peers, educators, and society. These concepts become our version of reality, as concrete as our perception of a house or a car. Our brains create an interpretation of essentially everything. That is why true awareness is impossible, as each person perceives their view of life as correct — positive or negative.

ASSIGNMENT

1. Please list any negative experiences you had as a child as you remember them.

2. How did those experiences make you feel?

3. Do you understand how the negativity of the environment helps shape your brain?

4. Do you understand the term, "Anything less than nurturing is trauma?"

5. Do you understand "implicit memory?"

6. Do you understand "mirroring?"

7. Do you want to get well?

CHAPTER 5
A Positive Environment

A Positive Environment

The Book of Manning, an SEC-storied documentary, had me completely enthralled as I watched it on television. I watched a young boy who went to the University of Mississippi and had to come home because his father had died of suicide. His mom and sister insisted he return to the university and not stay and help support them. He later met Olivia there, and they fell in love with Ole Miss, who later was the folk hero quarterback and the homecoming queen. The film tells the story of the hero worship that Manning endured until it went away, of how Archie and Olivia settled down and raised three boys in New Orleans as normally as they could, right down to the VHS camera on Archie's shoulder.

It is also a story of how those three boys — Cooper, Peyton, and Eli — followed in their dad's footsteps and signed to play football in the SEC.

"I get invitations to go speak," Manning says. "They want to put a title on there: 'How to Raise an All-American.' No, no, no, no, no, no… we tried to raise kids, not NFL quarterbacks."

Archie and Olivia managed to do both. Peyton became an All-American at Tennessee. Eli went to Ole Miss like his dad and became the first pick in the NFL draft like his brother. But you know that. Everybody knows that the Mannings have lived their lives in the public eye without being cuddled by the attention.

If it were easy, every NFL player would do it.

"I really don't think I have lived my life as an open book," Manning says. "It's just the boys are so high profile. People ask questions. Things are out there… we've just been blessed. But I know Ryan Leaf used to call Peyton, 'Peyton Perfect.' Well,

Peyton wasn't always Peyton Perfect, and Cooper wasn't always Cooper Perfect, and Eli wasn't Eli Perfect. There are always hills there in raising kids, and we've had ours. We've just been fortunate to get through them."

The Mannings have had their hills. Only after Archie's mother passed away did he begin to speak publicly of the suicide of his father, who ran a farm machinery business in Drew, Mississippi. Elisha Archibald Manning Sr. had health and business problems, and in small-town Mississippi in the late 1960s, men did not ask for help.

"He was stubborn," Manning says. "People knew him as someone who was tough. A stroke happened to him! And he didn't go to the doctor for two weeks! He smoked, like everybody. Smoked Chesterfields. He wore a pair of khakis and a shirt to work every day. And he had to have two front pockets. If you gave him a birthday present with one front pocket, it would never come out of the wrapper. One pocket is for his pens, and one is for his Chesterfields."

In the film, Cooper's chin quivers as he talks about how the discovery of a congenital spinal condition swept away his football career at Ole Miss before he ever played a down. The hate mail that Peyton got from Rebels fans when he signed with Tennessee, the public drunkenness citation that turned Eli's career around at Ole Miss...the hills are apparent.

It may sound not very sensible, but a man known for humility agrees to take part in a documentary about his life. Archie turned down the film. Then he said yes. Then he pulled out of it. Six months later, Olivia asked him how the documentary was going.

"I nixed it," Archie says.

"Well, you're going to call them back and tell them you're going to do it," Olivia says, "because your grandchildren need to see your story."

The rest is SEC history.

As the film progresses, you see the love of Archie and Olivia, and then the first son, second son, and third son are born, and how the father and mother are involved in their lives. Archie did not take his pro football problems into the home; when he got home, the family was uppermost. You see that in his and Olivia's participation with each son and together. Archie comments on the film, highlighting the significance of embracing, cherishing, and kissing boys. You see the fighting between the brothers, the love between them, the individual confidence and well-being, and their unbreakable bonds. They maintain healthy marriages, and although they keep many aspects of their private lives hidden, it is widely acknowledged how close this family is to each other. You do not see jealousy and envy; you see togetherness.

For a child to develop "healthy affect regulation," the child needs:

- Soothing

- Being held softly and securely

- Comforting warmth

- Loving words

- Non-stressful times in sleep, hunger, and stimulation

- Repeated experiences of emotional transitions from times of distress to calmness

- An atmosphere of positive emotional states between parents and the child

A child may not remember these experiences, but they shape the neuropathways in our brain's infrastructure and have a lifelong influence on us. Face-to-face interaction is vital to the child's development. It affects the development of the nervous system, increases oxygen consumption, increases energy metabolism, and affects the child's expressions. Be reminded that immature brains, which are the child's, solely depend upon their caregivers for their well-being. These attachment patterns are powerful and profoundly influential for a lifetime!

Just imagine how a loving and caring home nurtured the little brains of each son, with the voices they heard, the love they received, and the robust network of neuro-activity taking place. Although Archie said it was not perfect, no home is, they overcame the negatives with many positives: love, correction, boundaries, discipline, words of affirmation, etc. Also, this is an example of a positive atmosphere and a product of it. Archie himself made a commitment and promised to do what he did not get for his sons. Archie Manning made a *CHOICE!* That took focus and determination; in doing so, he built new neuropathways and became comfortable with them. It beset me with tears of joy as I watched this. It spoke volumes about what I did not get, and with so many counselees that I have had the privilege of serving, men in Battle Lines never received it. I had tears for them. I did not get certain things that I should have. Still, I received a lot, which we will talk about later, to help me overcome and somewhat be successful in life and personal healing.

As you reflect on this story or watch this film on the Manning family, what hit you about yourself? How does it speak to you? What are you feeling? What hit you about yourself as you reflect on this story or seek to watch this film on the Manning family? How does it speak to you? What are you feeling? You can be healed from the negativity of your past and build patterns and feelings in your life that you never had before, just like the three Manning brothers did not get. It takes work but know this: *YOUR PAST DOES NOT HAVE TO DETERMINE YOUR PRESENT and YOUR TOMORROWS. However, YOUR CHOICE alone* determines if you want a healed life.

ASSIGNMENT

1. When you read the Manning story, how did it affect you regarding your own family? Please write down your feelings in detail.

2. As you processed the story, is there a feeling of loss that came that you did not get and should have gotten?

3. As you moved through the story and heard about the father/son relationship, how did that make you feel about your father?

4. What was your relationship with your father as a child and now as an adult?

5. What is your relationship with your children as a father?

6. Do you understand how a positive environment affects the brain and its development?

7. Do you see any patterns of behavior repeated from your family of origin to your present wife and children?

8. Do you want to get well?

CHAPTER 6
More About Attachments

Before we move forward, let's revisit attachments. A child's attachment motivates an infant to seek closeness to their parents (caregivers) and seek to communicate with them. The emotional exchanges of secure attachment involve a parent's ability to be emotionally sensitive to the responses to the child's signals, which magnifies the child's positive emotional state and effectively regulates the negative state. Repeated experiences become encoded in the implicit memory as expectations and then as mental models of attachment. John Bowlby calls this a "secure base" in the world.

How attachment relationships are developed serves to provide the infant with protection of many kinds and is crucial in organizing ongoing experience and the neurological growth of the developing brain. These serve as anchoring points in the memory, emotions, things that are represented, and the state of mind of the infant as it develops. It appears that **secure attachment** forms emotional resilience, and an **insecure attachment** may create a significant risk factor in the child's development. I am reminded of these verses from the Bible:

According to Matthew 7:24–27:

> *24 Anyone who listens to my teaching and follows it is wise, like a person who builds a house on solid rock. 25 Though the rain comes in torrents, the floodwaters rise, and the winds beat against that house, it won't collapse because **it is built on bedrock**. 26 But Anyone who hears my teaching and doesn't obey it is foolish, like a person who builds a house on sand. 27 When the rains and floods come, and the winds beat against that house, it will collapse with a mighty crash."*

Parents must raise their children on the bedrock of physical, emotional, relational, environmental, and Godly solid bedrock attachments. If you did not get that as a child, healing can take place for you if there are issues in your life that have not been dealt with through appropriate therapy. In addition, if you have children, it is never too late to bring about changes in your life and your marriage and bring about health for your children. Remember, our brains have plasticity. It may take a while for the changes to take place, but **consistency brings about consistent growth!**

When children develop secure attachments to their parents, they seek to explore the world around them and develop relationships. In the beginning, children need proximity to their parents, which gives them a sense of security and a "safe haven!" John Bowlby calls this a "secure base" that comes about eighteen months of age. This image of attachment figures forward in their minds, which helps comfort them. These neurosensory images — faces, voices, smell, taste, place, touch, etc. — are mental representations of their relationship. I reminded myself of my daughter when she was being raised.

My wife brought her into the kitchen early on as an infant when she was not in her baby's bed or when no other activities were happening. She also placed her child's rocker on the floor on a blanket, looking at individual black and white pictures (which were rotated around) and/or laying her on the blanket. My wife did what needed to be accomplished there in the kitchen. As my daughter grew, she had her playtime in the kitchen, moving from the blanket to her crawling. As she checked out territories in the kitchen and beyond, she went so far as to look back at Mom and return. Later, she slowly ventured a little further, always looking back at Mom for security. Not only was the bond there, but there was safety as well. Although Em could not yet talk, she felt safe inwardly. This, my friends, is called "bonding."

My daughter developed connectivity there, and it was her safe haven. As she began to crawl and explore, we had safety latches on all drawers and doors except one, and that was where the Tupperware was. In this area, she connected to bowls and lids apart from other toys on the floor. She ventured out from the kitchen area, but not much further from where she could turn and see Mom, and Mom made sure she could see her.

Our daughter had our upstairs safety to crawl around in, from room to room, except the stairs, where we had a child safety barrier. She was in a positive atmosphere and was not fear-based by us, her parents, as she explored. She was not only attaching to us in this environment; she was building neuropathways in her experiences. She got a tiny pat on her bottom if she went beyond the "This is a no, no" repeatedly. This brought about her inner being about boundaries and brought forth safety and security for the environment in which she lived. I would call this the external and internal working model of attachments. She also got hugs and kisses and "I love you" after those rare little pats on her bottom.

Our daughter later had a child's table and two chairs in our kitchen, where she and her little friends played. I had tea parties with her there. She would, later in age, come down the stairs with her beautiful party dress bought at a toy store and the request to put her arm into my arm. We enjoyed talking and having proper tea or just playing like it. And this time together is all about attachments, safety, love, etc., that built neuropathways she operated from later. I got perhaps more out of it than she did! I know I miss it now that she is approaching thirty.

Some parents think expensive toys, if they have the financial ability, express love. Still, parents may not be engaged in the child's life. Those toys are meaningless to the healthy development of a child. I remember so well my wife's father (Gramps) getting on the floor with Em, under the coffee table, dancing to the '50s music in her toy store '50s dress and having a ball! Gramps got down the floor eye-level to Em.

When Gramps and Grammy came into town from Georgetown, Texas, they called when they reached 610 and 290.

Emily went out on the sidewalk and sat, and when they drove up in their prominent "aircraft carrier" — the four-door Lincoln — Gramps hopped out and jumped up and down, as would Em! That is connecting. That is love.

I was married before and had two beautiful sons I loved with all my heart and beyond the universe. As *YOU* were meant to be, *BOTH* of my sons were meant to be, and my *DAUGHTER* was meant to be! However, my sons grew up in a conflicting home during the sixteen years of my first marriage. I'm making a point here without any form or fashion of blame. But the truth is, they did not receive boundaries, a verbally safe and loving environment, rules, regulations, consequences, etc. I sought a voice, but children "learn to go the path of least resistance." I never knew from one day to the next if I was married or divorced over those sixteen years. I even sought a move to Fayetteville, Arkansas, to save the marriage from Houston, Texas.

Little did I realize there was a garbage trailer behind our cars, filled with issues that just followed us to Fayetteville, Arkansas. My stay there was only four years as I was unsuccessful in saving my marriage. I returned to Houston, Texas, which I knew was home, as I did not want to see my ex-wife living with another husband. My sons faced no consequences or responsibility, and I was silenced every time I tried to voice my concerns. Following her divorce from that husband, my ex had other men enter her life. My sons had to deal with this as they moved into adulthood and beyond. Flash forward to my youngest son committing suicide at the age of thirty-eight, and my oldest son at forty-nine is an alcoholic and divorced from his wife.

CASE IN POINT

An eleven-year-old daughter grew up in an unhealthy environment characterized by screaming, secrets, and no love. As I write this, she does not want to see her father again. That which is described above is *TRAUMA!* The person can heal from trauma, but they have to make a choice to seek treatment, find a competent counselor, and maintain focus and discipline throughout a long period. The person can create new neuropathways. I might add here that this is a fact, and I will share actual examples of lives that were healed, changed, and transformed.

Again, I remind you that it is ONLY THROUGH CHRIST that real healing can occur! You CAN experience being set free, healed, and transformed. You do the work, develop a relationship with HIM, and HE will do the work you cannot do. Guess what? It is on HIS timetable. Others will notice a change in you before you do! That is Christ doing the work.

I will add it separately here, again, as a reminder. SHORT TERM COUNSELING for people with addiction and those with trauma is not an answer, and it takes long-term counseling to be healed and transformed. Additionally, it's important to note that the intensity of the therapy can be reduced after a certain point. After every counseling session, there is work that the client needs to attend to. I might also add that what works for one person does not necessarily work for another. Just because a friend processed a specific counseling theory method does not mean it will work for you. I know what I am talking about here, personally!

So, do not let anyone tell you that you must have the treatment they specialize in. It must be for you! You must do your own due diligence. The counselor's job is to build trust with you, and a course of direction occurs from that. You work on it in the counselor's office and come back and do it repeatedly. Also, you must do the work, go to the group, and read outside the counseling office. It takes work, and I will repeat that consistently. If the counselor's specialty is not registering and functioning as the therapist seeks to give evidence, then leave that counselor. Also, if a counselor has not had issues in their own life, it is challenging for them to connect and have empathy with you. They are more of a TEXTBOOK counselor.

Just because that therapist uses this method in most of his/her sessions with other clients does not mean it will work for you! Be willing to speak up. Sometimes, no, in fact, many times, therapists jump on a new bandwagon of a new technique discovered, but let me say, it is not an all in all. There are hundreds of theories out there. Be careful who you choose as your counselor. Probe them to see if they are the one for you. If they have not had issues, if they do not give you homework, if they are unlearned in the issues that you have, say goodbye to them.

In the last fifty-plus years, the Western world has been a way of life in the breakup of the traditional family system, where the mother could stay at home as a choice and be there and raise babies into children at least until they started school. A variety of social, economic, and self-actualization drivers and goals created most of this change. The increasing demand for raised living standards and materialistic consumption also creates the need for the family system to be underpinned by two parents' incomes. As a young child, most of my aunts and uncles, including my grandparents, lived nearby. In my generation, people started moving away to more distant cities and out of state for increased income and, thus, longer distances from our hometown network. I did not get to know my cousins, and they became less connected to grandparents, aunts, and uncles themselves. Disconnect leads to less accountability and, many times, divorce. Divorce has exponentially increased since I was a child in the United States, I believe because of the disconnect.

This was prime territory for making a disconnect. That opened the door for no accountability, and divorces happened more often. The nuclear family breakup rapidly took place because those divorces caused wounds to the couple and big time for their children. Wounded children, in time, brought about the same pattern as what they grew up under, and thus, more divorces occurred. The children of divorce become traumatized; no matter how you slice the break, they become victims. Many parents say, "Oh, they will be okay," which I have heard a thousand times when they share they want a divorce and have children.

I stop the parents, and I look into their eyes in counseling and state, "You are wrong, and issues will show up in your children. Just remember what I say because it will come about!"

The attachment bonding processes of baby/infant years are also significant in the later adult years, in ways during adult forms of attachment via relationship and intimacy. Attachment patterns formed in intimacy usually remained relativity stable throughout childhood and adulthood, which means the same way of connecting or not connecting!

The key to supporting healthy brain development is nurturing and responsive care for the child's body and mind. Positive or negative experiences can add up to shape a child's growth and can have lifelong effects. Parents and caregivers need support and the right resources to nurture their child's body and mind. The proper care for children, starting before birth and continuing through childhood, ensures that their brains grow well and reach their full potential.

Children are born ready to learn and have many skills to learn over many years. It is of utmost importance that the parents are informed and educated about this importance. If they are not, and they come from adverse backgrounds themselves, they will repeat the same pattern they grew up with in most cases. Safe environments are the best places to learn, where they are protected from neglect and extreme or chronic stressors and have plenty of opportunities to play and explore.

Parents and other caregivers can support healthy brain growth by speaking to, playing with, and caring for their child. Nurturing a child by understanding their needs and responding sensitively helps protect children's brains from stress. Spending quality time is the key, and that means TIME, not minutes! Also, speaking with them, reading to them, exploring with them, stories that are made up and fun, and songs help strengthen children's language and communication, which puts them on a path towards learning and succeeding in school. We placed a CD in our daughter's room each night, playing soft Christian music or having God's Word process in a quiet voice. Remember, we are talking about brain development and how the healthiness of the mind is developed.

In the same way, I questioned God concerning my previous family and the breakup I might not understand, and let me confess I do not, with the COVID-19 virus! I have to accept that my God is in control. You may wonder, How did Benno get healed (considering all the stories and/or stories that have been written here and/or have not been told)? That will be further shared and discussed in a different chapter. Again, as a reminder about dripping faucets, I will add that here: it is all about CHOICE!

I have been married now since February 1989, and the home environment, far from perfect, has produced a child who has experienced health, again far from the ideal home environment. There were hugs, kisses, affirmation, storytelling, Christian upbringing, the church, the friend's parents having healthy couple friendships, and our daughter being friends with many of those children in those couple relationships. Also, prayer and the Bible were and are a part of our home; our daughter saw this from day one. Our daughter was born on April 25th and was in church on May 14th, Mother's Day. She met most of her friends in the children's area of our church when she was still in diapers. Our daughter went through her teenage years with her mom, perhaps more difficult than others, then again not as difficult as some.

We ensured that our daughter's friends were being raised like she was being parented. She grew up with five others, and they all graduated together. She, of course, had other friends outside of them, but patterns were being established. I must add that we were far from perfect, for sure! Parents must have positive environments around them from DAY ONE of their child's conception! Remember, parents, you are responsible for your child's development, as were your parents. Keep in mind, our main concern is the child's development, and this book encompasses more than just you.

Healthy brain development relies on appropriate nutrition as well. Remember, the brain is being wired, as millions of brain cells or neurons communicate with each other in the learning experiences by carrying chemical messages over tiny spaces called synapses. The brain creates more links and neural pathways by repeating these messages. These connections develop at a swift pace. That is why it is so important what a child experiences in the environment, from parent to child, parent to parent, and other caregivers, and being fed to them through healthy eating habits.

Remember, children mirror and repeat what they know. This affects the child's ability to learn a language, interact with people, read, play, etc. What influences did you grow up under regarding your environment? You are "evidence" in your physical and emotional health right now, as is related to your childhood? How did you get along with others in your youth and adulthood? Reflect on this. This is another opportunity not to blame but to take a personal and honest inventory of your past.

Children do not need expensive toys; they need their parents! Watching TV and other electronic devices are passive. Babies need to interact with their parents and other people in their lives and explore their world. Talking to a child is very important, and it is equally important to have a kind and caring voice. It is also about bonding and making a child feel safe. Hugs and kisses are so essential for proper brain development.

Children need a human touch. As adults, we need a human touch. We need this at every stage of our lives, and if we never got it, we can learn to receive it and stay there and not remove ourselves from that touch by another, no matter how uncomfortable you are, as, in time, you will enjoy it and look forward to it. I will never forget a call I got at the office some years back from a man with a New York accent asking about Battle Lines, and I shared with him from the beginning to the end of each meeting what we were about. I shared that in the end, we get in a big circle and put our arms over each man's shoulder or waist, and we have a prayer.

He said, "I do not like hugs!"

I responded, "That's okay. You can just stand there and be next to a brother, and I will shake your hand in the beginning when welcoming you, if that's okay?"

He said sure. Much later, tall and robust, this strong man welcomed my hugs as he came into the room for a meeting, as I did to other brothers. He made sure he got a hug each time he came! He later got married, and our Lord changed his life. What an amazing man!

If you are a parent now, how much affection are you showing to your children? Are you reflecting the same as what you grew up under? That reminds me here: one night, we had about fifty or so men in the group, and I asked them to share their first name and their relationship with their fathers growing up. Boom, it went around the circle. Almost without exception, the relationships were all negative. I told them I didn't want a novel or paragraph to be shared but a short sentence or two. Then, I asked them to go around again and share their first name and relationship with their children if they had any. Boom... the answers are nearly identical, suggesting a less-than-satisfactory relationship. This exercise was conducted to prove how patterns are repeated from our study's subject matter that night.

Childhood abuse, a study from UCLA suggests, is a hostile environment of the home and abuse or lack of parental affection. It takes a mental and physical toll that can last a lifetime. Childhood neglect increases the adult risk for morbidity and mortality. Always question: "Do I eat healthily? Do I exercise? What do my eyes see regarding movies and TV, and where does my social life come from?" As you reflect again here, what do you come up with in an honest inventory of your life?

When a child experiences stress, the hypothalamus (above the brain stem) releases a hormone that rushes to the neighboring pituitary gland. The pituitary gland then mobilizes a second hormone production that swims via the bloodstream to adrenal bands above the kidney. The adrenal glands activate adrenaline and cortisol. Adrenaline accelerates the child's heart rate and elevates blood pressure. Cortisol pumps up the blood sugar level, raising the child's muscle and memory power and boosting the pain threshold. Our fight-or-flight stress reaction is designed for emergencies, like life-or-death situations, not everyday life! When the brain experiences stress for extended periods, stress hormones flood our bodies for days, not just a few seconds.

Research shows that cortisol chews up the brain if it stays there long-term. Long-term stress has also been found to affect the neuron branches in the hippocampus and decrease the length and branch numbers. Again, this is where new learning takes place, and this type of injury to the brain, under chronic stress, will cause learning new things and committing new material to memory an issue. It's a major issue! It has also been shown that children under extreme pressure have lower IQ levels. Additionally, studies have shown that this negative type of atmosphere has a strong negative biological impact on health later in life.

One definition of "shame" is a condition of humiliating disgrace or disrepute. For instance, IGNOMINY is the shame of being arrested. Another definition is to bring shame to DISGRACE or shame the family name. Shame is toxic! Children believe what is told them is true, so they keep silent, even if they feel bad. Suppose a child is being bullied or humiliated by a grown-up or peer. In that case, it's unacceptable for that child to speak up and dismantle the abuse. Shaming is inappropriate at any time. It speaks to the child's soul, of their worth and value! Besides, it is demeaning in the worst kind of way! Children are to be built up, not to be torn down. What did your parents do for you? Mine were silent.

It's important to note that our brains have plasticity, allowing us to change our thinking, and experience both physical and emotional healing, even if we were raised in a harmful or abusive environment. Many experts report that physical exercise can help stimulate hippocampus growth, which fosters neuron development, especially in team sports. Maintaining regular physical activity is one way to help promote both stress resistance and stress resilience, as reported by Monica R. Fleshner, PhD, an integrative physiologist at the University of Colorado. Thus, I always ask, "Do you exercise?"

I thought it would be neat to show the attached image concerning the development of a child's brain:

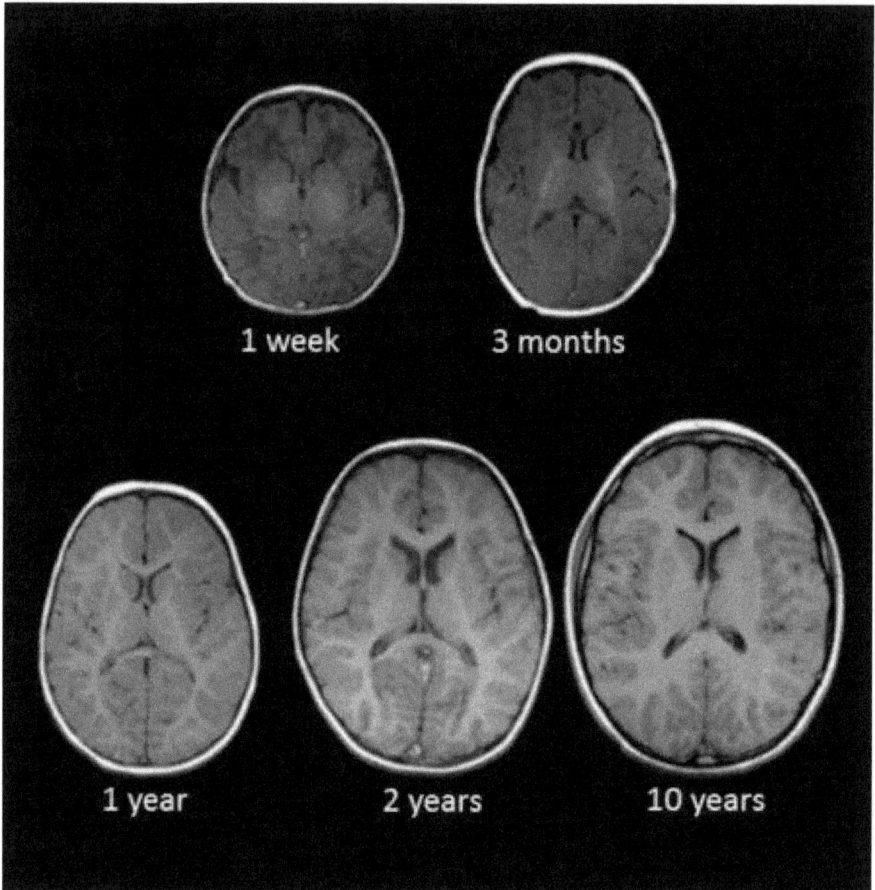

MRI scans of human brain development

As you look at it, consider for yourself those years of development and how you think your brain was shaped and molded, so to speak, as you move from year to year, from birthday to birthday.

Now, get in touch with trauma and how that affects a child's brain from an actual scan:

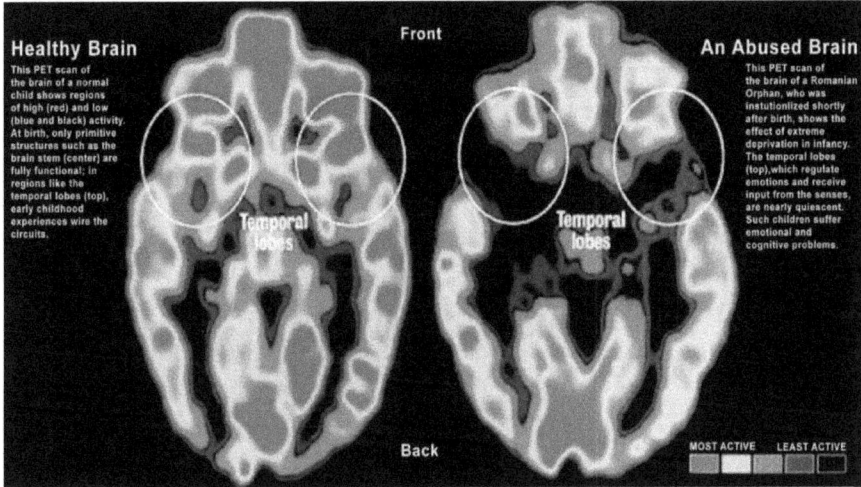

4 Ways Childhood Trauma Changes A Child's Brain and Body

Where do you see yourself? More on trauma will be discussed later, but for now, let's get in touch with this journey of healing, change, and transformation.

Childhood Trauma Can Alter the Developing Brain and Create a Lifetime of Risk.

Shall we continue? Yes, we will concentrate on the development of a child! The next chapter will be on ***trauma***. We have noted it in this chapter, but I want to get into the specifics of this concept.

ASSIGNMENT: Genogram of Your Family

Draw your own genogram for both sides of your family — do so on something like a butcher sheet of paper because there will be a lot of detail. Following is a sample:

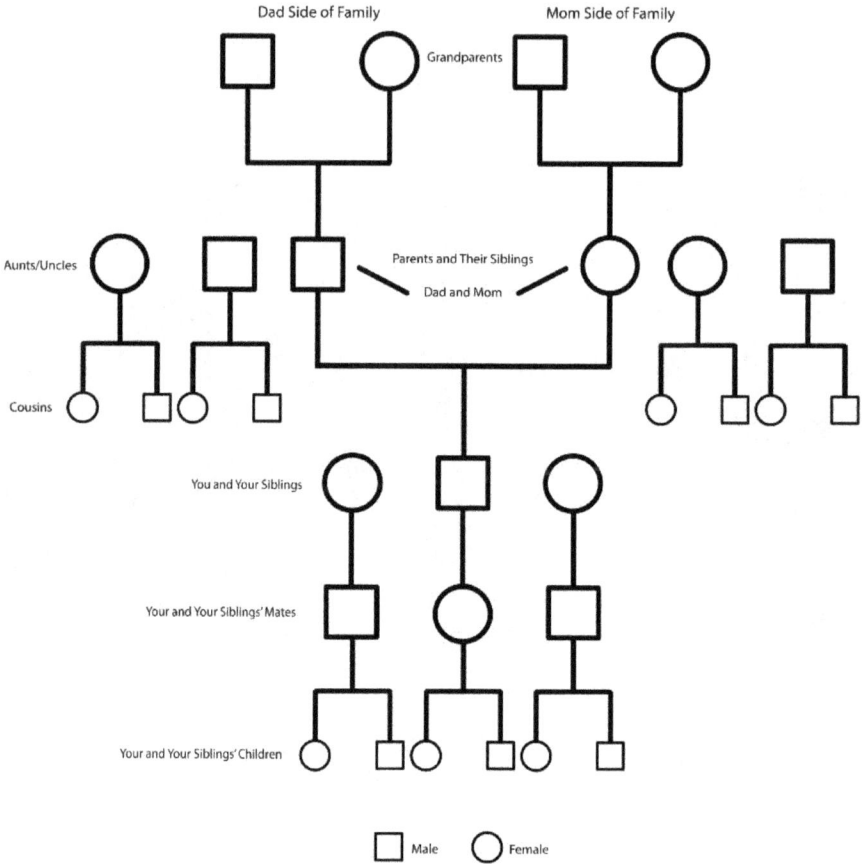

1. Your first step is to identify your grandparents (we could go further back, but I rarely request such)

   a. Write using a number system. I would suggest on a separate sheet of paper the type of grandfather and grandmother you had on both sides of your family. Were they really hugging, loving, touching, yelling, ignoring alcohol issues, drug issues, workaholics, encouraging, speaking down to you or others, etc.?

   b. Your parents' relationship with each grandparent, individual and what they heard in their homes, as children, as best you can describe it.

    c. If your grandparents were married before or divorced, show that and remarriage. Draw all this out.

2. The second step is to identify each child from each of the grandparents:

3. Your parents

    a. As much as you know, share what you know about your father's childhood, and also share about your father. Write positive and negative hurts, pains, rejections, drug issues, alcohol issues, anger issues, whatever.

    b. Then do so with your mom, as you sought to do with your father.

    c. Their siblings

    d. Write about each show on the genogram, male and female. Then, answer as you sought to describe your parents as per the above. Also, write out if there have been any divorces, remarriages, etc.

    e. Next, write about your parents' siblings and mates, again as you seek to describe your parents.

    f. Write next to your cousins on each side of the family, and describe their lives as you know them, again as the above.

4. The third step is to write about your siblings and how you all related growing up and now.

    a. Again, as per the above, what are your siblings married, what are those marriages like, and if there have been any divorces, etc?

5. The fourth step is to write about your parents and the home life you had growing up and to identify good, bad, and indifferent things about your relationship with:

    a. Your father is first

    b. Your mom is second

6. In the fifth step, write out the details of your marriage and your mate, following the instructions above.

7. What is the purpose? To get in touch by your drawings and writing things out — what emotions are being generated within you? The ultimate goal is to recognize patterns in your family and perhaps your mate's family that you have.

This is exhausting. Yet, it should be interesting and revealing to you.

1. Your mind is deceptive. Your mind easily distorts things. That's a blessing and a curse. If you write things down, you change perspective. Now, you are looking at it on paper. Does it still make the same sense as it did in your head?

2. Think on paper. When it's on paper, you can look your challenges in the eyes and slice them down to size. Your mind is powerful when it can more objectively look at things instead of swirling them around in your head.

3. It sinks in better. Writing it down creates a little more of an experience, and that helps it stick.

This assignment was not just to do so; it was to seek to find a pattern, but it also helps connect with the first two chapters for you personally and the environment you grew up in. It will also prepare you for what lies ahead in the future chapters.

What do you see in your family structure that has helped shape you positively and negatively? And it means all relationships, their patterns, personal lives, how they live, their belief systems, etc.

You can say, "Oh, that is just how I was developed," and leave it at that if there are many negative influences. You can also do something about it for yourself; change can occur if you are married and have children. How, by CHOICE!

ASSIGNMENT

1. As you get in touch with your family of origin after completing the genogram and doing all that is asked of you, the significant question is: DO YOU WANT TO BREAK NEGATIVE FAMILY PATTERNS? Again, list all of them that you see and that you have brought forward in your life. Rewriting what you have written for the genogram helps you genuinely recognize what change has to take place for you.

2. The great question: Do you want to get well?

CHAPTER 7
Do You Really Have a Relationship with the Lord?

Jesus came to set the captive free, and that means "free." However, there are conditions to what Jesus says in setting the captive free: you must have a relationship with Him. A *relationship* is described as follows at merriam-webster.com:

> *1: The state of being related or interrelated studied the relationship between the variables;*
>
> *2: The relation connecting or binding participants in a relationship: such as a: KINSHIP, b: a specific instance or type of kinship;*
>
> *3a: A state of affairs existing between those having relations or dealings had a good relationship with his family, b: a romantic or passionate attachment.*

In counseling and Battle Lines over the years, I always ask, at some point, "Tell me about your relationship with the Lord." Here are some of the answers, which are certainly not all-inclusive:

- I was baptized as an infant

- I was baptized at a beach retreat when I was 15 years old

- I walked the isles of the church at 12, and my father baptized me

- I read the Bible

- I believe in Jesus

- I believe that God's Word in the Bible, even though I do not understand it

- I grew up in a Christian home

- I went to a Christian school from K-12.

I sit there and listen, and when they are through, I tell the group, "You did not tell me one thing about your relationship with the Lord."

WHAT YOU MUST BELIEVE ABOUT OUR LORD TO BEGIN TO HAVE A REAL RELATIONSHIP WITH HIM

Belief #1

John 3:17 states, "For God did not send his Son into the world to condemn the world, [a] but that the world should be saved through him."

Belief #2

Luke 19:10 states, "For the son of man came to seek and to save the lost."

Belief #3

Philippians 2:5–11 also states:

> 5 Have this mind among yourselves, which is yours in Christ Jesus, 6 who, though he was in the form of God, did not count equality with God a thing to be grasped, 7 but emptied himself, by taking the form of a servant, [c] being born in the likeness of men. 8 And being found in human form, he humbled himself by becoming obedient to the point of death, even death on a cross. 9 Therefore, God has highly exalted him and bestowed on him the name that is above every name. 10 So that at the name of Jesus, every knee should bow, in Heaven and on earth and under the earth. 11 And every tongue confess that Jesus Christ is Lord, to the glory of God the Father.

Belief #4

Matthew 1:18–25 states:

18 Now, the birth of Jesus Christ[e] took place in this way. When his mother Mary had been betrothed to Joseph, before they came together, she was found to be with child from the Holy Spirit. 19 And her husband Joseph, being a just man and unwilling to put her to shame, resolved to divorce her quietly. 20 But as he considered these things, behold, an angel of the Lord appeared to him in a dream, saying, "Joseph, son of David, do not fear to take Mary as your wife, for that which is conceived in her is from the Holy Spirit. 21 She will bear a son, and you shall call his name Jesus, for he will save his people from their sins." 22 All this took place to fulfill what the Lord had spoken by the prophet, 23 "Behold, the virgin shall conceive and bear a son, and they shall call his name Immanuel (which means God with us)." 24 When Joseph woke from sleep, he did as the angel of the Lord commanded him: he took his wife, 25 but knew her not until she had given birth to a son. And he called his name Jesus.

Belief #5

Luke 23:26–43 states:

26 And as they led him away, they seized one Simon of Cyrene, who was coming in from the country, and laid on him the Cross, to carry it behind Jesus. 27 And there followed him a great multitude of the people and of women who were mourning and lamenting for him. 28 But turning to them, Jesus said, "Daughters of Jerusalem, do not weep for me but weep for yourselves and for your children." 29 For behold, the days are coming when they will say, "Blessed are the barren and the wombs that never bore and the breasts that never nursed!" 30 Then they will begin to say to the mountains, "Fall on us," and to the hills, "Cover us." 31

For if they do these things when the wood is green, what will happen when it is dry? 32 Two others, who were criminals, were led away to be put to death with him. 33 And when they came to the place that is called the "Skull," there they crucified him and the criminals, one on his right and one on his left. 34 And Jesus said, "Father, forgive them, for they know not what they do." And they cast lots to divide his garments. 35 And the people stood by, watching, but the rulers scoffed at him, saying, "He saved others; let him save himself, if he is the Christ of God, his Chosen One!" 36 The soldiers also mocked him, coming up and offering him sour wine 37 and saying, "If you are the King of the Jews, save yourself!" 38 There was also an inscription over him, "This is the King of the Jews."

39 One of the criminals who were hanged railed at him, [d] saying, "Are you not the Christ? Save yourself and us!" 40 But the other rebuked him, saying, "Do you not fear God since you are under the same sentence of condemnation? 41 And we indeed justly, for we are receiving the due reward of our deeds, but this man has done nothing wrong." 42 And he said, "Jesus, remember me when you come into your kingdom." 43 And he said to him, "Truly, I say to you, today you will be with me in paradise."

Belief #6

Jesus rose from the dead after three days. What is the significance of this? Here is what you need to understand, as best as possible, through faith and the Word: There are several significant reasons, including that Jesus was dead for three days before His resurrection. First, resurrection after three days of death proved to Jesus' opponents that He indeed rose from the dead. It is significant Jesus was dead for three days before His resurrection. According to Jewish tradition, a person's soul/spirit remains with his/her dead body for three days. After three days, the soul/spirit departed. If Jesus' resurrection had occurred on the same day or even the next day, it would have been easier for His enemies to argue He had never indeed died. Significantly, Jesus waited several days after Lazarus had died before He came to resurrect Lazarus so that no one could deny the miracle (John 11:38–44).

It was important for Jesus to be dead for three days to fulfill biblical prophecy. Jesus personally claimed He would be dead for three days (Matthew 12:40; 16:21; 27:63; John 2:19). Also, some point to Hosea 6:1–3 as a prophecy of the Messiah's resurrection after three days: "Come, let us return to the LORD. He has torn us to pieces, but He will heal us; He has injured us, but He will bind up our wounds. After two days, He will revive us; on the third day, He will restore us so that we may live in his presence. Let us acknowledge the LORD; let us press on to acknowledge Him. As surely as the sun rises, he will appear; he will come to us like the winter rains, like the spring rains that water the earth." This may also be the passage Paul refers to in 1 Corinthians 15:4, which says, "Jesus was raised on the third day according to the Scriptures."

The three days were significant in other ways as well. Jesus died on a Friday, Nisan 14, the day when the Passover lamb was sacrificed. His death represents the death of a perfect, unblemished sacrifice on our behalf. His resurrection on the third day took place on the first day of the week, illustrating a new beginning and new life to all who trust in Him.

Why was it necessary for Jesus to be dead for three days before His resurrection?

- So, the unbelieving Jews could not deny that Jesus had indeed been dead.

- Because three days is what Jesus Himself prophesied.

- Aside from these two reasons, the Word of God does not explicitly state the reason for the necessity of three days between Jesus' death and resurrection.

Belief #7

Acts 1:3 states, "He presented himself alive to them after his suffering by many proofs, appearing to them during forty days and speaking about the Kingdom of God."

After Jesus rose from the dead, he appeared on earth for 40 days in many places. He walked and talked in places where His ministry had been; He was seen in His restored body by thousands; He healed many; He continued to preach. He continued to love. And then He ascended to Heaven, taken up in the sky, which also was witnessed by others.

Belief #8

Acts 1:6–12:

> *6 So when they had come together, they asked him, "Lord, will you at this time restore the kingdom to Israel?" 7 He said to them, "It is not for you to know times or seasons that the Father has fixed by his own authority. 8 But you will receive power when the Holy Spirit has come upon you, and you will be my witnesses in Jerusalem and in all Judea and Samaria, and to the end of the earth." 9 And when he had said these things, as they were looking on, he was lifted up, and a cloud took him out of their sight. 10 And while they were gazing into Heaven as he went, behold, two men stood by them in white robes, 11 and said, "Men of Galilee, why do you stand looking into Heaven? This Jesus, who was taken up from you into Heaven, will come in the same way as you saw Him go into Heaven."*

Belief #9

Not only are you to believe the above and that the Bible is genuinely the Word of God, but you must come to that place of repentance, as Jesus said in Luke 13:3, "No, I tell you; but unless you repent, you will all perish as they did." Jesus also said in Luke 13:5, "No, I tell you; but unless you repent, you will all perish just as they did." Matthew 4:17 states, "From that time, Jesus began to proclaim, 'Repent, for the Kingdom of heaven has come near.'"

When John the Baptist began his public ministry, the first word out of his mouth was "Repent." In those days, John the Baptist appeared in the wilderness of Judea, proclaiming, "Repent, for the kingdom of heaven has come near" (Matthew 3:1–2).

Repentance is a heart attitude that is brought about by godly sorrow over our sins. Second Corinthians 7:10 says, "For godly grief produces a repentance that leads to salvation without regret, whereas worldly grief produces death." Repentance is the desire to turn from our vile sins and be cleansed by the pure, precious blood of Jesus Christ. A gospel message that does not include repentance (turning from sin) is not valid. Many false gospel messages are coming forth today by churches that tell the lost that they do not have to turn from their sin to be saved. They tell people, "God will accept you just the way that you are." That is a statement like Satan made in the Garden of Eden to Eve that has some truth and some lies, thus making it all a lie. When you are deceived, you do not know you are deceived. You can be deceived right into hell itself. Anything less than the truth is a lie. Also, this is why it is so essential for YOU to study God's Word for YOURSELF.

The truth is that we cannot clean up ourselves and make ourselves acceptable to God. In that sense, we can only come to God "as we are." Romans 5:8 says, "but God shows his love for us in that while we were still sinners, Christ died for us." Thus, God's standard is absolute holiness. Matthew 5:48 says, "You therefore must be perfect, as your heavenly Father is perfect. We have all come far short of that standard." Romans 3:23 says, "For all have sinned and come short of the glory of God." So, we cannot make ourselves acceptable to God because we are vile sinners with nothing to offer to pay for that sin. Only pure, sinless blood could do that, and we were born in sin.

Secondly, the false part of that statement is saying that we can come to God with the attitude, "Well, God, if you will accept me the way that I am and not expect me to change, then, sure, I will receive you as my Savior." That is a false gospel, and that is exactly what is being told to a multitude of people out there today.

That is not yielding to God. That is trying to make God yield to man and come down to His level. Salvation comes about when we humbly yield to God. Matthew 18:3–4 says:

> *At that time the disciples came to Jesus, saying, "Who is the greatest in the kingdom of heaven?" And calling to him a child, he put him in the midst of them and said, "Truly, I say to you, unless you turn and become like children, you will never enter the kingdom of Heaven. Whoever humbles himself like this child is the greatest in the kingdom of Heaven."*

Repentance is a heart moment that indeed comes with grief, sorrow, and a contrite heart to HIM and only HIM. Only in true repentance will there be a change of actions.

There is a new way of thinking about God, about sin, about Jesus Christ, and a changed disposition and a new way of thinking about holiness and doing things God's way! This Godly sorrow is a pain deep within that only HE can bring about, but it brings you to your knees and to HIM to confess all, not just doing it by checking it off or walking the isles of a church and "joining." This is a deep work of God. A cleansing takes place as you empty your sins before HIM. This is real stuff, and you feel relieved afterward.

> *I will hurry, without delay, to obey your commands.*

Psalm 119:60

Repentance is necessary for salvation, men! Not joining a church and being on its rolls is not repentance! This will get you into one place, and it will not be eternal life.

God desires for you to come to HIM and REPENT!

Belief #10

We are also to forgive. No matter how small or big the offense is, we must forgive. Forgiveness operates in the realm of sin — your sin to another or the other person's sin to you. God forgives people based on the sacrifice of Christ. "Bear with each other and forgive one another if any of you has a grievance against someone. Forgive as the Lord forgave you" (Colossians 3:13). Those who refuse to forgive betray that they do not understand how much of their sin they need to have forgiven. Christians should be willing to forgive people who have sinned against them. Every person has wronged God far more than other people have wronged them. Jesus illustrates the point in Matthew 18:21–35:

21 Then Peter came up and said to him, "Lord, how often will my brother sin against me, and I forgive him? As many as seven times?" 22 Jesus said to him, "I do not say to you seven times, but seventy-seven times."

23 Therefore, the Kingdom of Heaven may be compared to a king who wished to settle accounts with his servants. 24 When he began to settle, one was brought to him who owed him ten thousand talents. 25 And since he could not pay, his master ordered him to be sold, with his wife and children and all that he had, and payment to be made. 26 So the servant fell on his knees, imploring him, "Have patience with me, and I will pay you everything." 27 And out of pity for him, the master of that servant released him and forgave him the debt. 28 But when that same servant went out, he found one of his fellow servants who owed him a hundred denarii, and seizing him, he began to choke him, saying, "Pay what you owe." 29 So his fellow servant fell down and pleaded with him, "Have patience with me, and I will pay you." 30 He refused and went and put him in prison until he could pay the debt. 31 When his fellow servants saw what had taken place, they were greatly distressed, and they went and reported to their master all that had taken place.

32 Then, his master summoned him and said to him, "You wicked servant! I forgave you all that debt because you pleaded with me. 33 And should not you have had mercy on your fellow servant, as I had mercy on you?" 34 And in anger, his master delivered him to the jailers until he should pay all his debt. 35 So also my heavenly Father will do to every one of you if you do not forgive your brother from your heart.

The NECESSITY OF FORGIVENESS!

I like what C.S. Lewis gives about helpful insight on forgiving others, as found on the C. S. Lewis Institute website (cslewisinstitute.org/resources/reflections-january-2007/):

As regards my own sins, it is a safe bet (though not a certainty) that the excuses are not really so good as I think; as regards other men's sins against me it is a safe bet (though not a certainty) I think that the excuses are better. One must, therefore, begin by attending to everything that may show that the other man was not as much to blame as we thought. But if he is absolutely fully to blame, we still have to forgive him, and even if ninety-nine percent of his apparent guilt can be explained away by really good excuses, the problem of forgiveness begins with the one percent of guilt which is left over. To excuse what can really produce good excuses is not Christian charity; it is only fairness. To be Christian means to forgive the inexcusable because God has forgiven the inexcusable in you. This is hard. It is perhaps not so hard to forgive a single great injury. But to forgive the incessant provocations of daily life — to keep on forgiving the bossy mother-in-law, the bullying husband, the nagging wife, the selfish daughter, the deceitful son — how can we do it?

Only, I think, by remembering where we stand, by meaning our words when we say in our prayers each night, "Forgive us our trespasses as we forgive those that trespass against us." We are offered forgiveness on no other terms. To refuse it is to refuse God's mercy for ourselves. There are no hint of exceptions, and God means what He says. In comparison to sins like adultery, murder, theft, etc., unforgiveness might seem relatively minor. But Christ does not see it that way. Of all the serious sins he could have possibly mentioned in the Lord's Prayer, Jesus focused only on forgiveness (Matthew 6:12, 14–15). He knew that offenses come to each of us regularly and that we are prone to rationalize and justify our unforgiveness of the offender. He also knew that when we do so, we erect a barrier of sin between us and God which blocks our own forgiveness, as well as our prayers and fellowship with him, and leads to backsliding. Unforgiveness is a spiritual abscess that poisons the soul; the only remedy for this is forgiveness, no matter how difficult it is. Men, you must forgive all from the heart. The best way to forgive takes time and thought; as we live, we are to forgive from our hearts new offenses.

God can and will help you change your life. One of my clients left Houston, went to New Mexico, and borrowed his aunt's 4-wheeler. He went up into the mountains, spent two nights and three days grieving and forgiving, and left it all behind. It changed his life. Yes, God wants to change YOUR LIFE as well.

HAVING A RELATIONSHIP

What is having a relationship with your wife like for you? Do you spend time with her, to delight in her, and to enjoy her company? Or do you ignore her and have a void of silence between you? If we were to go around the room in Battle Lines and ask the men to tell me about their married wives, the group and I would hear different stories. Some met as teenagers; others were further along in life. Some were looking for a mate when they met their wives, and others met by chance or introduction and had no plans or thoughts to get married soon. For some, it was love at first sight, and for others, it was a process.

It is the same with your relationship with Christ! Your introduction was made by having been invited to a church by a friend, and that very day, words were spoken by the pastor that caught you, and you gave your life to the Lord that very day. You may have been in a crisis, and that crisis caused you to call out to Him, and He met you right then and there. Whatever means you met the Lord, to know HIM, you know Jesus Christ personally, or you do not know Him at all.

You can say, "Christ is my Lord." Just as Paul said, "Indeed, I count everything as loss because of the surpassing worth of knowing Christ Jesus my Lord. For his sake, I have suffered the loss of all things and count them as rubbish so that I may gain Christ" (Philippians 3:8).

You can know a lot about someone without knowing that person yourself. I know about James Baker, the ex-Secretary of State. I have read his autobiography. I wrote a letter telling James Baker how much I enjoyed his book and hunting. He was kind enough to write me a letter back, thanking me for the note and commenting on hunting. I do not know James Baker, I know about him. It takes time and effort to know someone by being around that person.

I am not in the place of really knowing either man. We do not have a personal relationship. All this to say that you can know about God, believe in God, know about Christ, believe in Christ, but not "know" our Father and His Son, Jesus Christ of Nazareth. Knowing is about a real relationship. What are you spending your time on? Is there time spent getting to know all about Him? Is your time with Him a duty or a pleasure? Is He another one on your "check-off list" every day? When there is no closeness, there cannot be intimacy with Him. Jesus stated in

John 14:21, "Whoever has my commandments and keeps them, it is He who loves me. And my Father will love him who loves me, and I will love him and manifest myself to him."

In the most successful relationships, partners not only afford each other the benefit of the doubt; they take active, supportive steps that foster a powerful sense of being on the same team. Research shows that in order to maintain a relationship over the long term, the *connection* provides individuals with a solid emotional base for pursuing their dreams and bouncing back quickly when they encounter setbacks.

In healthy relationships, our partners see us more positively than anyone else in our lives — perhaps more thoroughly than we view ourselves — and we can use their belief in us to get closer to our ideal selves. This is known as the "Michelangelo phenomenon" because just as the great sculptor could look at a slab of stone and see a perfect hidden human form, our partner's complimentary messages and signals of support can help us flourish.

Being in a healthy relationship should lead to personal growth, or "eudaimonia," the tendency to strive to be the best that you can be. Research shows that with the enthusiastic support of a partner, people bounce back better from stress or trauma, are more appreciative of life, and are more open to new things.

Although the term is often used as a euphemism for sex, the sharing between two people define **intimacy** as not exclusively a physical connection, and it is not exclusive to romantic relationships. **Intimacy** involves the risk of putting yourself out there. It tends to begin cautiously in conversation-sharing. Something emotionally meaningful with a new partner but evolves into a connection with someone we believe genuinely understands us. Once a **bond of intimacy** is established, it can become the bedrock of deep friendship and physical desire. Do you have that bond of familiarity with the Lord?

Having a relationship with the Lord is not about "religion." It is about a relationship! The natural man cannot understand this (1 Corinthians 2:14). Having a personal relationship requires one person to have a relationship with another person.

God uses the relationship (a healthy one) between husband and wife as an example of how our relationship should be with the Lord in having oneness with HIM! Scripture speaks of marriage as "the two shall become one." Just think of your wedding vow, and after the marriage is announced, you become ONE with that person. When your mate hurts, you hurt; when your mate has joy, you have joy, etc. When there is a divorce, one reason it is so hard is the tearing apart of one flesh. You will always have part of you with the other person.

In Scripture, when you have sex with another, you become one with them in the flesh. Note that I Corinthians 6:16 states, "Or do you not know that he who is joined to a prostitute becomes one body with her? For, as it is written, 'The two will become one flesh.'"

At Pentecost's time, there was an outpouring of Christ in spirit to those who believed in Him (1 Corinthians 15:45). The truth is, as Christians, we cannot honestly explain to the individual who has not accepted Christ what a genuine relationship with Christ is about until that person receives Christ Himself. Following in the Scripture, 2 Corinthians 5:17 states, "Therefore, if anyone is in Christ, he is a new creation. The old has passed away; behold, the new has come."

Like any relationship, once you have met, you must cultivate that relationship. As you meet the girl of your dreams, you must spend time with her to get to know her, and she to you. You get to know one another through conversation and shared experiences. You learn about her family background, her grandfather's stories, her parents, brothers and sisters, and other family traditions, and you know about her likes and dislikes.

In today's world, there is this word, "Churchianity," and this is a term that is used not as a personal relationship with Christ but as a member of a particular "religion." That specific religion can be a member of a Bible church, a Baptist Church, a Lutheran Church, a Pentecostal Church, etc. In one research, the phone may be answered at the church as "the church of the good news!" Those who attend or who may be interested are introduced to the "programs" and not what a relationship with Christ is about in many churches of today! Being a member or attending is far more important than a relationship with Christ Himself, it would seem. When was the last time, if you attended church, that you heard the word "repent?" You can become a member without even understanding the word "repent!" Many are presented with a "fire insurance plan" instead of a dynamic and personal relationship with Christ is about who is the Living Lord Jesus in the present!

John 14:1–21 states:

> *1 Let not your hearts be troubled. Believe in God; believe also in me. 2 In my Father's house are many rooms. If it were not so, would I have told you that I go to prepare a place for you? 3 And if I go and prepare a place for you, I will come again and will take you to myself, that where I am, you may be also. 4 And you know the way to where I am going. 5 Thomas said to him, "Lord, we do not know where you are going. How can we know the way?" 6 Jesus said to him, "I am the way, and the truth, and the life. No one comes to the Father except through me. 7 If you had known me, you would have known my Father also. From now on, you do know him and have seen him."*

> *8 Philip said to him, "Lord, show us the Father, and it is enough for us." 9 Jesus said to him, "Have I been with you so long, and you still do not know me, Philip? Whoever has seen me has seen the Father. How can you say, 'Show us the Father?' 10 Do you not believe that I am in the Father and the Father is in me? The words that I say to you I do not speak on my own authority, but the Father who dwells*

in me does his works. 11 Believe me that I am in the Father and the Father is in me, or else believe on account of the works themselves. 12 Truly, truly, I say to you, whoever believes in me will also do the works that I do; and greater works than these will he do, because I am going to the Father. 13 Whatever you ask in my name, this I will do, that the Father may be glorified in the Son. 14 If you ask me anything in my name, I will do it. 15 If you love me, you will keep my commandments.16 And I will ask the Father, and he will give you another Helper, to be with you forever, 17 even the Spirit of Truth, whom the world cannot receive because it neither sees Him nor knows Him. You know Him, for He dwells with you and will be in you.

18 I will not leave you as orphans; I will come to you. 19 Yet a little while and the world will see me no more, but you will see me. Because I live, you also will live. 20 In that day, you will know that I am in my Father, and you in me, and I in you. 21 Whoever has my commandments and keeps them is He who loves me. And he who loves me will be loved by my Father, and I will love him and manifest myself to him."

Is being a Christian about doing your best, or is it about a relationship with the Living Christ? To "know" God is about being a Christian — not about having a religion! You can be a member of a church but not have a relationship with Christ! God reveals Himself through the Word (the Bible). God has chosen to reveal Himself through His Son Jesus Christ.

God reveals Himself through prayer, your transparent conversations with Him, and also, as stated, through Scriptures, where His Word is proclaimed. When the "body of Christ" comes together, those true believers, Christ is in the midst of them. Being a reader of books about Christ from noted theologians who indeed exhibit or have exhibited their relationship with the Lord is another way to get to know Christ, like Francis Shaeffer, Bonhoeffer, J. I. Packer, etc.

The more of you that let go of your life and trust His life, the closer you come to know Him and trust Him. God speaks through His Word and the Holy Spirit. Can you capture your mind in His presence and listen to Him speak? He challenges us with His Truth if we'd just "but listen!"

Do you have love? Do you love your neighbor as yourself? If you do not have love, you do not have Christ! John 13:35 states: "By this, all people will know that you are my disciples if you have a love for one another." This is challenging, is it not? Love is the "mark" of a Christian!

Do you aspire to be like Christ? What is your benchmark? Your highest goal? When there is less you and more Him, you will not see it; others will! To know Christ, you must surrender all to Him! You must die to self so that He can live through you. One of my favorite Scriptures is the following, John 15:1–11, which states:

> *1 "I am the true Vine, and my Father is the vinedresser. 2 Every branch in me that does not bear fruit he takes away, and every branch that does bear fruit he prunes, that it may bear more fruit. 3 Already, you are clean because of the Word that I have spoken to you. 4 Abide in me, and I in you. As the branch cannot bear fruit by itself unless it abides in the Vine, neither can you unless you abide in me. 5 I am the Vine; you are the branches. Whoever abides in me and I in him, It is He that bears much fruit, for apart from me, you can do nothing. 6 If anyone does not abide in Me, he is thrown away like a branch and withers, and the branches are gathered, thrown into the fire, and burned. 7 If you abide in me, and my words abide in you, ask whatever you wish, and it will be done for you. 8 By this, my Father is glorified, that you bear much fruit, and so prove to be my disciples. 9 As the Father has loved me, so have I loved you. Abide in my love. 10 If you keep my commandments, you will abide*

in my love, just as I have kept my Father's commandments and abide in His love. 11 These things I have spoken to you, that my joy may be in you, and that your joy may be full" (John 15:1–11).

Just imagine in your mind that God is the "roots," Jesus is the "vine," you are the "branch," and grapes are the "fruit."

The fruit is Galatians 5:22. A branch only gets its life source from the vine and only the vine. It is focused, abandoned, trusts, depends, abides, and other words like that in its life source. You cannot produce the fruit; only Christ, through you, can the fruit be produced.

Many think that being a Christian is about not having strife in their life. Strife is about shaping and molding, as James 1:1–5 speaks. We learn obedience through suffering, or we turn away from that and seek out our own path.

We cannot know about the Triune God except through prayer, His Word, and Him revealing Himself to us. You can never know him through philosophy or speculation. We cannot know Him through our imagination or feelings. We cannot know Him through ideas about Him or the experiences of others. We can only know Him as He has chosen to reveal Himself to us. That revelation comes through His Written Word, the Bible, and through His Son Jesus Christ.

DENY SELF

Let's stop for a moment and discuss "death (Deny) to self" and "alive to Christ." What does that mean? Most of your life, if you analyze it, was and is about YOU. Oh yes, you care about your wife and children, but most people are "self-focused." They are interested, as you are, in the "I" of life! You can never walk into a deep relationship with the Lord being "I" focused, and you can never step into freedom from your addiction, being "I" focused.

The essence of a being's "existence" has to do with the fact that it is a "living reality." If one no longer has the functions of vitality, they are said to "no longer exist." So, the essence of "death" is the absence of "life." Therefore, when one dies, "one ceases to exist." That is pretty simple to understand, is it not? To carry the argument into the spiritual realm, when someone "spiritually dies to self," the self ceases to exist — that is, the SELF IS NO LONGER THE REASON FOR ONE'S EXISTENCE. As such, the individual is no longer concerned with "his own will or happiness" because he is no longer in the picture. He is no longer the center of his little universe, and he no longer continues to arrange the world around himself. In concept, I think this is pretty easy to understand; in reality, it is indeed another thing to do. The addictive man is self-centered about himself and his needs. He may not admit he is self-centered, but the fact that he is caught up in addiction makes a clear and unargumentative statement that he is.

Advertising, store displays, billboards, magazines, etc., are focused on having you "think about you." God's Word says you must die to yourself! In Luke 9:23, "And he said to all, "If anyone would come after me, let him deny himself and take up his cross daily and follow me." What did Jesus do at the Cross? He denied Himself!

Selfish thinking is what the world says mostly, and when I say, "the world," I mean secular beliefs. What do selfish people do? Some of the traits of a selfish person are as follows:

1. Are excellent manipulators

2. Are uncaring towards others

3. Plot and scheme against you

4. Are arrogant and self-centered

5. Find sharing and giving difficult

6. Put their own goals ahead of other people

7. Do not show weakness or vulnerability

8. Don't accept constructive criticism — they are not teachable

9. Believe they deserve everything

10. I would add, finally, they are fearful

In effect, selfish people's eyes are turned inward. It is all about "me, me, and me." I would further state that they are "actors," as they cannot be genuinely themselves because they want to control everything. They have to control everything; otherwise, they would have to face their fears and not let their guard down.

To die (DENY) to self is exceedingly difficult; it is excruciatingly painful. To deny ourselves is something that Christians find hard to do. In this world where there is pressure on all sides to replace the love of God for something lesser, to die to oneself is something that nearly every believer is averse to doing; since we live in a world of instant gratification, dying to oneself is a concept that is both foreign and unacceptable. Yet, this is one thing that Jesus insisted upon. Essentially, the Christian life is an ongoing process of denying self and living for Christ — seeking His will and Kingdom and righteousness rather than our own.

But as fallen humans, we are hard-wired to pursue our own will above anyone else's. We want our way in life. We all tend to see things from our perspective and define the world by how we see it. Though most people deny their self-centeredness, most men, by nature, are very self-centered and self-interested.

We were not born good or "others oriented." ***Our fall stemmed from "wanting to be like God"*** (Gen 3:5). Thus, many aspects of pride that characterized the first man also describe us! And "pride" keeps us from receiving God's love. We are so full of ourselves that we are inclined to think that our need for God is not that great. Because we are proud, we chase after other lovers to please ourselves, and that is the essence of idolatry. Idolatry takes many forms — a relationship we value more than God, the desire for material wealth that is greater than our love for God, and the desire to draw attention to ourselves rather than directing the attention of others toward God.

The world is full of idols that dethrone God from our hearts. **Anything** that causes one to have a "self-focus" rather than a "God-focus" is a form of pride and is abhorrent to God. The two things that keep us from God and the two main reasons why we need to die to ourselves are PRIDE (Self) and IDOLATRY (Desire).

We are not dead; we are alive. We died with Christ on the Cross with our sins when we accepted Christ as our Lord and Savior and believed the truths about Him. We are to be dead to sin and deny ourselves to those temptations that are not of God. How do we deny ourselves? We are to put Christ first and self second. It's about putting God's will over our will. It's about putting Christ first above everything else, no matter what it costs us. It's the realization that we are His servants, and as such, our goal is to live for Him and glorify Him in everything we do. When we came to Christ, we chose to make Him our Lord and invited Him to come to live in us. In doing so, we decided to give up our will for His. Since we decided to become His child and servant, then we must die to ourselves every day, every hour, every minute, every second — the greatest hope for each of us as believers is to die (deny) to self that we might **live** for Christ.

To deny ourselves is to know Him and His ways through His Word, through prayer, and the Holy Spirit is prompting us in life experiences, where we find ourselves fighting old habits of being about "me." We are being sensitized to do the opposite, doing things God's way, even though it does not feel right. That sensitizing, if you will, is the Holy Spirit, "Do not do it the world's way; do it my way, not your 'old way.'"

The individual who seeks to "deny himself" understands that God created him for a reason, that he is a part of God's plan for the world. To be used by God, one must understand the essence of who he now really is and how God can use him. Every genuine child of God wants to be used by God to accomplish His purposes in the world. Jesus said, "By this, My Father is glorified, that you bear much fruit, and so prove to be My disciples" (John 15:8).

That is the essence of God's plan; we are saved to bear fruit, created in Christ Jesus for good works (Ephesians 2:10). We bear fruit when Christ lives His life in and through us (John 15:5; Galatians 2:20), as I shared earlier. The apostle Paul said, "For me, to live is Christ, and to die is gain" (Philippians 1:21). The Lord wants us to live a godly and spiritually productive, happy life.

Obedience is not easy. Sometimes, our carnal mind doesn't like the idea of God having His way and us obeying it — it is the nature of man to "want things to go his way." When things don't go as we planned, when it rains on our parade, when someone says something unbecoming to us, when our world turns upside down, when difficulties and circumstances tax us too much, when we get turned down for a promotion, when we don't get what we worked so hard to acquire, and the long and short of it all is, "It bothers us! It rubs us wrong! It makes us angry!"

Here's the real rub: just because we live a life of obedience doesn't automatically make our situation better. Most believers think that by being obedient, the clouds will go away, and the skies will turn blue; their financial problems will disappear, and their little nest egg will grow again; their physical infirmities will go away, and their health will once again return. Sometimes, these things may happen, but at other times they don't. Is God still good? Absolutely. We will also conclude that being in God's will is far better than being outside His will. The secret to a "joy-filled life" doesn't lie in the absence of pain or in demanding our way but in "dying to self" and embracing God's will.

Submission to the will of God in your prayer life may be expressed in words like this: "Lord, YOUR way, not my way. Lord, YOUR will, not my will. Lord, You know me better than I know myself. You know my innermost being, and I submit all of me to You and trust that You will take care of me."

Only when an egg is broken can it be used. When a seed is cracked, can it bring forth the life of a plant? Jesus said, "Truly, truly, I say to you, unless a grain of wheat falls into the earth and dies, it remains alone; *but if it dies, it bears much fruit*" (John 12:24).

The world's philosophy says LIVE FOR SELF... **but God's Word says DENY SELF!** Many people came to Jesus and asked to be His disciples, but most of them turned away because they were not willing to give themselves to Christ, i.e., make themselves a "slave of Christ" (Luke 14:26, 33; 16:13; Romans 12:1; 1 Corinthians 6:19–20; 1 Peter 1:18–19). Jesus said, "He who loves his father or mother or himself more than Me, he is not worthy of Me" (Matthew 10:37–39).

The would-be follower of Christ must "deny himself," that is, he must disregard his interests and die to the willful, selfish, sinful parts of himself. He must let go of his plans and what he wants to do. The issue of dying to self is a process of stripping away layers of sin encrusted with selfishness — it is an integral part of sanctification. The disciples' instinct was to preserve their own lives, which caused them to flee from Christ at His arrest, but self-preservation resulted in spiritual loss (Luke 9:24–25). The disciples learned that the Christian life was not about them; it was all about Christ. It is about putting God's will over our will! It's about putting Christ first above everything else, no matter what it costs us. It's the realization that we are His servants, and as such, our goal is to live for Him and glorify Him in everything we do.

When we came to Christ, we chose to make Him our Lord and invited Him to come to live in us, and in doing so, we decided to give up our will for His. Since we chose to become His child and servant, then we must die to ourselves every day, every hour, every minute, every second! The greatest hope for each of us as believers is to die to self that we might live for Christ. An excellent question: "Did you come to Christ for eternal life (an insurance policy), but with exclusions in the fine print?"

With Christ as your Lord, it is either all in or all out. He cannot and will not stand being lukewarm! *"I know your deeds that you are neither cold nor hot. I wish you were either one or the other! So, because you are lukewarm, neither hot nor cold, I* am *about to spit you out of my mouth. You say, 'I am rich; I have acquired wealth and do not need a thing. But you do not realize that you are wretched, pitiful, poor, blind, and naked.'"* (Revelation 3:15–17).

Dying to self is never portrayed in Scripture as something "optional" in the Christian life. As believers, we are to "take up our cross daily" and follow Christ. It is our "daily cross" that makes us weep more than any other thing. And this makes us cry out like Jesus, "Father, why is this?" This can cause us to run to Christ and put our arms around Him. This can make us sick of the earth and self and give us a longing for Heaven. In 1 Corinthians 15:31, Paul said, "I die every day!"

The goal of death to self and daily cross-bearing is "fellowship with Christ." The purpose of life for the believer is to "seek God" and make Him their all in all, their last end, of all ends! Jeff Alexander suggests the following five ways that we embrace the Cross:

1. **Humiliation:** This is the essence of the Christ-life. Here, God uses reproaches, abuse, poverty, loneliness, persecution, distress, seeming failure, disappointments, and the like. These things succeed when they cause us to lose our own will and let God take charge.

2. **Rejecting the praise of men:** Self thrives on praise and adoration; self-esteem is the hotbed of self-life.

3. **Embracing simplicity and child-likeness:** Self feeds on things grand and glorious; Christ-likeness is childlike and straightforward.

4. **Living by pure faith:** Self depends on outward assurances; living by pure faith trusts the Word of God even when there is no indication of God's presence or

blessing.

5. **Seeking our nothingness and His all-ness**: We must make a daily habit of distrusting ourselves, our wisdom, and our strength and look to Christ alone for what we need. Men, we cannot do this in and of ourselves, as it can only occur if Christ is our all in all! Is Christ yours all in all?

Paul said, "I have been crucified with Christ; it is no longer I who live, but Christ lives in me" (Galatians 2:20). How can Christ live "in you?" Jesus said on that day, "I will be in you, you will be in Me, and I will be in the Father" (paraphrased by Benno). John 14:18–20 states, "I will not leave you as orphans; I will come to you. 19 Yet a little while and the world will see me no more, but you will see me. Because I live, you also will live. 20 In that day, you will know that I am in my Father, and you in me, and I in you." *Note verse 20!*

When He ascended into the heavens, He came in You through His Holy Spirit. Christ is in YOU, YOU are in HIM, and HE is in the FATHER. You walked into the eternal life when you truly, truly accepted Christ. This is hard to fathom! Some call this "Exchanged life." It is based upon Isaiah 40:31. English translations refer to those who wait on or hope in the Lord as being able to "renew" their strength. Many commentaries and study Bibles that deal with this verse note that the Hebrew word's literal translation for "renew" is "exchange." Those who wait on the Lord will exchange their strength for His strength, as stated in verses 25–30.

Here are some great resources on this subject: Hudson Taylor's *Spiritual Secret* (Moody Classics); *The Marvelous Exchange: Discovering the Power of Spiritual Union with Christ, An Exposition of Romans 6:1–14; Classic Christianity: Life's Too Short to Miss the Real Thing; Handbook in Happiness.* I always tell people to search for the truth for themselves.

I studied in Atlanta in the fall of 1993 at the Ministry of the

Exchanged Life, and it was a truth that I had not seen before, and I used it a lot in counseling. It helped in my life and my journey of change. Again, to point out clearly, God is still and will always be at work in me to chisel the old away and bring in the new if I continue to focus on Him. Paul said the same thing, as he shared Christ in the ministry that God placed upon him.

The term "Exchanged Life" is directly related to the believer's discovery of their new identity in Christ. The believer is a new creation, one born of God. What was once true is no longer true. J. Hudson Taylor made the English term "Exchanged Life" popular through his testimony of how God made him a new man (from Chapter 14 of Hudson Taylor's *Spiritual Secret*).

PRAYER

C.S. Lewis' literary demon *Screwtape* has something insightful to say. He tells his young nephew that humans rarely pray for the thing God wants them to pray for. They want enough grace to see them through some moment or time of trouble; they conjure up a vision of the future they want and appeal for that outcome. They persist in wrapping their anxious hands around life's steering wheel as if "it's going to work this time if only they clutch it more tightly." The most challenging prayer for us to voice is, ***"Not my will, but Thine be done."***

Our conversations with God regularly leapfrog over our intellectual resolve not to "ask for stuff" and land squarely on the bargaining and pleading table. The best we seem to be able to do is arrive at a compromise between what we know to be right intellectually and the howl of protest that lies within us. When we look at the Bible, there is a beautiful guide that Jesus uses to teach us how to pray. You can pray with the exact words. But did you ever know that our Lord's Prayer is also a structure of how we should pray? Jesus used this to teach us how to talk to God, our Father.

Why don't we pray the most well-known prayer in the world that Jesus said? After this manner, all who follow me should pray in this way. Do you all know what it Is? It is the book of Matthew 6:9–13.

Did you know that He didn't ask us to repeat that prayer? Neither were they the exact words we should always use, but instead, He said to follow this pattern in this manner. What I mean is it is more of a structure of how we should pray.

Did you know that the Lord's Prayer is a beautiful framework? It starts well.

Let's just say the first line goes like this: "Our Father who art in heaven hallowed be thy name." Let us stop at that and look at it. Do you know what that just was? All prayers first start by focusing on who God is and acknowledging His position.

He's our Father, He's in Heaven, and He is hallowed. The second part of the prayer is what Martin Luther called the terrible petition. The next line is, "Thy Kingdom come." Now, the first part is saying I want to focus on who you are.

Do you know what the second petition is telling you? When it says, "Thy Kingdom come," it is saying *God, I want you to control me.* That's why Martin Luther said it's terrible. He said, "Do you understand that if you ask God to control you, He's going to change your life?"

So, the Lord's Prayer is focused! Acknowledge God on who He is, then let Him control your life and trust that you are safe in His hands, just like you trust a pilot on a plane.

You don't need to see the pilot while you are seated at the back; you know the flight is risky, but you trust the pilot. Do the same with God. Let God fly you through this life, for that is what He does best if you board His plane.

The thirst portion in the Lord's Prayer says that "thy will be done." Do you know what that is? That means that you should be asking God to lead you. It means that you should let God's will be done at His pace as long as you trust in Him. You are putting God in charge and giving Him power since you trust He will never fail you.

Up to that point, we notice that Jesus, through the Lord's Prayer, is guiding us in three steps:

The middle petition of the prayer states, "Give us this day our daily bread." This means that you are asking God to supply. Notice it's in the middle. Up to this point, Christians should note that we don't ask God for stuff until we first have focused on Who He is, worshiped Him, surrendered to Him, and said I want to do Your will.

That's why Jesus said, "Anything you ask My Name, I'll do." You don't ask until you get to the middle of the prayer after already focusing on God, submitting to Him, and following him. Only then will He give you everything that you pray for.

Most people don't want to submit, follow, and do all that. They just want to say, "I like this, or I want this job or this grade or this person or whatever."

The last three steps of our Lord's Prayer are fascinating. It says, "Forgive us." Jesus says here, "Forgive us our trespasses as we forgive those who trespass against us."

What is that? Well, that cleanses me, Lord. I don't want to have any unconfessed, broken relationships or sins in my life. Cleanse me! This stage is translating that you should ask God to purify you after acknowledging His position, submitting to His will, and accepting that He should control you.

The next petition number six is "and lead us." This is important when you want to pray effectively and correctly. It says, "And lead us not into temptation but deliver us from evil." That means that you are asking for God's protection.

"Protect me from temptation; protect me from the evil one, Satan." Do you see why the Lord's Prayer is not just some words that we should mumble and leave it at that? It is a perfect way to pray, and it is the best way for beginners to learn to pray. It is a very effective way to pray to God and have our prayers accepted.

The Lord's Prayer is inviting God to:

FOCUS ME ON WHO HE IS.

To Control My Life,

To Lead Me Through Life as He's Leading Me, Supply Me,

Cleanse Me Constantly So I Don't Grieve Him,

Protect Me.

Then what's the ending of the Lord's Prayer? Here it is, "For thine is the kingdom and the power forever, amen." Do you know what that part is? That's the best part of the prayer. The ending, the seventh petition, is the best. It translates to "Empty me, so you get all the glory."

What does 1 John 5:14 say? "And this is the confidence that we have toward him, that if we ask anything according to his will, he hears us." We are to pray appropriately. I should not have to add, do not pray selfishly, but I will since that is the way many pray or have prayed.

Men, prayer is a must! Prayer is a must in your relationship with the Lord. You must spend time here, and you cannot give it tokenism. You must make it a priority in your life! Prayer is also about being quiet and seeking to listen to that still, small voice of the Holy Spirit. Prayer is a discipline; it must become a part of your day! A priority part of your day! Prayer is our way of communicating with God by talking to Him, but it's also a time to be still and listen for His guidance. Instead of simply running through our list of requests and moving on to the day's duties and activities, we need to *learn to be still* for a while to see if He has anything to say to our hearts. Quieten our day, let our minds relax and move toward silence as we seek to listen to Him after we pray or fill in the gaps in our prayer time. We must be disciplined.

Prayer is a Christian discipline, and we should practice and make prayer a habit. Adding structure, such as having a place, a time, a pattern, or a partner, encourages consistency and growth. You need your alone time, but it is certainly appropriate to pray with your mate or a buddy at times. Your mate cannot know your heart unless you reveal your heart. What better place to do it when you pray as a couple, revealing you're all before the Lord and her? You must be transparent to the Lord and to your wife. Intimacy can only take place with complete transparency. Holding back hurts God, who already knows you through and through, but your wife knows you and senses that you are holding back. It is part of that oneness mystery of being one flesh.

Let's look at Psalms 51, a prayer of David:

> *1 Have mercy on me, O God, according to your steadfast love; according to your abundant mercy, blot out my transgressions.*

> *2 Wash me thoroughly from my iniquity, and cleanse me from my sin!*

> *3 For I know my transgressions and my sin is ever before me.*

> *4 Against you, you only, have I sinned and done what is evil in your sight, so that you may be justified in your words and blameless in your judgment.*

> *5 Behold, I was brought forth in iniquity, and in sin did my mother conceive me.*

> *6 Behold, you delight in truth in the inward being, and you teach me wisdom in the secret heart.*

> *7 Purge me with hyssop, and I shall be clean; wash me, and I shall be whiter than snow.*

8 Let me hear joy and gladness; let the bones that you have broken rejoice.

9 Hide your face from my sins, and blot out all my iniquities.

10 Create in me a clean heart, O God, and renew the right spirit within me.

11 Cast me not away from your presence, and take not your Holy Spirit from me.

12 Restore to me the joy of your salvation, and uphold me with a willing spirit.

13 Then, I will teach transgressors your ways, and sinners will return to you.

14 Deliver me from bloodguiltiness, O God, O God of my salvation, and my tongue will sing aloud of your righteousness.

15 O Lord, open my lips, and my mouth will declare your praise.

16 For you will not delight in sacrifice, or I would give it; you will not be pleased with a burnt offering.

17 The sacrifices of God are a broken spirit, a broken and contrite heart, O God, you will not despise.

How did David pray, men? What we should be focusing on? When we're praying according to His will, we know that He hears us with surety to grant us our desires.

In verse number 1, David said: "Be gracious to me, O God, according to Your loving kindness. It's about knowing God's disposition towards you."

God desires to be favorable to you because he loves you. In verse number 2, David said this: **"Wash me thoroughly from my iniquity and cleanse me from my sin."**

Let's continue with verse number 6: **"Behold, you desire truth in the innermost being, and in the hidden part, You will make me know wisdom. Purify me with hyssop, and I shall be clean; Wash me, and I shall be whiter than snow."** Men, you cannot hide anything from God, so you might as well let God see the truth, and He wants you to reveal all to Him. You can only receive from Him if you are clean inside. "Make me hear joy and gladness. Let the bones which You have broken rejoice. **Hide Your face from my sins and blot out my iniquities."**

I want to focus on this deep longing in *David to be washed of his sin. "Wash me, he said, and I shall be clean. Wash me with hyssop."* David wanted to be clean before the Lord, before his seeking God in prayer!

Let us get serious right now: if we're not washed inside, get this now. If we're not cleansed on the inside, we cannot know God. The Bible says who shall ascend to the house of the Lord, but who has clean hands and a pure heart? Hidden sin does not work before God! It is not hidden from Him; you just think it is.

In other words, what God is saying here is that we can't walk in fellowship with him unless we have clean hands and a pure heart. Unless our nature is purified, we can't walk with God. It's called the law of similarity, that the more we become like Jesus, the more that we're washed on the inside. More of Jesus, less of ME!

Jesus said, "Blessed are pure in spirit, for they shall see God." The more we're washed, cleansed, and purified on the inside, the more connected to Jesus. His presence can be manifested within you and through you only as you are surrendered to Him and walk in His ways.

But we need to know a Jesus that's here, that's now, that's in us. Christ is in you, the hope of glory. So, we're not going to know him in us. We're not going to know Him within us in a way that will bring us deep satisfaction unless we are washed inside. This is so important! The only way is to REPENT specifically of all and name that specific sin or sins. To be forgiven takes place in an instant. The instant we receive Jesus, we're legally forgiven. When we surrender all to the Lord, believe in all who He is, and repent for our sins. *But to be washed is a process. The Bible speaks of transformation, and that is a process.* It's a process of cleansing *old ways of thinking and old ways of relating.* "Make me hear joy." And so, again, this is a prayer that we should continuously be lifting to the Lord: "Create in me a clean heart and renew a right spirit in me." Let's just pray to the Lord right now through that song. This is a deep calling because as we're washed and cleansed, and as his clean heart is created within us, we're brought into deep intimacy with Jesus. David wanted to be as white as snow. Do you want to be white as snow inside? What freedom that brings when we are!

Deep intimacy with Jesus is something that will satisfy us. *Things on the outside, although they're blessings, can never be satisfied.* "You see," Jesus said, "life consists not in the abundance of things." *The only thing that will satisfy us is when we become like Jesus because then we'll know him.* **Eternal life is about a relationship.** And so, when we look at this man of God's heart, when we look at David's heart, first of all, we find he has confidence in who God is, that God has goodwill for him, and that God desires to bless him.

Remember, the Lord said, "I know the plan I have for you."

Jeremiah 29:11–14 states:

> *11 "For I know the plans I have for you,"*
> *declares the LORD, "plans for welfare and not*
> *for evil, to give you a future and a hope. 12*
> *Then, you will call upon ME and come and*
> *pray to ME, and I will hear you. 13 You will*
> *seek ME and find ME when you seek ME with*
> *all your heart. 14 I will be found by you,"*

declares the LORD, "and I will restore your fortunes and gather you from all the nations and all the places where I have driven you." The LORD declares, "And I will bring you back to the place from which I sent you into exile."

So, David knew God in this way. He knew this was who God was. He didn't think that God was far away, but he thought that the Lord was kind of toward him. Men know this: God has a plan for you, not to harm you, but to bless you. And when YOU seek HIM with all your heart, He will make Himself known to YOU and deliver YOU from captivity! There are always conditions based upon promises in God's Word spoken to us by our Father.

David wanted to be clean before the Lord. Do YOU want to be clean before the Lord? It is a condition of God that you be so!

You see, we have a choice as to whether we're going to put ourselves in God's beam of light upon our lives. His LIGHT is SO BRIGHT, and there is no darkness with HIM shining that light on you. Many people are running from the conviction of the Holy Spirit, and the Bible says it's the goodness of God that leads to repentance.

It's only through the conviction of the Holy Spirit that we can come before our Lord and repent; otherwise, it has no meaning. That repentance comes from deep remorse regarding our sins and how they offended not our Father but ourselves and others!

The Bible says he's faithful to forgive us and to cleanse us from all unrighteousness. So David said, "Cleanse (wash) me." But we also have to realize that to be cleansed, we must cooperate with the Holy Spirit, and that means walking God's ways!

David said, "Cleanse me." But the Bible also says, "If we confess our sins, He's faithful and just to forgive us and cleanse us." So, this should be a deep longing in our hearts. We must confess! We must do it out loud. There is something about praying out loud that stirs the Holy Spirit, and we feel His presence when we do so!

I am telling you that with your prayers having this focus, such as David did, God will bring about transformation in your life over HIS TIME, not YOURS! You will not notice the transformation, as others will see it before you even feel it because your eyes are focused on the Lord and not yourself.

It will bring you into deep waters in your walk with God in terms of knowing Jesus and the river of living water that will come forth from your life as you're walking in a state, brothers, of being cleansed and purified. God desires us to move from wading to walking into the deep. God has so much for us, deep things of Him, and depending upon Him, trusting in Him is where He wants to take us into the DEEP. God desires to break forth within us, as Psalms says, "And that goodness of our Lord is released to the innermost part of our beings!"

It is in the matter of the heart that God operates. And this is where deep touches deep. And with this, as we walk His ways, seek Him in prayer, and read His Word, that transformation takes place from the inside out, and we become a new creation! In addition to this, He renews our minds, as our ways become His ways, and our thoughts are His thoughts because the Living Word abides in us, and we desire to please only HIM! And with this, our neuropathways change in our physical brain because we are DOING THINGS DIFFERENTLY! Watch your thoughts. They become words. Watch your words. They become deeds. Watch your deeds. They become habits. Watch your habits. They become characters. Your character reflects Christ when you walk this way. Another way to say it is: "Watch your thoughts, they become words; watch your words, they become actions; watch your actions, they become habits; watch your habits, they become character; watch your character, for it becomes your destiny."[xli] Do you have a focus on where you want to go and be? That is your destiny, whatever you so choose!

Men, nothing comes on a silver platter; we must do, as James speaks of in Chapter 2: *"Obedience is the key to the Kingdom of God."*

> *14 What good is it, my brothers and sisters, if someone claims to have faith but has no deeds? Can such faith save them? 15 Suppose a brother or a sister is without clothes and daily food. 16 If one of you says to them, "Go in peace; keep warm and well fed," but does nothing about their physical needs, what good is it? 17 In the same way, faith by itself, if it is not accompanied by action, is dead. 18 But someone will say, "You have faith; I have deeds." Show me your faith without deeds, and I will show you my faith by my deeds. 19 You believe that there is one God. Good! Even the demons believe that-and shudder. 20 You foolish person, do you want evidence that faith without deeds is useless? 21 Was not our father Abraham considered righteous for what he did when he offered his son Isaac on the altar? 22 You see that his faith and his actions were working together, and his faith was made complete by what he did. 23 And the Scripture was fulfilled that says, "Abraham believed God, and it was credited to him as righteousness," and he was called God's friend. 24 You see that a person is considered righteous by what they do and not by faith alone.*

Unless you develop a deep and abiding relationship with our Lord, you can never be healed and set free; all other ways are through human effort and mindset that will not last. Unless you're walking in The Spirit, you are walking in "the flesh." The flesh wants its way to do things, and that is why addicts stay addicts, why anger lingers, why self-centeredness is the focus, and the therapist who does not bring Christ in just cements self-back into self. If Christian therapists do not bring forth great techniques founded on those in the secular world, they fall short in ministering to clients.

WHAT ARE YOU GOING TO DO ABOUT YOUR PRAYER LIFE?

Christ must be your focus and role model, which requires us to walk as Jesus did. His virtues are found in the Bible, and you can know those virtues; it is all another thing to walk in them. Unless your eyes are heavenly focused, as I described, looking to the Vine and surrendering to HIM, you cannot walk out those virtues daily. You know already the testing that takes place, and as you truly surrender to Him, the evil one wants to come and steal all away. This walk is a daily step-by-step walk. Our hearts must be focused on Him, as Ephesians 3: "16 In addition to all this, take up the shield of faith, with which you can extinguish all the flaming arrows of the evil one. 17 Take the helmet of salvation and the sword of the Spirit, which is the Word of God."

Your morality is evidence in some respects of cleaning up your life. However, it can also be a flesh thing, where you are fighting and depending on your strength to live, and not live being surrendered to the vine. Others will know your demeanor before you do. They will see the Holy Spirit shining through you before you are aware of it because you cannot see it; you are looking to the Lord. Your eyeballs of your inner man cannot be focused on two places at once. This self-control comes through the strength of the Holy Spirit. To have self-control, you have to persevere and fight the temptations that come before you, as they undoubtedly do well. God does something in His time that you cannot explain in your being transformed. He is doing something in your life spiritually that you cannot do.

Godliness will begin happening in your life; again, it is something that you cannot do in and of yourself. One couple, whom I called "the Power & Light Company," were missionaries to Guatemala for over sixty-five years and were some of the wealthiest people I have ever met. In money, they had nothing, but spiritually, they were beyond description. They had calloused knees from prayer. They traveled by mule in the early years, and he was responsible for over 3,000 minsters coming into being.

They had to raise their support here in the US as required by the Assembly of God Missionary offices in Springfield, Missouri. They just glowed with the love of the Lord, and at the same time, had common sense and enjoyed life to the fullest, with his love of fishing and her love of her things, which included, I believe, eight children and grandchildren. When they retired, they interpreted Spanish at the Houston Memorial Southwest.

What is the greatest commandment? Luke 10:27 states: "Love the Lord your God with all your heart and with all your soul and with all your strength and with all your mind." And "Love your neighbor as yourself." You are to love YOU not in a self-centered way but acknowledging that He fearfully and wonderfully made you — and can make you anew. You are to love others, and again, unless Christ is the focus of your life, you just cannot do so in and of yourself.

Faith is where you must rest because we cannot understand all that God is about. Satan will want to shake your faith and believe me, you know so. In faith, we focus on Him, we trust in Him, and we hope in Him. We do so because we choose to trust Him. You will be tested on that faith as you are on this journey, but you can become like steel as He works in and through you.

In this journey of a real relationship with Him, you must allow the Holy Spirit to gradually work through you as He prompts you with His Word as you walk each day. He will remind you, and you must choose to listen to that voice. The more you give in to Him, the more readily you will hear that voice of His in a much louder way because His Word is the bedrock of which you choose to walk.

HOMEWORK

Have you discovered how amazing your life in Christ is meant to be? This list reveals the truth about who God created you to be and how He wants you to live! HE wants you to receive these truths deep down in your soul. YOU are to LIVE these TRUTHS OUT, no matter how you feel!

- I am complete in Him Who is the head over all rule and authority of every angelic and earthly power (Colossians 2:10).

- I am alive with Christ (Ephesians 2:5).

- I am free from the law of sin and death (Romans 8:2).

- I am far from oppression and will not live in fear (Isaiah 54:14).

- I am born of God, and the evil one does not touch me (1 John 5:18).

- I am holy and without blame before Him in love (Ephesians 1:4; 1 Peter 1:16).

- I have the mind of Christ (1 Corinthians 2:16; Philippians 2:5).

- I have the peace of God that surpasses all understanding (Philippians 4:7).

- The Spirit of God, who is greater than the enemy in the world, lives in me (1 John 4:4).

- I have received abundant grace and the gift of righteousness and reign in life through Jesus Christ (Romans 5:17).

- I have received the Spirit of wisdom and revelation in the knowledge of Jesus, the eyes of my heart enlightened so that I know the hope of having life in Christ (Ephesians 1:17–18).

- I have received the power of the Holy Spirit, and He can do miraculous things for me. I have authority and power over the enemy in this world (Mark 16:17–18; Luke 10:17–19).

- I am renewed in the knowledge of God and no longer want to live in my old ways or nature before I accepted

Christ (Colossians 3:9–10).

- I am merciful, I do not judge others, and I forgive quickly. As I do this by God's grace, He blesses my life (Luke 6:36–38).

- God supplies all of my needs according to His riches in glory in Christ Jesus (Philippians 4:19).

- In all circumstances, I live by faith in God and extinguish all the flaming darts (attacks) of the enemy (Ephesians 6:16).

- I can do whatever I need to do in life through Christ Jesus, who gives me strength (Philippians 4:13).

- I am chosen by God, who called me out of the darkness of sin and into the light and life of Christ so I can proclaim the excellence and greatness of who He is (1 Peter 2:9).

- I am born again-spiritually transformed, renewed, and set apart for God's purpose through the living and everlasting word of God (1 Peter 1:23).

- I am God's workmanship, created in Christ to do good works that He has prepared for me to do (Ephesians 2:10).

- I am a new creation in Christ (2 Corinthians 5:17).

- In Christ, I am dead to sin; my relationship to it is broken and alive to God living in unbroken fellowship with Him (Romans 6:11).

- The light of God's truth has shone in my heart and given me knowledge of salvation through Christ (2 Corinthians 4:6).

- As I hear God's Word, I do what it says, and I am blessed by my actions (James 1:22, 25).

- I am a joint-heir with Christ (Romans 8:17). I am more

than a conqueror through Him who loves me (Romans 8:37).

- I overcome the enemy of my soul by the blood of the Lamb and the word of my testimony (Revelation 12:11).

- I have everything I need to live a godly life and am equipped to live in His divine nature (2 Peter 1:3–4).

- I am an ambassador for Christ (2 Corinthians 5:20). I am part of a chosen generation, a royal priesthood, a holy nation, and a purchased people (1 Peter 2:9).

- I am the righteousness of God — I have right standing with Him — in Jesus Christ (2 Corinthians 5:21).

- My body is a temple of the Holy Spirit; I belong to Him (1 Corinthians 6:19).

- I am the head and not the tail, and I only go up and not down in life as I trust and obey God (Deuteronomy 28:13).

- I am the light of the world (Matthew 5:14).

- I am chosen by God, forgiven, and justified through Christ. I have a compassionate heart, kindness, humility, meekness, and patience (Romans 8:33; Colossians 3:12).

- I am redeemed-forgiven of all my sins and made clean through the blood of Christ (Ephesians 1:7).

- I have been rescued from the domain and the power of darkness and brought into God's Kingdom (Colossians 1:13).

- I am redeemed from the curse of sin, sickness, and poverty (Deuteronomy 28:15–68; Galatians 3:13).

- My life is rooted in my faith in Christ, and I overflow with thanksgiving for all He has done for me (Colossians 2:7).

- I am called to live a holy life by the grace of God and to declare His praise in the world (Psalm 66:8; 2 Timothy 1:9).

- I am healed and whole in Jesus (Isaiah 53:5; 1 Peter 2:24).

- I am saved by God's grace, raised up with Christ, and seated with Him in heavenly places (Ephesians 2:5–6; Colossians 2:12).

- I am greatly loved by God (John 3:16; Ephesians 2:4; Colossians 3:12; 1 Thessalonians 1:4).

- I am strengthened with all power according to His glorious might (Colossians 1:11).

- I humbly submit myself to God, and the devil flees from me because I resist him in the Name of Jesus (James 4:7).

- I press on each day to fulfill God's plan for my life because I live to please Him (Philippians 3:14).

- I am not ruled by fear because the Holy Spirit lives in me and gives me His power, love, and self-control (2 Timothy 1:7).

- Christ lives in me, and I live by faith in Him and His love for me (Galatians 2:20).

TRANSFORMATION!

In the Bible, transformation means "change or renewal" from a life that no longer conforms to the way of this world to a life that seeks to please God, as HE is the GREAT "I AM" (Romans 12:2). In this transformation it will show itself in your outward actions, and to those closest to you, will see it first. Still, you will not if your eyes are on Jesus. They may not be believers, but they may see a change. Get your eyes on HIM!

You can only draw near to HIM and only through the blood of Christ. And the evidence of true transformation within you and me is seen in the way we reflect the likeness of Jesus Christ.

Apostle Paul said, "You, however, are controlled not by the sinful nature but by the Spirit if the Spirit of God lives in you. And if anyone does not have the Spirit of Christ, he does not belong to Christ." The transformed life mirrors the attitude of the Apostle Paul: "I have been crucified with Christ, and I no longer live, but Christ lives in me. The life I live in the body, I live by faith in the Son of God, who loved me and gave himself for me" (Galatians 2:20, one of my favorite Scriptures)!

Also, without the gospel message of Christ, you cannot be transformed. It is the gospel that brings salvation, which is the Word of God, because it is the power of God for salvation for each believer. Men, you have to immerse yourself in the Word.

God's Word says, "Do not be conformed to this world, but be transformed by the renewal of our mind" (Romans 12:2). In your mind, I pray you desire to be transformed and renewed. You cannot do this separate from God; it is your walking HIS and doing HIS Word, and as you do his, plus prayer. God does something within you that you cannot do yourself! Of course, REPENTANCE and FORGIVENESS have to be part of this transformation journey! Surrendering to HIM must be part of this journey like a branch does in connecting to the vine (John 15).

God gives us the revelation of sacred Scripture so you and I can change our minds so we can begin to think like Jesus. Remember, when you accept Christ, HE (the Holy Spirit) comes in YOU. Sanctification and spiritual growth are all about this. If you just have it in your mind and you don't have it in your heart, YOU DON'T HAVE IT! But you cannot have it in your heart without first having it in your mind. We want to have a mind (don't you?) informed by the Word of God.

The Christian's character is marked by kingdom-minded, humble service. Humility is not a choice; it is one of the fruits of the spirit in Galatians 5:22. God produces it as we put our eyes and hearts upon Him, in surrendered, abiding, and abandonment to Him, again the branch to the Vine (Jesus).

Merely imparting information (in the world and church of today) to a human mind is insufficient! Knowledge apart from the love of Christ is nothing but "puffed up PRIDE!"

In Romans 1:18–32, the darkened mind continually shifts the boundaries of God's standards, moves, slips, and slides further into darkness. In today's world, unless you are absolutely blind and dumb, the treasonous revolution against the CREATOR is in full swing! Self-appointed, self-determined rights in pursuing dignity and liberty supposedly trump any outside influence, wisdom, or authority. LOST IS THE TRUTH that men are image bearers of God, created in knowledge, righteousness, and holiness.

What choice do you want to make, walking according to God's Word and HIS WAYS, or the watered-down, secular message to the church and society of today? The first, you get captured into darkness, and second, you get captured into THE LIGHT!

Unless the gospel fuels the way you and I live, we live by the flesh and the world. It is living according to the gospels that the transformation of our lives has taken place by the RENEWAL OF OUR MINDS.

The renewed mind is marked by reliance upon God's Word, the Bible, the only infallible rule for faith and practice. IT IS TOTALLY SUFFICIENT! Through the LIGHT of SCRIPTURE, we understand God's holy character, realize our sinfulness, and discover why we long to turn from the world to the fellowship of God Almighty. This is a process, but it is also the process of transformation. Our old desires become less of the past, and our current desires and future are to please and honor HIM. Again, this is a process of change, as Paul the apostle was in that process until his life was taken.

My question to you is, do you want this kind of life?

PRAYER SUGGESTIONS

In time, develop your own prayers from your heart! Pray

always out loud! Pray from the depths of your being!

Heavenly Father, I pray that You forgive me of all my sins of commission, sins of omission, and any unknown sins according to Psalms 19:12. Heavenly Father, I repent for all of my sins, and I ask You to forgive me of all my sins, iniquities, trespasses and transgressions and to cover them with the blood of the Lord Christ Jesus, and to cleanse me of all unrighteousness. I ask You to do this in the Name of the Lord and Savior Jesus Christ according to Your Word, 1 John 1:9.

I am thankful for this day, for this is the day that You have made. I will rejoice and be glad in it. I am thankful that Jesus died on the cross for me, knowing it cleanses me from all unrighteousness according to 1 John 1:9 and allows me to come boldly to the throne of grace according to Hebrews 4: 16. I am thankful for the power in the blood of the Lord Jesus Christ to protect, cleanse, heal, deliver, sanctify, redeem, justify, and to make all things new.

I declare and decree that where the Blood of Jesus Christ is applied, Satan cannot enter, according to Hebrews 10:4–23. I confess now that Jesus is Lord over my family, church, finances, businesses, jobs, and possessions.

Thank You, Heavenly Father, for Your Holy Spirit. Thank You for always being present with me. Thank You for the gifts of the Spirit: Heavenly Father, I praise and thank You for everything You have done, for everything You are doing, and for everything You are going to do. Blessed be to You, Lord.

Heavenly Father, I know that my battle is not with flesh and blood but against principalities, against powers, against the rulers of darkness of this age, against spiritual wickedness in high places. Therefore, I put on the whole armor of God so that I may be able to withstand an evil day, and having done all to stand. I will be strong in You, Lord, and in the power of Your might, according to Ephesians 6:10–13. I have Christ in me, the hope of glory, according to Colossians 1:27, so I shall prevail because the battles are not mine, but Yours Lord, according to 1 Samuel 17:47.

Heavenly Father, I now put on the breastplate of Righteousness according to Ephesians 6:14. I crucify my flesh now according to Romans 8:13, as I die daily from self-desires and live to do Your desires according to 1 Corinthians 15:31. In the name of Christ Jesus, I command the mind of my flesh to shut up: Don't talk to me about sin for I am dead to sin, according to Romans 6:2. Don't talk to me about condemnation, for there is no condemnation in me because I am in Christ according Romans 8:1; I walk after the Spirit and not after the flesh according to Romans 8:4. I have been healed by the stripes of Jesus according to Isaiah 53:5. I have been redeemed from the curse of the law according to Galatians 3:13; I am blessed when I come in and blessed when I go out. I am blessed in the city and blessed in the country. Let everything I touch be blessed and prosper, according to Deuteronomy 28:3–6. All these blessings shall come upon me and overtake me because we obey the Voice of the Lord our God. Thank You, God, that You did not give us the spirit of fear, but of power, and of love, and of a sound mind, according to 2 Timothy 1:7.

Heavenly Father, I now put on the Helmet of Salvation. I declare that we are spiritually minded according to Romans 8:6 and have the mind of Christ according to 1 Corinthians 2:16. I take off the carnal way of thinking according to Romans 12:2. When I put on this helmet, I no longer allow my five carnal senses to affect the way that I think. I exercise my spiritual senses, spiritual hearing, spiritual sight, spiritual touch, spiritual taste, and spiritual smell according to Romans 8:14. I thank You for being my God of peace, Jehovah Shalom, according to Judges 6:24. (You should pray this prayer every morning before you begin your day!)

Heavenly Father, I now gird my loins with Your belt of Truth. I am set free from bondages and strongholds according to II Corinthians 10:4. I now operate in discernment according to Hebrews 5:14 that I may continue to be free. I take off all dependency on the flesh and dependency on anything in this world or this world system. I trust and depend completely on You, Jesus, according to Psalms 31:1. I thank You that You are my Healer, Jehovah Rophe, and You are my Provider, Jehovah Jireh.

Heavenly Father, I now cover my feet with the preparation of the Gospel of Peace Sandals, enabling me to walk in the spirit so I won't fulfill the lust of the flesh according to Galatians 5:16. I thank You that the spirit leads me, and I walk in the light, as Jesus is, the light according to 1 John 1:7. As I cover my feet with this preparation, I take off vanity, pride, darkness, and ignorance according to Colossians 3:8–10.

Heavenly Father, I now put the shield of faith, which protects me from all fiery darts of the enemy, according to Ephesians 6. As I put on the Shield of Faith, I will take off all fear, mistrust, unthankfulness, unfaithfulness, and disobedience.

Heavenly Father, I now put on my hands the sword of the Spirit, the Word of God, which I choose to use against all forces of evil. I declare that I will defeat the enemy with the Word of God as the Spirit of God leads me, according to Revelation 19:11–16. I put away all murmuring, complaining, condemning, and criticizing. I now take the Sword of the Spirit and use the authority that God has ordained me with according to Luke 9:1, for I have been given all authority over all powers and principalities according to Luke 10:19. In Jesus' name, I pray in faith in Christ Jesus. Amen.

THE SECRET OF THE BELIEVER'S LIFE

The Vine and the Branches (John 15)

15 I am the true Vine, and my Father is the gardener. 2 He cuts off every branch in me that bears no fruit, while every branch that does bear fruit he prunes[a] so that it will be even more fruitful. 3 You are already clean because of the word I have spoken to you. 4 Remain in me, as I also remain in you. No branch can bear fruit by itself; it must remain in the vine. Neither can you bear fruit unless you remain in me.

5 I am the vine; you are the branches. If you remain in me and I in you, you will bear much fruit; apart from me, you can do nothing. 6 If you do not remain in me, you are like a branch that is thrown away and withers; such branches are picked up, thrown into the fire, and burned. 7 If you remain in me and my words remain in you, ask whatever you wish, and it will be done for you.

The only place the branch gets its life is from the vine. In effect, it does the following for its "life support:"

1. Focuses on the Vine
2. Depends on the Vine
3. Trust in the Vine
4. Abides in the Vine
5. Abandonment to the Vine
6. Surrendered to the Vine
7. etc.

The branch ***DOES NOT*** DERIVE ITS LIFE SOURCE from the "sun," the "rain," the "farmer," the "sky," and the "fertilizer." ***The only place the branch gets its life source is***

from the Vine.

THE VINE IS JESUS — this is the only place that you can get your life source, and that is Christ and Christ alone! He is the VINE, and without HIM, you can do nothing. Fruit is Galatians 5:22; however, you cannot produce it. Christ can only produce it through you as you abide in HIM.

To have that relationship with the Lord, you must become a "branch," totally focusing on the vine. Not church, not acts of doing, not being in the right zip code, not with titles and monies, etc.

ASSIGNMENT:

1. Do you really have a deep and abiding relationship with the Lord? Explain how that is?

2. Do you not have that personal relationship with the Lord? Explain where you are with this question. And you have to be honest! There is no judgment from anyone, so do not receive any guilt or shame.

3. The key to true healing will only come from HIM in HIS time, as you take part, work, counsel, read, group, accountability, seek HIM, and choose to walk new ways! Do you believe this?

4. I want you to reread this chapter three times and see how it registers with you!

5. Are you ready to surrender your life to the Lord? This is a simple prayer, but it has to be prayed not with intellect but from the heart:

   Jesus, I believe you are the Son of God, that you died on the cross to rescue me from sin and death and to restore me to the Father. I choose now to turn from my sins, my self-centeredness, and every part of my life that does not please you. I choose you. I give myself to you. I receive your forgiveness and ask you to take your rightful place in my life as my Savior and Lord. Come reign in my heart, fill me with your love and your life, and help me become a truly loving person like you. Restore me, Jesus. Live in me. Love through me. Thank you, God. In Jesus' name I pray. Amen.

6. DO YOU WANT TO GET WELL? Explain!

CHAPTER 8
Trauma

Again, to remind you, some define trauma as anything less than nurturing, and I agree. Throughout my counseling and in leading Battle Lines, childhood issues were prevalent to a very high percentage of men who attended. Many times, and I would again say a high percentage, they could not identify with the word "trauma." Still, as we peeled back the "onion" layers, they started to have more in-depth insight and understanding of how adverse childhood experiences affected them and their well-being.

Many think that trauma is being in a war and experiencing horrifying events, losing a loved one at an early age, or being in a terrifying car wreck. These are a trauma for sure, but the effect of childhood trauma is no less the same.

Sharing about a man named "61." As a child, he was a happy, curious kid who earned excellent grades, and as a child, he loved the outdoors, and because of that, he joined the Boy Scouts. But those camping trips soon became terrifying. On the pretense of separating a boisterous group, the scoutmaster brought this young, innocent, and naïve boy into his tent. He then sexually abused him. The child was frozen and taken captive in his trauma, as most children are. For this individual, it frequently happened over four years.

Besides a brief mention to his wife years later, counting it as nothing, he told no one else. This was his "secret," bedded in "shame & guilt."

There is a lot of shame with that, as noted, for this victim, and the thinking is no one will understand this. The shame always comes back to, "Was it my fault?" Many victims share these thoughts, and I've heard similar stories for years, albeit in different forms.

Not long after the abuse started, the child will seek ways to "kill the pain" and may sneak alcohol from his father's liquor cabinet. The child could withdraw and build emotional barriers or become heavily involved in sports, excel academically, read extensively, or become engrossed in computers to unintentionally escape. Let us say he married his high school sweetheart. However, after a while, she could not put up with his bouts of anger and continuous drinking issues.

After she left and they divorced, this man got help and cleaned up his act. He went through chemical abuse treatment, and the couple remarried. However, he knew he still had not dealt with the deep wound of sexual abuse.

"It takes a lot to come to terms with this," this man might say. "I worked hard on myself to be a better person and understand who I was."

"Adults age fifty and older are far less likely than younger people to reveal a childhood trauma of any kind," said Michael Barnes, clinical program manager at CeDAR, the Center for Dependency, Addiction, and Rehabilitation, at the University of Colorado Hospital in Aurora, Colorado.

"I think some of that is generational and the view of counseling," he said, "and there's a significant difference between men and women." Women are more likely to tell others. Barnes said men are socialized to be stoic and not complain. He estimated that thirty to ninety percent of the patients seen at his addiction program on any given day had some childhood trauma.

Scott Easton of the Boston College School of Social Work has studied how childhood sexual abuse affects men in later life. In one study, which received a federal National Institute on Aging grant, the men who were sexually abused as kids waited an average of **twenty years** before telling a single person about the abuse. It took **them twenty-eight years** to give a fuller account to someone else.

"The longer they waited, the worse their mental health," Easton said.

Children don't know how to process a traumatic event or environment. According to the Australian abuse support group Blue Knot Foundation, children who experience childhood abuse or trauma often grow to distrust others due to being betrayed by the very adults who were supposed to teach, nurture, and protect them.

A study titled "Long-term effects of childhood abuse on the quality of life and health of older people: results from the Depression and Early Prevention of Suicide in General Practice Project" and published in the *Journal of the American Geriatrics Society* found that more than 21,000 child abuse survivors aged sixty and older in Australia reported a greater rate of failed marriages and relationships. Abuse survivors were more likely to rate themselves "not happy at all" or "not very happy." The rate of attempted suicide was four to five times higher among abuse survivors compared to those who had not been abused.

Others with a history of childhood trauma may later experience problems such as these, according to experts:

- Anxiety
- Sadness and depression
- Hypervigilance
- Drug or alcohol abuse
- Addiction to gambling or shopping
- Feelings of alienation
- Feelings of hopelessness
- Low self-esteem
- Adult relationships with abusers

Another common trait among trauma survivors is the need for *control.*

"Control can look one of two different ways: 'I'm going to

control everyone and everything around me, so I can feel safe,' or 'I'm going to withdraw from everything and control by *not* participating,'" Barnes said. "So, many older folks are underemployed (or) they may work in very independent kinds of work."

Many times, as a child or a young adult, they make a vow, "I will never allow anyone to hurt me like that again!" Unknowingly, they put up an emotional wall where no one can penetrate it. They cannot realize the impact of that vow, originating from the depth of their soul, on themselves and on everyone involved in their relationships. Vows, as such, become self-fulfilling prophecies!

Regarding sexual abuse, which is one trauma that is blatant in its reality, here are some other stories:

- As a child, this young boy's stepdad would come into his room at night, and the child pretended to be asleep as his stepdad fondled him and had an orgasm on him.

- As a young child, with his father being a pastor, two different youth pastors molested him; he kept it a secret and did not let anyone know about it until he found out about his having an affair at 48. He told his wife that for the first time. This man acted out with women, transvestites, and men. After his wife became aware of his latest affair at 48, he confessed it to his wife for the first time. Subsequently, he sought counseling, took part in my addiction group, embraced the teachings of the Word, practiced accountability, and dedicated himself to studying and following God's Word. His commitment and transformation led him to become one of my leaders in Battle Lines.

- As a young boy, his mom would walk around in her underwear and bra or no clothes. Later, this boy, as a teenager, began acting out sexually.

- As a child, his parents moved to the United States and left him and his brother to live with an aunt. The aunt had a TV in her home that had rabbit ears. By accident, he found if he manipulated the antennas, he would somehow come up with scrambled TV and see sexual TV shows. As he grew older, he accidentally noticed the neighbor's home was receiving adult movies on their TV. He went and spliced the TV line also into his aunt's house and continued to flood his mind with porn and masturbation. He felt abandoned by his parents, and he did not see them again for twelve years.

- This young boy, in another country, his father would take him to strip clubs and see his dad have other relationships, which is "part of the culture," where he began early on sexually acting out. His mother whipped him with a whip with multiple leather strings at the end, with knots tied into them at the tip of the lines. His sister became a prostitute, and his parents kicked him out of the home at thirteen to make it independently. This man became self-reliant, highly intelligent, and resourceful. He never acted out in marriage but did so before marriage. But because of his eyes wandering, looking at other women, and his wife knowing about his past, she became very suspicious of him, and he would be under constant questioning; later, in their marriage with children, she separated from him. He experienced a transformation in his life through counseling, group support, accountability, and a genuine relationship with the Lord, which ultimately resulted in the healing of their marriage.

- On a mission trip to Mexico with the youth group, a pastor molested the young teenage boy there. The boy kept the secret with shame. He acted out sexually by masturbating and looking at porn.

- As a child in a home of many children, next to the youngest, he remembers lying on the floor of the kitchen crying. His mother would not pick him up but did so for the youngest child. His dad was verbally and physically abusive. This man (client) became a perfectionist who excelled in athlete education in his compulsory school (K-12) and university. He became a multimillionaire, married a beautiful lady, and had children. His dark secret was his sexually acting out with women, but also with men. His secret came to light, leading to his wife divorcing him. He always felt inadequate and unloved, had low self-esteem, etc. Yet, beyond successful in the corporate world. In Battle Lines, he would weep, weep, with the cost of his addiction.

I frequently became the first person to learn about their sexual abuse or other forms of trauma. And note that I would have never known if I had not taken the history of their lives. Many felt shame as they shared it, and I would let them know, in no uncertain terms, that as a child, they did not have the mental capacity to process it all. I shared how our brain develops, with the last part being around twenty-four. I also had them look me in the eye and share that they were the child and an adult did this to them. I told them that our Lord fearfully and wonderfully made them and that the shame they carried was "false shame," nevertheless, it did not make their shame hurt less. They did not know. Educating clients is a big part of the therapist's responsibility. Few therapists do that in counseling and in support groups. To tickle your brain, I'll add that without vulnerability and transparency in counseling and in groups, healing will be challenging to achieve. Trust is a thing the sexually abused person will not have toward others or from others.

Since I brought up the word abandonment above, let us talk about that in the scope of trauma. A parent can be in the home but has abandoned the child emotionally, as they may be perhaps so caught up in themselves with their work, their golf, etc. They never engage with the child, play with them, see how their school day went, etc. You will recall how Archie Manning made sure he was connected to his three boys. He did so based on each son's personality. Love and affection were a significant part of that almost daily connection. The three sons did not doubt that they were loved. When you do not have this, that is abandonment.

When a parent leaves through a divorce, and there is limited and/or no connection to that child, and most times stays with the mom, they feel abandoned. That, my friends, is trauma! We live in a world of disconnect today. Divorce after divorce carries forward to the next generation. Abandonment issues run high among those who are now adults and who were once children. It is a pandemic in our society today!

The above paragraph describes this as emotional abandonment resulting from a significant person discarding, dismissing, devaluing, or not acknowledging you. This type of invisible injury causes great harm to the recipient. The term "recipient" is ironic because the recipient often receives nothing, which is the problem. Can you imagine not being noted? That you are invisible?

Receiving nothingness from a "supposed" loved one is an emotional abandonment that cuts deeply into the person's heart. No one sees it, and it goes underground in terms of abuse. Victims feel empty, invisible, and alone.

Victims of overt abuse may not initially comprehend how it feels to be invisible because they often wish they could hide and become unseen. How ironic is that? However, it is a mistaken belief that being invisible to a significant other or even a non-significant other is good. People need to feel that they matter to others.

Being invisible to your loved one is an existential wound. It causes you to feel that you don't matter and question your right even to exist. Research has found that one of the primary ways to injure a person is to remove them from significant human contact, particularly communication.

The silent treatment is a standard weapon of narcissists and other emotional abusers, and it causes deep feelings of abandonment in the recipient. Recurring silent treatment incidents so hurt some people that they turn to substance abuse, anti-depressant/anti-anxiety medication, or even suicide to escape the emptiness.

An absent parent can also cause an abandonment wound. When one of your parents has chosen not to be in your life, this cuts deeply. Those who've been abandoned by a parent can't find a simple explanation. Some try to make the best of the situation, ignoring that they don't have this parent in their lives, but the damage is still the same. There are lifelong consequences of parental abandonment.

People learn to cope in different ways. Some pretend it doesn't matter; some question their worth; others may be openly angry. With abandonment comes defense mechanisms.

For healing to take place for those abandoned, there is only one immediate solution: grief. Being abandoned, whether permanently or temporarily, causes you emotional pain. The only way to heal an emotional hurt is to grieve. Grieving wounds, and when it comes from the depth of your soul, you are not in a place to do that without guidance, which comes through counseling. To weep, sob, and feel the pain is getting things out; I almost describe it as "vomiting!" It's important to note that grieving is not a one-time event. It also does not mean you will never be hurt when you think about it. I can talk about my son Chad and do it.

Then again, tears will come into my eyes around someone, in sharing about him, or I may cry when alone. Chad took his life on June 2, 2011, and the pain is indescribable; no one can understand, only God can! A person may have empathy, but understanding can never occur, even to the other person who has lost a child themselves. *Your feelings are YOUR FEELINGS!* It was a process for me and will be until the Lord determines my life here on this earth has ended. However, with all this said, you can heal, move on in life, and enjoy it. You deserve to enjoy life! God wants you to! He will also use your experiences of negativity to help others. Second Corinthians 1:4 states: "Who comforts us in all our troubles so that we can comfort those in any trouble with the comfort we receive from God." God certainly works in mysterious ways; does He not?

God allowed me to help others; I pray productively with the pain and losses I have experienced. I often knew where they were "at," in some shape or form of human words by me. They were amazed, and that brought about connectivity and trust from the client, whether in counseling or Battle Lines. I certainly was not a "textbook and no experience of life counselor."

What are some of the signs and symptoms of being abandoned in adults? The following are a few:

- Always wanting to please others (being a "people pleaser")
- Giving too much in relationships
- An inability to trust others
- Pushing others away to avoid rejection
- Feeling insecure in romantic partnerships and friendships
- Codependency
- A need for continual reassurance that others love them and will stay with them
- The need to control others
- Persisting with unhealthy relationships
- The inability to maintain relationships
- Moving quickly from one relationship to another
- Sabotaging relationships
- Lack of emotional intimacy

I might note that as adults, some individuals who experienced abandonment in childhood may find themselves drawn to people who will treat them poorly and eventually leave them. When this occurs, it reinforces their fears and distrust of others. It is like a self-fulfilling prophecy.

In children, here are some possible signs of abandonment issues:

- Constant worry about being abandoned
- Anxiety or panic when a parent or caregiver drops them at school or daycare
- Clinginess
- Fear of being alone, including at bedtime
- Frequent illness, which often has no apparent physical cause
- Isolation
- Low self-esteem

In some children, there can be more extreme signs of abandonment issues, which could be some of the following:

- Addiction
- Disordered eating
- Lashing out at others physically or verbally
- Self-harm

It should be noted that we cannot explain why some individuals have no issues of abandonment that manifest internally or externally while others, despite having similar experiences, do.

I want to add that God can heal you and show you how beautiful you are, and YOU WERE MEANT TO BE. No matter your past and circumstances, this is true, and God's Word is TRUTH!

I also want to add that tragedy can be a springboard to

transformation! This goes against what you or those around you may think. However, it is an accurate statement! I can tell you for sure that there were places in my life where the pain was so great that I would have rather died than continue another moment, as I saw no possibility of a future for me. I can also share with certainty that I do not wish for tragedy! I also want to add trauma is not an illness that a doctor can heal! It is not an illness! Also, do not let a therapist label you with PTSD! So many of these days use that as a "catchall phrase!" You have a responsibility to become well, but you are the only one who can CHOOSE that, and that pathway will walk you into healthiness.

You can begin your healing journey; don't say you can't. You have the choice to be resilient despite the constant pain of trauma, whether recent or from childhood. You can choose to turn the tragedy of all sorts into victory and growth, and when you look back in time, you can see, if you bring God into the equation, and see that John 1:2–5 is real:

> *2 Count it all joy, my brothers, when you meet trials of various kinds, 3 for you know that the testing of your faith produces steadfastness. 4 And let steadfastness have its full effect, that you may be perfect and complete, lacking in nothing.*
>
> *5 If any of you lacks wisdom, let him ask God, who gives generously to all without reproach, and it will be given him.*

God used adversity to bring about growth in my life. I used to hate the above Scripture, as there was "another pain" to go through. I would not be where I am today, I am convinced, if I had not had that pain in my life. I hurt for my sons. I wish that they had not experienced divorce, a new father, no boundaries, and a lack of discipline. I cannot get in touch with my older son's pain in the loss of his brother. All that came from childhood and how they were raised. I, too, was affected. I learned that I was unique and fearfully and wonderfully by Him. I did not know that. I depended upon others too much in seeking to please them. I was super hard on myself, a perfectionist, and with OCD, a lot of that would be repeated in my mind. I never took a vacation; I worked from dawn to dusk and, in the beginning, at night at my office, on the phone and paying bills with subcontractors because it was only me, myself, and I. I sold my soul to do so, and when you do that, you begin to die! In the darkest times, I might add, there was crying and praying, and God's Word, literally three-dimensionally, jumped off the page and spoke to me. It was food for that day, that night, and the next day and tomorrow. I fought to go beyond. You have to fight to go beyond.

I never jogged, but in June of 1985, I began jogging at Memorial Park in Houston, a three-mile circle. At first, I walked and jogged. I met my sister, who is fourteen years younger, there. Initially, she moved on in her running and left me behind. By August, I was doing three, six, and nine miles, and at that time of day, with the sun facing you and the pressed gravel running path, the sun rays would bounce back into you at one hundred degrees many days. It was an accomplishment for me. That spoke to me. I was healthy in the body, and it released the positive effects of endorphins into my brain, which helps fight depression.

The fastest I ever ran as a forty-one-year-old was seven-minute miles, trying to keep up with a twenty-year-old young man. I could only do that for three miles, and then I slowed down. That fueled some positivity in me. However, if I had just gone in June once and in August once, what kind of advancement in jogging should I have expected? You can answer that. What does that mean to you? Do YOU want to GET WELL? That is YOUR CHOICE!

There were many beyond just this experience. Dr. Vjktor Frankl lost all his family in Theresienstadt's Nazi concentration camps. He alone was the only one that survived. After the war, he became one of the most influential psychologists of the twentieth century! Frankel wrote, "How a man accepts his fate and all the suffering it entails, how he takes up his cross, gives him ample opportunity, even under the most difficult circumstances, to add a deeper meaning to his life."

God wants to not only heal you, but He wants you to have a productive life! In the scheme of life, success, accomplishments, possessions, etc., there is nothing wrong with that. Still, I will tell you the most important aspects of life are: 1. Your intimate relationship with the Lord and His Word; 2. Your relationship with your loved ones and others. Notice that I put the word "relationship" in both critical aspects of life. What you leave inside someone and what they leave within you is the most important. Most importantly, this can only occur in healthy relationships.

Life has no certainties, from when we are born until we die. It would help if you grabbed the truth that life is uncertain. You have a responsibility to make your life choices. In today's world, you are without the excuse of not being informed as a child and growing up as I did, even though in the twentieth century, I did not know about life. Today, information is at your fingertip. You can acquire positives, or you can obtain negatives from that thing called the computer. But you are without the excuse of not being informed.

Short-term therapy, again, is not the answer for trauma, and you should pace yourself and be with a therapist who operates in that fashion. God's timetable for you is not about statistics of the medical world or therapists; it is His and how you become engaged in your healing journey.

I must note here your brain never forgets. Your conscious mind may fail, but your physical brain does not. According to studies, only eight to twelve percent of people who have experienced trauma ever reach the point of developing PTSD. It must also be noted that only a minority of people living with PTSD experience the long-term effects of this disorder.

Have any of you ever been near the seashore, walked or driven, and looked at the trees as the tree growth bends toward land? Over time, they just "bent with the wind," and they became resilient and continued to grow. Many times, they grew deformed limbs but thrived. Some trees grow straight along the seashore, but when strong winds come, they bend, and they, too, have become resilient.

I might add here where it may be appropriate. To walk into healing from trauma, you must face the pain and "walk through it." That is the only way healing can occur. Life is precious, and you are loved, and God wants you to have joy in life.

Romans 12:2 states, "Do not be conformed to this world, but be transformed by the renewal of your mind, that by testing you may discern what the will of God is, what is good and acceptable and perfect."

God wants to TRANSFORM YOU! No matter what, use your experiences to be transformed. Pain hurts; one gets angry at God and others. I have experienced that, and all that does is bring about cancer in the depths of your soul! We will talk more later about repentance and forgiveness, which must be processed from the center of your soul to be healed.

VERBAL ABUSE

Verbal abuse can be just as harmful, if not more, than physical abuse. A study by Akemi Tomoda, MD, PhD, and others points to literal structural change in the brain's gray matter in the presence of verbal abuse without proving causation. Thanks to MRI imaging, the question of whether verbal abuse changes how the brain functions is no longer in question: We know that abuse leaves behind a specific legacy.

Studies show that the circuitry for physical and emotional pain is the same. An experiment by Naomi L. Eisenberger showed that social rejection activated the same neural circuitry as physical pain. More expansively, Ethan Kross, experimental psychologist and neuroscientist, and his colleagues demonstrated the complexity of this connection in an experiment that used MRI scanning to see what areas of the brain lit up when individuals who'd recently experienced being left by a lover viewed a photograph of their ex. When a toxic amount of heat is applied to the forearm, guess what? The same neural circuitry was involved in the brain. The pain of social rejection is real. Also, *verbal abuse* is a social rejection expressed in **language.**

A child under the care of an abusive parent may be continuously flooded with feelings that further limit the growth of his or her emotional intelligence, a skill set built on identifying emotions and processing them. In the wake of continued verbal aggression, it's hard for a child to sort out whether they feel afraid, ashamed, hurt, or angry.

Finally, the messages' internalization — those diminishing, hypercritical, and shaming words and phrases — changes one's personality, self-esteem, and behavior. "Self-criticism," the common term for this, sounds far more benign than it is because it can verge dangerously on self-hatred and be hobbling in the extreme. This is the habit of mind that ascribes every glitch, setback, or failure to ingrained flaws in character, leading someone to think, *I failed because I'm too stupid and worthless to do anything else.* Or, *No wonder my wife left. Who could ever truly love me?* It must be noted that as a child, the child most times believes what the verbally abusive parent is telling them. How are they to know differently from early childhood with that constant verbal abuse in their everyday life? There is a hole in the depths of their soul that says, **"You are worthless!"**

PHYSICAL ABUSE

Physical abuse to a child and the effects may last a lifetime and can include brain damage and hearing and vision loss, resulting in disability. Even less severe injuries can lead to the abused child developing severe emotional, behavioral, or learning problems. Injuries to a child's growing brain can result in cognitive delays and intense emotional issues that could forever affect their quality of life.

The primary, or first, effects of child physical abuse occur during and immediately after the abuse. The child will suffer pain and medical problems from bodily injury and even death in severe cases. The physical pain from cuts, bruises, burns, whipping, kicking, punching, strangling, binding, etc., will eventually pass, but the emotional pain will last long after the visible wounds have healed.

The age at which the abuse occurs influences how the injuries — or any permanent damage — affect the child. Infant victims of physical abuse have the most significant risk of suffering long-term physical problems, such as neurological damage that manifests as tremors, irritability, lethargy, and vomiting. In more severe cases, the effects of child physical abuse can include seizures, permanent blindness or deafness, paralysis, mental and developmental delays, and, of course, death. The longer the abuse continues, the greater the impact on the child, regardless of age.

Remember that our brains do not fully develop around the age of twenty-four. If there are fifteen years of physical and emotional abuse, which some of my clients experienced, it takes a long time to heal and walk into "the newness of Christ and how they feel about themselves." In all my years of working with individuals, mostly men, I am thankful that external physical damage was not done to them by their caregivers for those who were physically abused. Nonetheless, the inner wounds and messages were within them.

Many abused children may find it difficult to form lasting and appropriate friendships. They may not trust others in the most basic of ways. Children who have suffered long-term abuse may lack the necessary social skills and cannot communicate naturally as other children can.

The physically abused may also tend to over-comply with authority figures to use aggression to solve interpersonal issues. The social effects of child physical abuse continue to influence the adult life of the abused child negatively. They're more likely to divorce and develop drug and alcohol addictions.

Adults who were physically abused as children suffer from physical, emotional, and social effects of the abuse throughout their lives. Experts report that victims of physical child abuse are at greater risk of developing a mental illness, becoming homeless, engaging in criminal activity, and unemployment. These create a financial burden on the community and society because authorities must allocate funds from taxes, other social welfare programs, and the foster care system.

SEXUAL ABUSE

There are many forms of childhood sexual abuse. Sexual abuse can involve seduction by a beloved relative, or it can be a violent act committed by a stranger. It's hard to define because of the many different forms it can take on, the different frequency levels, the variety of circumstances it occurs within, and the various relationships that it may be associated with. Here's one definition from Wendy **Maltz**, LCSW, DST, and author of *The Sexual Healing Journey: A Guide for Survivors of Sexual Abuse*: **"Sexual abuse occurs whenever one person dominates and exploits another through sexual activity or suggestion."**

Kathleen L. Ratican, Certified Professional Counselor, defines **childhood sexual abuse as any sexual act, overt or covert, between a child and an adult (or older child, where the younger child's participation is obtained through seduction or coercion.**)

Irrespective of how childhood sexual abuse is defined, it generally has a significant negative and pervasive psychological impact on its victims.

The majority of sexual abuse happens in childhood, with incest being the most common form. The impact of childhood sexual abuse varies from person to person and from case to case. Research shows that the extent of sexual abuse, a higher number of sexual abuse experiences, a younger age during the first sexual abuse experiences, the perspective of the victim, the victim's internal resources, and the victim's level of support all affect the amount of damage to a survivor.

Although not all forms of childhood sexual abuse include direct touch, it is essential for therapists to understand that childhood sexual abuse can occur in many different ways that still exploit the victim sexually and cause harm. The perpetrator may control the child by introducing them to pornography prematurely, assaulting them through the internet, or manipulating them into taking pornographic photos. Other forms may include invasion of privacy, such as just barging into the bathroom by the adult while the child is taking a bath/shower or going to the bathroom.

Childhood sexual abuse infringes on the fundamental rights of human beings. It is an invasion of privacy, which the child has no control over, most times because an adult controls them, and the child has learned over a short period of their life or a more extended period of life to obey the adult. Children should have sexual experiences at the appropriate developmental time within their control and choice, the experts say. However, God would argue that children are not to be in sexual relationships. Marriage is the only place where sex is to occur.

When a society moves away from God, society crumbles. We live in a crumbling society, with the Bible and the relationship with the Lord being found antiquated, as each year passes, by our schools, universities, and, in some cases, different dominations themselves. The nature and dynamics of sexual abuse and sexually abusive relationships are often traumatic. In counseling and Battle Lines, I have seen that when the sexually abused secrets are revealed, they have all been traumatic! When sexual abuse occurs in childhood, it can hinder average social growth and cause many different psychosocial problems.

Childhood sexual abuse has been associated with higher depression levels, guilt, shame, self-blame, eating disorders, somatic concerns, anxiety, dissociative patterns, repression, denial, sexual problems, and relationship problems. Depression is the most common long-term symptom among survivors.

Survivors may have difficulty externalizing the abuse, thus thinking negatively about themselves. After years of negative self-thoughts, survivors have feelings of worthlessness and avoid others because they believe they have nothing to offer. Symptoms of child sexual abuse *survivors' depression* include feeling down most of the time, having suicidal ideation, having disturbed sleeping patterns, having disturbed eating habits and having a negative body image or body dysmorphia.

Survivors often experience guilt, shame, and self-blame. They might take personal responsibility for the abuse. When an esteemed trusted adult sexually abuses children, it may be hard to view the perpetrator negatively, thus leaving them incapable of seeing what happened as not their fault. Survivors often blame themselves and internalize negative messages about themselves. Survivors tend to display more self-destructive behaviors and experience more suicidal ideation than those who have not been abused.

Stress and anxiety are often long-term effects of childhood sexual abuse, which can be frightening and cause residual harm long after the experience or experiences have ceased, such as chronic anxiety, tension, anxiety attacks, and phobias. A study by Judith A. McNew, PhD, LISW, and Neil Abell, PhD, ACSW, LCSW, compared the posttraumatic stress symptoms in Vietnam veterans and adult survivors of childhood sexual abuse. The study revealed that childhood sexual abuse is traumatizing and can result in symptoms comparable to war-related trauma.

Some survivors have *dissociated* or had out-of-body experiences to protect themselves during childhood sexual abuse (a coping and/or self-defense mechanism) and may still use this coping mechanism as adults when feeling unsafe or threatened. Dissociation for survivors may include feelings of confusion, feelings of disorientation, nightmares, flashbacks, and difficulty experiencing feelings. Denial and repression of sexual abuse are believed by some to be a long-term effect of childhood sexual abuse. Symptoms may include experiencing amnesia concerning parts of their childhood, negating the results and impact of sexual abuse, and feeling that they should forget about the abuse, according to Kathleen L. Ratican, Certified Professional Counselor.

Ratican also shares that survivors of sexual abuse may experience difficulty in establishing interpersonal relationships. Symptoms correlated with childhood sexual abuse may hinder the development and growth of relationships. Common relationship difficulties that survivors may experience are difficulties with trust, fear of intimacy, fear of being different or weird, difficulty establishing interpersonal boundaries, passive behaviors, and getting involved in abusive relationships.

Can survivors forget past childhood sexual abuse experiences and later recover those memories? This is a controversial topic. Some therapists believe that sexual abuse can cause enough trauma that the victim forgets or represses the experience as a coping mechanism. Others believe that recovered memories are false or that the client is led to create them. Elizabeth Loftus, PhD, discusses this topic on an American Psychological Association podcast.

Wendy Maltz, LCSW, DST, has shared a list of the top ten sexual symptoms that often result from experiences of sexual abuse: "Avoiding, fearing, or lacking interest in sex; approaching sex as an obligation; experiencing negative feelings such as anger, disgust, or guilt with touch; having difficulty becoming aroused or feeling sensation; feeling emotionally distant or not present during sex; experiencing intrusive or disturbing sexual thoughts and images; engaging in compulsive or inappropriate sexual behaviors; experiencing difficulty establishing or maintaining an intimate relationship; and experiencing erectile, ejaculatory, or orgasmic difficulties."

It is essential to point out that although research has shown there to be significant relationships between long-term effect variables and childhood sexual abuse, ***each victim's responses and experiences will not be the same.*** Although it is often viewed as a traumatic experience, there is no single symptom among all survivors. Clinicians need to focus on the client's individual needs. Let me add here that children are indeed VICTIMS!

THE TRAUMA TEMPLATE

Often, based on the way a person was sexually abused, the victim later on "mirrors" that behavior in their sexually acting-out addiction. Let me give you some examples, if I may. When there is trauma taking place, there is what is called the "trauma template." What is a trauma template? In simple terms, the same way the victim was sexually abused, later in their sexual addiction, they "unknowingly" act out in the same manner they were taken advantage of sexually.

I was sharing this one night in Battle Lines many years ago, and it struck one gentleman with new understanding. His uncle sexually abused him in roadside park restrooms, and he acted out sexually with his sexual relationships in roadside park restrooms! For the very first time in his late forties, he understood. He could not figure out the "whys" until that night. This gentleman sought counseling elsewhere, closer to his home; he surrendered his life to the Lord and His Word and developed a deep relationship with Christ. He became educated on the issues of sex addiction, its causes, and its effects. Like General George Patton, his education brought him to the place where he became an overcomer, walking into victory, being transformed by our Lord, and having been free from captivity. Work at it, he did, and he became that warrior that God speaks of in the Bible, King David.

I want to note here that no matter what abuse issues you have experienced, God can heal you from them. Your brain has not forgotten, but you can go beyond memory and live life. At times, I am not going to say that pain may come forth from memory or sharing with someone about a particular subject in this regard, but it is a dim memory.

I explain it this way. In Houston, Texas, is our 610 Loop. On the west side, between Bellaire and Interstate 10, it exceeds 69 (Southwest Freeway). When traveling from the south to the north, having traveled so much, I know where exits are ahead. But let us say on this particular day, I hit fog early in the morning at the very top of 610 over Southwest Freeway. So, with great caution, I slowly pulled over to the side with my blinkers on. I just sat there and could barely see the end of the hood of my car. I knew that there is an exit up ahead to San Felipe, but I could not see it. I knew it is there, but I could not see it! I repeat that because with trauma of any kind, you "KNOW IT HAPPENED, BUT YOU CANNOT FEEL IT!"

Again, there may be times when sensitivity shows up, but you don't live there in the scheme of things. You live in the present. I can personally vouch for this truth. Now, am I big enough to just "forget?" No, I am not, but something happens when you work on the issues that are particular to you, and you have that relationship with the Lord and His Word, and have a true prayer life, that HE DOES SOMETHING THAT YOU CANNOT DO! I might step on some toes here, but I am noted in doing so at times, and that is, many counselors will not agree with what I just shared, whether they are true Christian therapists and duly trained or secular therapists and highly skilled also. I have seen it happen in men's lives in Battle Lines and in counseling with me, and I have experienced it myself.

With what I have experienced in life, I often wonder how I could truly live life, yet I have, and I am not saying and hearing myself out here; I do not see glory in that. I would not want one person to walk through what I have. I am in wonderment at times about what I have been able to do. I look at others, not in envy, but "if only," at times, with healthy children and grandchildren. This has not been totally afforded to me. However, I have been highly blessed, and I am in wonderment about what God gave me: my wife, Jan, and my daughter, Emily.

It is your choice, once again, if YOU WANT TO GET WELL. No one can choose that path except you! You can wallow in self-pity, or you can be victorious. Our REDEEMER lives, and He is the same yesterday, today, and forever!

It is another great exercise, and again, it is identifying those who have hurt you. Again, get butcher paper, lay it on a table, and draw the most enormous egg you can. Now, I realize that not everyone who is dealing with sexual addiction is also dealing with trauma, but the percentages are high.

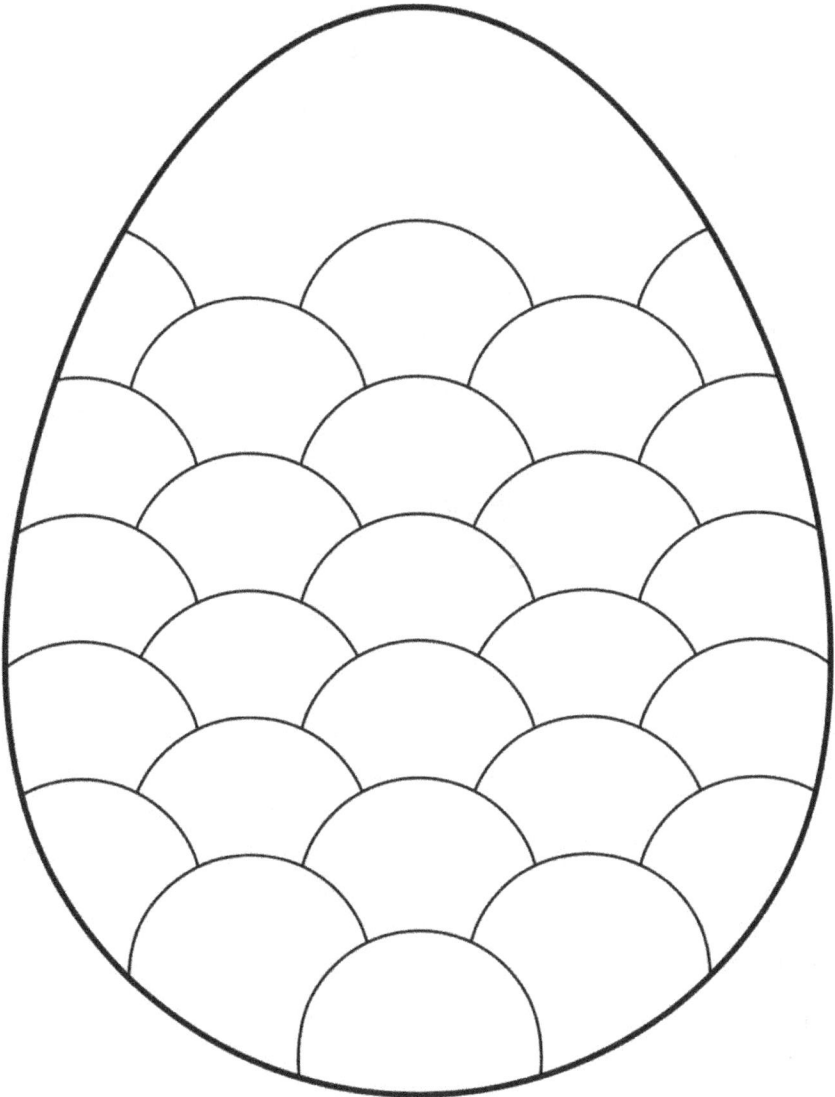

You take your time but draw your earliest memory of hurt and pain. You seek to feel that pain. For the example shown on the previous page, number it in sequence as best as possible, then describe what happened to you and how you felt, etc. You draw on the egg, as best you can, the situation.

For example, the earliest memory is below.

1. I am a little boy, around two years of age or so, and my dad is chasing me to beat me; I am yelling in terror, seeking to hide, and this is a typical occasion.

2. I have an older sister who molested me.

3. It was Christmas time. I don't remember my age, but Mother and Daddy got into a fight; it seemed fueled by drinking and ruined Christmas. I have never liked Christmas since then.

4. My aunt chewed me out at my younger sister's birthday when I was around four or so, and I always felt she favored my sister. I never told anyone. It made me feel less than.

5. My father is driving away in a pickup when I was around four or five, and I yell for him not to leave. "Come back," "Come back," "Come back," I yell! It was the last time I saw him in my life.

6. I must have been in kindergarten. Some boys pinned me down on the school ground and peed on me.

You do this to the present day and age, taking your time. This is all you do: sit back, pray, write down, and draw. You may have tears flowing at times. Just take a breath and then continue. I want this to be an all-day project for you. Take some breaks and eat lunch, but then begin again. You may be a BIG GUY and say, "Those things did not affect me," but they did, BIG BOY!

You can review this with your counselor and let him or her decide how to proceed with their professionalism.

You can also do what the one gentleman did: take all and go up into the mountains, forgiving and feeling each hurt and blessing the offender or offenders who hurt you.

This is a powerful exercise of eventual cleansing if you do your work and truly forgive from your heart, as well as truly feeling each pain as you do.

Men, this is another example of covering all the bases of your life and your healing from sexual compulsivity. As you process and allow things to surface, they are no longer buried and brought forward in the light so that you can work through them appropriately.

Allow God to do work in your heart as you deal with these deep and embarrassing pains that were placed upon you by those older than you, and remember you had no control over that; you were a LITTLE BOY! And again, as a reminder, this is an excellent opportunity to process with your counselor.

HOMEWORK

1. Have you experienced trauma in your life, including childhood to the present? Please explain in detail.

2. Have you gone to any counseling or groups for your trauma?

3. What resulted from the counseling for the group for you?

4. Did you ever process forgiveness as the subject processed it in the true story?

5. If you have never gone to counseling or a group, why is that? What has kept you from it?

6. Do you want to get well?

CHAPTER 9
Your Wife

For the married, and you cannot ever understand and/or feel what your wife has experienced in betrayal, so do not insult her by saying that you do. You cannot because you cannot get inside of her.

I am beginning with the following to grab your attention:

First, take your eyes off yourself and focus them on the Lord and your wife.

Discovering an affair and/or any sexual betrayal can lead the offended spouse to experience grief that could last several months or much longer than that. It is the emotion of loss and includes struggles with feelings of sadness, hurt, anger, confusion, guilt, depression, and loneliness. Grieving individuals try to make sense of a great disappointment, which violates trust, yet their emotional expressions vary widely.

For example, two women compared notes regarding discovering their husband's affairs. One expressed anger, bordering on rage, that her husband would be so "low down" as to degrade himself in such a forbidden relationship. She railed against this lack of gratitude for the many chores she did for him daily and her constant availability whenever he expressed a need for sexual intimacy. Realizing she had been played for a fool, she resolved to let him know that she would ensure a nasty divorce, where she would ensure he lost everything.

The other woman was much more reserved in her reactions. She expressed great shame because she had not foreseen the affair. She felt extreme loneliness because she did not know how to express herself to her husband, and she was afraid of the possibility of becoming a divorcee.

They both felt a substantial loss differently. MEN, you need to look and develop not understanding but empathy for where your wife is hurting. She is an individual. She is fearfully and wonderfully made, and God created her!

For many, the immediate response is an affair, and/or one sexually acting out is in SHOCK and DISBELIEF. Engaging in an affair and/or other types of sexually acting out represents behavior outside the boundaries of normalcy. 99.9% of those getting married have an "expectation" of making their marriage distinct from all other relationships. When your wife learns that his exclusive sexual union is no longer unique, it is only natural to have this emotion.

NOTE MEN: IT IS ONLY NATURAL FOR YOUR WIFE TO HAVE THIS EMOTION! Reread this previous statement several times; hopefully, it will sink into your being! When your wife learns that her exclusive sexual union is no longer unique, it is only natural to have this emotion! In fact, a lack of shock might show an attitude of not caring toward the sanctity of marriage. WOULD YOU BE IN SHOCK IF YOUR WIFE, WERE YOU? BE REAL HERE, MEN, AND BE "IN TOUCH" WITH REALITY, AND DO NOT EXPECT YOUR WIFE TO JUMP THROUGH "YOUR HOOP" TO GET OVER IT!

When shock occurs, individuals may experience a temporary emotional numbness as they try to make sense of the newly revealed facts. A type of denial may emerge. Your injured wife may have such thoughts as:

- "I just cannot believe this is happening."

- "I was afraid of something like this, but now it seems too strange for it to be true!"

- "I've got to have some time for myself to come to grips with this."

- "I feel so foolish that I did not see this coming."

Men, let's just stop here for a second. Are you getting any sense of the reality of the trauma your wife has experienced?

Betrayal is trauma to your wife, period! Get it, men, and do not try to "fix her." She is hurting from the depth of her being. You have totally violated trust with your sexual acting out.

In a sense, the shock reaction serves as an emotional transition between a period of presumed normalcy and a period of turbulence. During this time, there is usually a **FLOOD OF THOUGHTS, OFTEN OBSESSIVE IN NATURE,** regarding the different courses of action that might be followed, the thoughts of your sexual liaisons that flood her mind, etc. Confusion is often a part of her journey because of the ever-changing nature of their obsessions. **AGAIN, MEN, WOULD NOT YOU NOT DO THE SAME IF THE ROLES WERE REVERSED? IF YOU DID NOT THEN I QUESTION YOUR HEART AND YOUR RELATIONSHIP WITH YOUR WIFE! MEN — SUCH CONFUSION IS N O R M A L!** It is as though you took **TASER** and shot it into her chest with a 50,000-volt electrical charge. And for you not to be patient and understand where she is at is uncalled for, and it is called **UNREASONABLE and LACKING SENSITIVITY!**

To expect your wife not to get **angry is also uncalled for, and not for her to be angry** would be "unhealthy." Jesus Himself expressed anger when exposed to people who presumed themselves to be above the laws of God or who showed blatant disregard for the worth of a human being in communicating anger, as HE threw the money changers out of the market of the temple. He publicly aligned Himself to the Father, hoping to make others MEASURE THEMSELVES against the standard of righteousness. An injured wife can **FEEL RIGHT IN EXPRESSING ANGER** as long as it is within the context of CONSTRUCTIVITY COMMUNICATING right convictions. This means that individuals can express their hurt and disappointment. Setting boundaries regarding the issues is also appropriate for her. And it is your responsibility to align with those boundaries set by your wife. If your wife was not angry, it would imply a lack of conviction of what a genuine marriage should be like under the Holiness of our Lord and of the sanctity of marriage. Where the two shall become one flesh!

Your wife may place upon herself **UNWARRANTED GUILT**, wondering what she could have done! Men, it is you who did the betrayal**, NOT HER!** This is another aspect of the **TASER** hit upon her. Your wife should never take on anything that is regarding your unfaithfulness. And men, you are absolutely wrong to try to place any guilt upon her. It was your choice to ACT OUT, not your wife's! Do not get in the position of "blame-shifting" so that you do not have to seriously look at yourself and your heart!

Another thing the **TASER** is that it places her in the spot of **LONELINESS**! She feels SO **ALONE and ABANDONED!** It is natural for her to feel lonely when illicit sexual relationships break the union of spirits. Loneliness is the emotion of isolation and seclusion, which includes a feeling of unfulfillment and incompleteness. It usually manifests itself in a mood of sadness. However, it may quickly regress into a state of fear and insecurity. There is a tremendous **EMPTINESS**! Men, your wife's pain is one that you cannot feel or understand!

A wife's anguish is a common part of her grief experience caused **BY YOU**, in **YOUR** acting out and her finding out! Her anguish stems from the great big "HOLE" you have created. Men, she got hit by your TASER, and she is in shock and may stay in shock and wander around aimlessly as though in a fog! It is as though she was waiting along the side of the road, enjoying the bluebonnets in the springtime in Texas, and suddenly she got hit by an 18-wheeler. All kinds of behaviors come from being **LONELY**! Men, are you gaining any insight into your beautiful wife's pain?

DEPRESSION can become persistent because of anger and loneliness. More than deep sadness, depression is an emotion of defeat and hopelessness. An inability to handle normal lifestyle requirements, unexplained crying spells, chronic fatigue, sleep irregularities, poor concentration, and a loss of motivation are manifested. Acute anxiety and nervousness often accompany depression. An inclination toward depression is a normal part of grief and deep pain.

The most distinguishing factor of depression is unresolved anger. The depressed person strongly believes that they should have been treated more fairly. Still, because they do not openly explore those ideas, they develop a sour disposition of depression.

Struggles with feelings of **INFERIORITY** also brought depression on! A sense of **DEVALUATION IS STRONG!** So are the feelings of **FAILURE** and **INADEQUACY.** The possibility of returning to a normal life seems so remote that it is easier to collapse in despair! The depressed person, which is your wife, will likely use the word **CAN'T** repeatedly.

Sometimes, a phenological issue occurs; gastrointestinal problems may appear, including constipation, headaches, irregular sleep, and rapid heartbeat, and the brain may be depleted of amines, norepinephrine, or serotonin (a chemical depression).

Men, I wanted to bring to the forefront for YOU to realize where your wife is at emotionally with the trauma that has occurred by YOUR betrayal. Your timetable may not be God's timetable., in the journey of healing for your wife. Your expectations might not match God's expectations. As I have already mentioned, our Lord individually and specifically created your wife as a person. SHE is not YOU! She is SHE! To win your wife's love and affection and for her to walk through the valley of death and into the light of day, choose if you will be part of the solution and/or continue to be part of the problem. Patience is the theme of the day for you.

James 5:7 says, "Be patient, therefore, brothers,1 until the coming of the Lord. See how the farmer waits for the precious fruit of the earth, being patient about it until it receives the early and the late rains."

You, also, be patient. Establish your hearts, for the coming of the Lord is at hand. Let's think about this for a moment. I have a dry land farmer friend out in West Texas. I have known him since 1967. What Don does on the thousands of acres is that he plows the ground, tills the soil, plants seeds (checking the world market for a price of goods, thinking and praying about it all, and chooses a certain seed to plant), and then he covers up the plants. Then what does it do? He waits for the rain. He is trusting for the rain at the right time. He is trusting the markets of the world for a great price on the crop he planted. Who is he trusting? He is trusting the Lord. My friend has the patience of JOB. He knows he is not in control; only God is in control. Men, you are not in control of your wife; thus, surrender her to the Lord, and you put your feet on the path to do the work that is particular to you.

One place to arrive for you is COMPREHENDERING. Another is being DESIROUS of winning her love by your DOING! YOU have to get your eyes off of your needs and place them upon her. To find out what her needs are, for you to do WHATEVER IT IS, SHE REQUIRES YOU TO BE on the healing journey. Get your eyes off of your PRIDE, your POSITION, your WAYS, and on to HIS WAYS, and delight in the WIFE OF YOUR YOUTH! You played the cards that brought you to where you are at now, and now it is time for you to play the cards that GOD WANTS YOU TO TAKE PART WITH and place any demands that you have on the upper shelf in "your bookcase," figuratively speaking. God can develop brokenness and humility for you here.

Have you wept with deep remorse before your wife, with a heart of repentance? If not, no wonder she is where she is at emotionally. Men, please take responsibility of your actions by doing whatever it takes, whatever it requires, whatever it is she wants you to do, to bring your marriage into a **Journey of Healing.** The responsibility is solely on you. YOU led your marriage into biblical counseling and prayer, into working on YOUR issues, and repentance, forgiveness and healing can take place. YOU are the one who can truly direct this ship into safe harbors by your efforts. And/or you can drive this ship upon "the rocks," and cause it to sink.

What do you want?

What hurts a committed wife the most is that the person she considers her oneness has shattered her trust and belief. For a healthy, attached wife, the experience of profound and unexpected betrayal can be incredibly traumatic, as mentioned before.

The trauma brought on by you, your wife, may manifest in one or more of the following ways:

- Excessive emotional reactions and mood shifts, from rage to sadness to hope and back again. She feels that she is on a roller coaster ride

- Hypervigilance can manifest in self-protective behaviors, such as doing "detective work." For example, you can check phone bills, look into your wallet, check bills, look at phone apps, credit card accounts, and your browser history, etc.

- Mind on trying to constantly figure all out

- Questioning any of your late coming home, too long at the grocery store, out with your buddies, looking at an attractive woman, turning off your computer quickly, etc. Men, just get it. She does not trust you at all. Her eyes are everywhere, and you have a choice to be patient and kind or be irritable. One choice is towards healing, and the other choice you make is to cause further damage.

- Not able to sleep, having nightmares, and focus issues during the day.

- Constant obsessing about the betrayal is a continuous invasion of her thoughts, and she cannot shake it.

- Avoidance of talking or discussing the betrayal. It hurts too much, so avoidance is a pain reliever to her, yet it is not.

- Isolation from you and her friends and family.

- Binging, compulsive spending, eating, exercise, etc.

- Intrusive thoughts about the betrayal

- Wanting to know the details of who, what, when, where, and HOW.

The betrayal blindsided the wife, and she became overwhelmed upon learning the full extent of your betrayal. And let me state here, most times *she "just knows the tip of the iceberg because most husbands withhold information."* Every time you give more information that you held back from being found out, it's like the original trauma of discovery for your wife. When you drip in information upon her, it is a new trauma each time. You are not helping yourself by withholding all the in information. Details of sexual behavior are not to be shared; it is all about who, what, when, where... no details! Why is this? Those stories are like worms that get into your wife's brain and infiltrate her. No is no on details!

She counted on you to "have her back," and now you have betrayed her. Her best friend, her husband, her protector, her lover, she NO LONGER KNOWS. You have ripped apart her emotional world and physical well-being. Is there any wonder by you regarding your wife's pain?

Often, your wife will question herself regarding your behaviors and blame herself for not being able to see everything as it was occurring (your betrayals).

Stopping right here for a moment, and let's state that your betrayal has been on porn sites, chat, etc. You masturbated with what was before you. Your thoughts were not on your wife (guaranteed) but on the image or images before you. Then, when your precious wife discovers you, this betrayal is not different in some ways from your physical betrayals (prostitutes, massage parlors, affairs, etc.). So do not lessen the pain of your wife, saying you did not really betray her. You did, and you were so caught up in porn that you often forgot the time spent, and then masturbation and ejaculation bring that chemical high you were in gone. She may have even caught you with your penis in your hand. That is trauma to her. Your pleasure was with you and the site and not your wife. You betrayed her. So, let's settle that right now, repeating that you traumatized her with porn — a major betrayal!

The most common of billboards or ads on TV can trigger your wife, such as being in the grocery store and your eyes looking at the woman on aisle nine or your eyes wandering to a woman on the sidewalk, etc. She may explode in rage, tearfulness, or any emotion when triggered by the simplest things. Men, your wife is fragile, and for you to say, "Just get over it," is like a spear into her heart. She just "cannot get over it," and it is that simple, so seek to be patient, kind, caring, helpful, etc.

Men, just so you "understand," someone has broken her trust, and it will take a year or longer for her to stay on this emotional roller coaster. The KEY for you is that you must get counseling, read books, have accountability, go to a group, get involved in a Bible-believing church, seek to read God's Word and pray. Your wife is watching YOU. As I have said, do not tell her what you are doing. Just do it! Zip your mouth and become that man that she can eventually trust again.

Sadly, many wives blame themselves as well. Perhaps she was unavailable. She sees that now. Regardless, you were unfaithful, and how she seeks out signs of betrayal. Why, why should she be looking in the first place? Spousal trust is the foundation of a marriage. If she is constantly suspicious, it is not a marriage that God will honor. A spouse is not meant to be a detective. If so, again, the marriage is not built upon trust. Guess who has to change that dynamic? YOU.

Sometimes, betrayed spouses will cheat back in retaliation, only to hate themselves for doing it. It's not unusual for betrayed spouses, even before finding out what's really been going on, to develop dependencies to fulfill their own unmet emotional needs and to soothe a deeply felt sense of frustration.

If you do not want a divorce, do whatever it takes over time to be a changed man. You serve your wife without expecting to "get anything back," even a thank you! If you are committed to behavioral change, then you must function in a realm of honesty, regaining personal integrity by going to counseling and going to group and having at least two strong accountability men. Be honest, patient, and kind. She'll see you reading books, educating yourself on the issues of yourself, but also seeking books to read about how you hurt your wife. In her eyes, despite her anger and devastation, this is good.

Finally, you find a solid Bible-believing church, join a Bible study, read the Bible at home, and surrender your life to Jesus. This is also good. Certainly, it's a must if you want to be set free, heal, and transform. That you cannot do alone, but HE can, in time! This also includes boundaries — what you see, who you see, where you go, what road you cannot go down, etc. You have to cut out all negative relationships in your life, including family. You have to cut off friends who are not well and/or live a different lifestyle.

Guys, staying on the right pathway is one step at a time. Blink your eyes; a year passes, and you wonder where it went. Same here. It may seem like a long time, one or two years, but blink your eyes, and boom, time passes that fast. You know it, and I know it, so do not go there. Do not say, "This is too much work!"

Do you love you? If you do, you will want change. Do you love your wife? Make the decision to win her back, and that takes time. If you have been lazy, passive, etc., throw those behaviors into the garbage can and begin a journey of disciplined choices.

If you immediately get help and she sees that, your efforts can facilitate healing for you, your wife, and your marriage.

Some men cannot restore trust; they cannot glue back together the expression "Humpty Dumpty" as far as their wife determines. Their marriage ends. Most men do not seek help after a divorce, but the wise man continues the journey for his own healing.

Betrayal represents a traumatic death of a relationship. As stated above, the wife will often experience all kinds of fallout because of the psychological and physiological trauma she has experienced. As you might suspect, men, she may experience a terrible loss of self-esteem, the rise of self-doubt, and a substantial inability to trust again. Each lady is an individual, and how she handles this can never be compared to how others process the same type of trauma. All women come from different backgrounds, different life experiences, etc. Any and all negative experiences will need to be processed in her own counseling journey and healing. So don't compare your wife to someone else and their healing! YOUR WIFE IS NOT THAT OTHER WOMAN!

To be wise here, there is no single way that betrayal trauma happens, looks, or affects someone, but it can be helpful to have some ideas as to what to expect, as mentioned above.

I must share here some hard facts:

- There are no such things as "steps to healing."

- There is no such thing as "stages to healing."

- There is no such thing as "stages or steps to grieving." (Believe me, I know this from the loss of a son). Run from the counseling room if this is stated.

There is work, work, work, depending upon you making that choice!

- Work is particular and specific to each individual and his or her background.

- Oh, did I mention work, work, work that is specific for you and your spouse?

Throughout this book, you are to educate yourself on the issues that are particular to you and are the same for your wife. In other words, you educate to be educated! And there is **SELF-**

EXAMINATION. Better yet, ask the Lord to look into your heart and your wife's to do the same. **Psalm 139:23–24 states:**

> *23 Search me, O God, and know my heart; test me and know my anxious thoughts. 24 Point out anything in me that offends you, and lead me along the path of everlasting life.*

And I promise you this. If you dive in and bring Christ into the equation, as with your wife, and do the work that is particular to each of you, then, finally, in couples counseling, God can do something you cannot do. And you'll find your love deeper, broader, and higher than ever, all because of HIM, our Lord. What Satan meant for bad to destroy each of you, God meant for good!

I want to put the word HOPE here for both you and your spouse. There is HOPE with and through our Lord in healing this marriage. There is no other way that will do what God can do. All other avenues are all self-effort, and you don' t have a partner, but with Christ, you have a partner, but you must surrender your life to HIM, as does your spouse. Oh, guess what? You cannot make her take this journey; that is her choice! What is your choice going to be?

Men, are you getting the picture of how much your wife has been hurt?

Betrayal trauma is a "brain injury," as Dr. Jill Manning, Licensed Marriage and Family Therapist, a Certified Clinical Partner Specialist (CCPS), a Certified Clinical Trauma Professional (CCTP), and a Board Certified TeleMental Health Provider (BC-TMH), explains, and occurs when someone we depend upon for survival or significantly attach to violates our trust in a critical way.

When such a word happens, the brain reacts by activating the limbic system, the "survival" part of the brain. When the brain's limbic system is ignited, "all logic goes out of the window." Get this, men! Rest on this for a moment. Look it up on the internet. Get informed. This is your beautiful wife, who you have hurt by your betrayal. The limbic system is programmed for survival, and it beats the pre-frontal cortex (thoughts and processes) every time. Compare this to the focus of the cortex — the control of voluntary movement, attention, learning, memory, motivation, planning decision-making, problem-solving, conceptual thinking, perception of sensory stimuli, language processing, visual processing and comprehension, and modulation of emotion.

All of these functions fly out the window because the LIMBIC system has taken over. The limbic system has registered with your wife that her spiritual, mental, emotional, moral, and financial relationships have placed her life in danger. In other words, your wife's mind is spinning in all kinds of directions. Her world has been placed upside down by your betrayal. She (limbic)) wants to run, fight back, protect, and do anything it can to help her survive.

With trauma, the brain has carefully regarded the exact details of every aspect of the situation. It released the limbic system EMERGENCY CREW immediately, blowing sirens and calling the dogs.

The trauma file in your beautiful wife's brain is not selective when something happens to "trigger" those feelings of fear, shock, terror, and anxiety, no matter how big or small it is connected to the images, emotions, and events that created the trauma in the first place.

Men, are you getting the picture?

All the above explains why women "overreact" and how those who have had trauma extended to them are triggered and set off so easily. For example, I had a couple whose husband betrayed his wife. He was really remorseful and working on his issues and read every book I passed his way. I saw them as a couple after a while before full disclosure. They were on their way to a counseling session, driving down a road with her as a passenger, and he was driving. Over on the sidewalk was this lady walking, and he put his eyes on her. Guess what? Yep, you guessed it, she was crying when they entered the office! She was triggered; his eyeballs got him into trouble, and she was relieving the original trauma. True story! I can also share that after full disclosure and several follow-ups, God transformed this man and this marriage and healed his beautiful wife, who was that beautiful externally but also on the inside from a biblical standpoint, spiritually! What a lady! What a gentleman that God created and transformed!

Trauma can cause the wife to cry constantly, have her sleep patterns interrupted, and take naps to escape the pain, seeking to sleep despite the nightmares she fears will come up because of the betrayal. Even suicidal thoughts can occur because the pain is so deep.

Men, are you getting the picture?

Rage is the other extreme! Rage with a capital "R" is a more accurate term. Men can help this by fully disclosing all, when appropriate, with a competent counselor and your wife at an appropriate time chosen by the counselor, knowing the sensitivity of all and when it would be appropriate to do so. Usually, this is a preparation that takes time to plan, and for the wife to seek separate counseling to prepare for full disclosure. We want it to be a safe environment for sharing, but the purpose of full disclosure, for me, is to pave the way for true healing and even, at some point, renewal of the marriage vows.

RAGE can be like a drug; it can offer a "brief release" for feeling completely worthless, although it is just a reprieve for the moment. She feels useless, has regrets, and is humiliated, embarrassed, ashamed, and guilty about how pathetic she has become. This is why, again, the sooner your ONENESS (your wife) competent counseling, the better. This is a must.

Trauma makes her feel like she is worthless! She will often stand in front of the mirror, looking at her body, comparing herself to what she imagines your betrayal was, and speaking lies about her beauty, worth, and value.

Trauma can place your wife into a fogged-like state, where her brain is not able to be alert, even to everyday tasks. Her everyday living is hard to connect to.

Husband (MAN), are you getting somewhat of an "understanding" of where your wife is at? You can never understand or feel what she is going through, so do not use those words with her. Those words are to be avoided at all costs!

Electricity in the air...can you imagine a current, a wiring carrying that current? Again, little things will trigger her emotions. This is the current of anxiety and fear FLOWING through her like a current of everything you hurt her with by your betrayal.

Some wives stay busy "doing" to escape the pain, yet they are burning both ends of their candles to the point that, at times, they collapse in exhaustion, as that candle burns out or the wiring (current) blows a fuse!

Let me say that I personally have firsthand knowledge that trauma can be healed. Healed despite betrayal, healed despite a son's death. However, the brain never forgets, and I can talk about Chad and not have tears, and then again I can talk about Chad and have tears. Even if some tears flow, God has healed me inwardly from betrayal and from a son's death. Did I do it? No! Did I put mind over manner? NO! God did something I could not do. It was a PROCESS! There are no steps! There are no stages! It is a process of walking with the Lord...His doing and my seeking Him.

Once again, it is crucial for both you and your wife to find a safe counselor or a safe and educational group for individual counseling and, eventually, couples counseling. Find a counselor who is primarily focused on marriage healing and not divorce (be cautious of therapists who support divorce).

Both you and your wife are adults. You both have choices to

make. Choice determines all. I know that God wants to heal the worse of the worse of issues. However, men, again, it takes time, effort, focus, and being intentional, determined, and committed to the process. Your wife is watching what you're doing. If you are vegging out in front of a TV instead of reading a helpful book, then your wife sees zero genuine effort. Show her genuine effort.

True story: I was counseling a man and his wife. They had been in their living room, their teenage children upstairs were doing their studying, and she was reading on one side of the L-shaped sofa. He was watching a Western. His wife said gently to him, "Didn't Benno say you need to be reading books?" He immediately cut off the TV without argument and picked up his assignment, which was a book. Actually, I had him reading eight books, going to group, seeing me, and making sure he had two accountability men who were mighty men of GOD! I might add that this marriage experienced healing and transformation! Not by me, but by God, as they both had to do a lot of work.

Men, you have an opportunity. What is that? It's the following:

VALIDATE YOUR BEAUTIFUL WIFE. VALIDATE HER FEELINGS. SAY THE FOLLOWING:

- Your feelings make sense. I have made you feel that way by my actions.

- I cannot fully understand, but I want you to know how sorry I am for the way I have hurt you.

- I hear you. I'm glad you told me how much I've hurt you.

- That sounds so troubling, how much I have hurt you.

EMPATHY

Sympathy and empathy both refer to a caring response to the emotional state of another person, but a distinction between them is typically made. While sympathy is a feeling of sincere concern for someone who is experiencing something difficult or painful, empathy involves ly sharing in the emotional experience of the other person.

WHAT ELSE TO SAY

- I can see how something has triggered you, and I am deeply sorry for hurting you in this way.

- It breaks my heart to see you this way because of my betrayal in the past; I take full responsibility for how you feel. What can I do to help you?

- I want you to know that I hate I did this to you.

- I realize you are angry for all the hurts and betrayal I did to you in the past.

TRUTH

Truth is:

1. The quality or state of being true

2. A true or accepted statement

3. The body of real events or facts

4. Agreement with fact or reality

Men, the truth is that you must walk beside your wife in healing! You cannot afford a quarter of the truth, half-truths, or three-quarters of the truth; you have to be walking. Correct?

As you and your wife process couple's counseling, start dating, and enjoy each other, consider the following:

In this story, probably three years in, a husband was found out. I counseled the man, the couple, and his wife at times. Her story was before the public, and she had to walk with her head held high and not flinch regarding all the pain and embarrassment her husband's sexual acting out caused. Every Sunday, she walked into church with elegance and grace, with a mindset that no one would defeat her due to what her husband had done, and the other participants were in the same church.

This man began Battle Lines and individual counseling and, at some point, couples counseling. It was not an easy highway to process with them, with her having so much pain. She was a strong woman in mindset, loving the Lord with all her heart, but divorce was on the table.

Eventually, little by little, things began to improve. He was faithful to the process, and I told them to do the following exercise when their hearts were ready, not before. But they had to get out of town to do it, a log cabin somewhere, where they would not be disturbed, as a suggestion.

They were to be in deep prayer beforehand, for days and weeks, and not do this as an exercise but from the heart.

Each was to write down the following on a pad:

I hurt you when… and spell it out one by one; day by day, week by week, month by month, year by year to the present (you can imagine how long the list might be if married thirty-five years — but this is the assignment).

When the couple was ready, these words were uttered face-to-face. It began with the husband doing two things, again, from his heart. He looked into his wife's eyes as he said these things. Again, not a checkoff, not a task, but a heart exercise:

- "I hurt you when —"
- "I repent that I did that to you —"

When he was finally through, he asked his wife, "Would you please forgive me?"

It was her choice to forgive or not. If she forgave everything, her husband planned to ask, "Honey, is there anything I left out?"

If she said, "Yes, there is," then he would write each down, taking his time to write thoroughly. He would take accountability for everything, responsibility for all of it, and not make any excuses.

Then he looked into his wife's eyes and told her, "I repent how I have hurt you here!"

1. When he was through, he asked his wife, "Would you please forgive me?"

2. She forgave him with all her heart.

3. Then it was her turn to do the same thing her husband did — again, as I have shared, all has to be done with the heart.

4. This was an all-day exercise and perhaps could go longer for other couples.

So, this couple had written all of this on paper and traveled out of town for a getaway. A cross rose atop a small mountain where they visited. They walked up and buried their paperwork at the foot of the cross. This is a true story. My wife, me, and their friends were invited when they renewed their vows.

Get this. One cold Christmas night at our church, after the Christmas Eve service, it was freezing outside. Everyone had on their coat, and this lady began talking to me on the way out. Thus, I introduced her to my wife, as I had no clue who she was, and then she said, "Oh, we met you were there when we renewed our vows!" Then I knew who she was, and her tall, handsome husband was walking beside her. Then she told me, "Guess where our retirement land is?" I told her I had no clue...

Boom — the place where they did the above exercise!

HOMEWORK

1. Write out in detail how you have hurt your wife emotionally, spiritually, and even perhaps physically. Seek to write in her terms, where you write from her pain.

2. How did that "feel" for you as you sought to write from her pain point of view?

3. Are you patient with your wife in this process of change?

4. Do you seek to "do" for your wife and seek to "do" right in helping her in the home and beyond? Expect nothing in return.

5. If you ever did, have you stopped saying to your wife, "Can't you see what I am doing?" A wife wants to see what you are doing, not being told what she is doing. She wants to see you doing it, in action!

6. As the spiritual leader of the home, are you asking her to kneel and pray with you every night in your bedroom? You pray to the Lord with vulnerability and transparency and only to Him. You say, "Lord, help my wife love me..." No words like that. She hears your heart in prayer. When you say Amen, it is her turn to pray to the Lord, and she cannot have any hidden words about you in her prayer. God tucks you in with HIS homemade Texas quilt of love in bed each night afterward. Be the leader.

7. Do you want to be well?

CHAPTER 10
True Stories of Healing, Transformation, and Setting the Captive Free

This chapter is being shared to encourage YOU that healing, freedom, and transformation can indeed take place for YOU "IF" you do the work that is necessary for you in counseling, group, and with the Lord, having a genuine relationship with HIM, choosing to walk according to HIS WAYS and walk along HIS PATHWAY, which is THE WAY, and YOUR bearing FRUIT, as it talks about in John 15. Without fruit, there is no Christ! Jesus is a "fruit inspector!"

Before beginning with true stories of truth, I wanted to share that none of what you read below has anything to do with me or my supposed talents, but only through the Lord are these stories told. My men's group, Battle Lines, began in my office with three men in May 2004. On June 30, 2019, 28,432 men attended Battle Lines. I also counseled full time, being on staff at Second Baptist Church, August 15, 1997. By the end of January 16, 2024, I had counseled over 19,000 sessions with 30 to 35,000 people (men and couples). For a season, I also visited the Medical Center every Wednesday. Patients of members, family members of members, or friends of members, and had over 5,000 visits.

As I mentioned in this book's introduction, I was a pastor/counselor, and around the year 2000, I started having cross "my desk," so to speak, men with sexual addiction issues and couples with their husbands having betrayed them. I knew I needed to learn more; thus, I bought books and went to workshops, seminars, conferences, etc., to learn more about this subject, which is deep because it is often childhood trauma, etc. The deeper I got with the deepening of understanding, the more I kept hearing the name of Dr. Patick Carnes, the expert of the experts on this subject of sexual addiction.

I was not a "certified counselor," but I already had seventy in my men's group with ten small groups in the early 2000s. I contacted IITAP to pursue certification and education, but they refused to train me because of my lack of licensure. My group was the largest in the United States; every Tuesday night, without a break, my group stayed in attendance. I kept knocking, and finally, Tami VerHelst, Vice President, in her consulting with Dr. Patrick Carnes, accepted me for training despite my lack of licensure. I was the first person without a license to undergo this training. It began in San Diego, California, and continued in Arizona, with sessions held in Tucson and Phoenix. At first, being with LPCs, psychiatrists, psychologists, and social workers wasn't very comforting. However, I knew much more than many because of Battle Lines and all the counseling I had been doing and reading every book I could get my hands on.

When I completed my training, a supervisor had to finalize my certification. Anna Valenti-Anderson, Clinical Social Work/Therapist, LCSW, LISAC, CSAT-S, CMAT-S became that for me. She is a wonderful lady who required such deep thinking during the challenges in my training. After her approval, I became a CSAT (CART) via IITAP.

I might add that I continued my training via conferences, workshops, symposiums, books, etc. Whether it was with IITAP, the American Association of Christian Counselors, or SASH, I continued on. I read between 800 to 1,000 books. In addition, I learned "The more you know, the more you do not know!"

In my group and in counseling, I could connect via my history of trials and tribulations, not in the addiction field, but in life. I was an apartment developer in Houston from 1969 to 1984 (when the economy crashed in '82). God sold all my apartments, which was a miracle because four months later, I could not hold my marriage of sixteen years together any longer. Throughout those sixteen years, I was unsure whether I would remain married or get divorced, all while raising two boys. How I survived, I do not know, but her betrayal throughout was like a knife into my stomach. I later lost a son to suicide, and another had significant issues, which were kept a secret.

God brought about another wife, Jan, who I mentioned has been with me for thirty-six years. I've also mentioned our beautiful twenty-eight-year-old daughter, who looks like her mom. God put this all together IN HIS TIME. Men, IN HIS TIME, GOD WORKS OUT ALL, IN HIS TIME, and HIS TIMING IS NOT OUR TIMING! God has much to teach during that time, and it continues until we take our last breath.

In the apartment building, which began with just me, myself, and I, I had to be tough, so in counseling and in Battle Lines, I could be tough if need be. Believe me, with people with an addiction, you have to have control, as they want to be in control. I had to let them know there was only one rooster in the barnyard, and it was me.

I will share some stories without names, so there is no ability to identify what has occurred through counseling with Battle Lines and me or with the men going to other counselors and Battle Lines. This is to honor confidentiality. ***These are actual stories about setting the captive free.*** They are not in sequential order, as they come to mind in writing this book. Therefore, these stories, in my own words, revolve around a few men over the years. I pray that they minister to you and those who have this issue, called sex addiction, can develop hope and faith that with the Lord, all things are possible.

STORY #1

This gentleman was around forty-eight when he came to Battle Lines. After his wife caught him in his acting out for many years, he became a broken man. He was receiving counseling somewhere else with a competent therapist. When his wife discovered his infidelity, she kicked him out of their home, and he lived alone in an apartment. He was so broken that he spent most days praying, reading the Word of God, and running his successful business from there.

He confided in his wife about two youth pastors who had molested him as a youngster, and they both kept that secret until the day he was found out by his wife. His wife was like an ice sickle to him; however, she insisted that he share his secret with his father and mother as a must, and there were no guarantees of reconciliation. This man, over many, many years, acted out with women, men, and transvestites. He shared with his pastor father and mother, and they loved upon him, their son. And this man is a man's man, yet there were many tears and brokenness taking place.

He became disciplined in prayer, reading God's Word, and meditating on it. His determination to seek help and do whatever was necessary was as serious as a heart attack. He lived in an apartment, and after many months, his wife finally allowed him back home, but it was freezing cold there with his wife. Many a day and night, he was on his knees in brokenness, sobbing, crying out to the Lord, and fighting to take his next breath. God had him in that position, as it was the only way change could occur. This man, in effect, was at the bottom of the barrel, and the only way was up. He started going to church regularly. He did all of this without knowing if he would ever get his marriage back. I have been there, where true brokenness cannot be humanly described. And God allows it as the avenue for change. You have a choice: fight for your life with HIM.

His father called him one day at this apartment and wondered if he could come over, and this gentleman did, and his dad came over. This man (addict) continued to work on his business from his desk, computer, and phone. After a while, with his father sitting on a sofa, he turned to his dad and asked, "Dad, you have said nothing, and you asked to come over; what's up?" His dad said this, and I will never forget these words, *"Son, I was not there for you when you were little (being molested), and I want to be there for you now."* What a father!

This man (addict) became the leader in Battle Lines. He held men's feet to the fire in being disciplined, structured, focused, with intention, and seeking for men to turn their lives over to the Lord, etc. His father came to the group several times, and he was a gentleman. One night, his father accompanied him to the big group meeting with his son. I could not allow him to attend the small group because of confidentiality. His son took his small group to a room (that is when I had ten groups) to meet. As I stood in the doorway visiting with this dad, his dad told me, just he and I, *"Benno, I have known my son all his life, and this is real with him!"*

This man (addict) said many times that divorce would be easier to go through than what he was going through with his wife. He kept faithful to his work in counseling, discipline, accountability, group, reading the Word, prayer + other books. One day, three years later, after being found out by his wife, he was leaving the house on a Sunday to go to church, and his wife said, *"Wait, I want to go with you!"* God transformed this man. God changed his marriage. This man had to forgive his offenders, one being a relative who had passed away. Thus, he, the person with an addiction, went to the gravesite to do so. He was in the process of getting rid of pain and seeking healing. Forgiveness is a must.

Through his church, Bible study at home, and volunteer work, this man (addict) became a fixture, which I cannot mention. Still, it was tremendous and a free-will offering to others, even when he was traveling out of state. This brother challenged me in regard to my walk and beyond in observing his journey. He told a man one time when another gentleman shared with this man whom God set free, seeking to help others, said, *"I cannot forgive...."* *(indicating that someone also molested him).* This brother shared, *"You cannot, but the Jesus in you can!"* I will never forget that statement.

I love this brother. He moved on in life, but I could call him right, and we would break bread somewhere together and be like no time had passed.

STORY #2

When this brother came to the group, he came because he got caught too many times, and he also was married and had two little children and a beautiful wife. He grew up in a Christian home but veered off track with drinking (he could consume nineteen beers in one sitting without getting drunk) and regularly engaged in inappropriate behavior with prostitutes, mostly.

His group leader became the brother in the Number 1 story above. As mentioned above, he was not easy on this man. This man, too, became immersed in the Word. I got to know his wife and him deeply in counseling and learned about her beautiful and forgiving heart. She wanted her marriage to work. It was difficult for him, as he would pass by specific locations because of his work. In his driving, he had boundaries and was not going to go down certain streets, etc.. He consistently upheld a strong sense of accountability. He fought the good fight and became a firm Believer with an in-depth knowledge of the Word. He, too, became one of my influential leaders. Even with limited hours, he made his presence known when he came, even in the later years. His big smile, physique, and the Holy Spirit shining through him truly revealed his identity.

His employment changed after twenty years, and he moved into another job. He and his wife homeschooled their children while monitoring the use of computers, and he built their new home with no TV. His children were cute as a button when I first met them at two years of age. Now, their children are growing up too fast, and I saw this man and his wife at my 80th birthday party at my home. We invited 115 people, with eighty percent of them being men from Battle Lines, along with some of their wives. They brought their fourteen-year-old children. The daughter is so beautiful, and his son is one handsome dude! I wanted to use this man and his wife from the counseling center in our couple's group as an authentic example of what God can do. Still, I was not afforded that opportunity, much to my regret, via my leadership above me. I had to apologize to them as they wanted to be used.

Again, I could call this brother up to meet somewhere for lunch, and he'd be like the brother in story number 1 — a solid example of transformation. I love this brother. His steadfastness, discipline, work ethic, etc., challenge me, as does his love of the Lord and his being such a FAMILY MAN!

STORY #3

When this brother came to the group, he was having affairs, married to a well-known family in the Houston area, with her family being very wealthy and having children. He is a member of a large Italian Catholic family.

Our pastor, Dr. Ed Young, sent him my way, as he knew him, and somehow, he shared his story with Dr. Young. This man is handsome, bubbly, outgoing, etc. He jumped into the group with both feet and met the challenge of what I was about with Battle Lines. He became inventive in different exercises he wanted to do later with our group; each one was special for that evening.

He turned his life over to the Lord and challenged fourteen men from Battle Lines to get baptized on a particular Sunday in May. There were clear blue skies as Dr. Young was baptizing in a pool outdoors. That day was perfect, as the Lord surely orchestrated it.

He also became one of my leaders, began dating, and honored that relationship in purity. He was a testimony and is a testimony for the Lord to the public and his large and extended family. He has kept his relationship pure, and the last time I talked to him last year, he was still single, running a family business successfully, and honoring God. When there are family functions, who do they call upon this brother, their son, grandson, nephew, or cousin, depending on whose home he is gathered in. They asked him to pray over the meal.

Every time we see each other, what happens? We hug! That's our greeting, and we sometimes kiss on the cheek! Wow!

STORY #4

What a story this is. When this man came to the group many years ago, he looked like a train wreck — like death warmed over. He had an accent, so it was hard to understand him at first. He was quiet and shared nothing.

He did not share or converse for over one year. Still, at some point, he was listening attentively as he always was, and he never saw guilt or condemnation placed on any man. However, this night was different, as someone was sharing, and it was as if the Holy Spirit was speaking to him. And that the night at home, he turned his life over to the Lord, and he woke up differently the following day. That does not mean work still had not to be done, but to him, it just began. From that meeting to the next Tuesday night, his life changed., He turned his life over to the Lord, he told his wife, and a new life began! What brought him to the group was that he had a child out of wedlock with another woman in another country, and he paid for that child's support, with his wife seeing that check sent out each month. This brother was a MUSLIM. The LIGHT OF CHRIST shone through him immediately, and his marriage later transformed. This man hungered and thirsted for God, His Word, and Prayer.

As this man's marriage and his family became transformed, he became one of my leaders at Battle Lines. He took on the position of a deacon. He always had a smile on and through him from the Lord. He was and is a man of peace and joy, and when he spoke, men LISTENED! I dined at his home and him at my house. He was and is such a wow!

He became one of my leaders on Saturdays. One moment he was one man, and the next moment, he became another.

His children were and are a delight. It has been years since I have seen them, but I know who they are and how they live their lives! This brother became the head of his home! A Godly husband and father he became! The last time with this brother and all the brothers that came to our last meeting of Battle Lines was in June of 2019, and I can't believe so many years have passed so quickly. Again, as I have mentioned above, this brother challenged me with God, His Word, and the walk we are to be about, walking according to the Word of God! This brother was and is a man of prayer. Having worked out of town and gone on a weekend and having to stay, he finds a church to attend! How many men do that may ask?

This man led his Muslim father to the Lord on a long and extended vacation. He is a kind gentleman, much like the soft, kind gentleman in the story of Number 1. A man that has a genteel heart! I miss this man and his son greatly.

This brother came up with some beautiful exercises for our group, and I will share a couple here that we used over the years.

We turned the lights down low and then wrote our worst sin on paper. When all were done, we folded them and placed them in a hat as it was passed. Then I shook the hat up, and each man drew a piece of paper, ensuring it was not his. We had previously set up an electronic paper shredder in the center of the room. We then, one by one, taking our time, read the sin. Then we quietly went to the shredder and shredded it. The shredding represented that man's repentance and forgiveness (where God forgot all about the past, and we should also). We took our time as we went around in a big circle. This exercise was over several hours, as it was a time of reflection, repentance, and forgiveness that was the evening's focus, and as always, it ended in a quiet but powerful Circle of Fire Prayer, where men put their arms around each other. One of us ended in prayer, and then we quietly departed.

Another time we had a cross built by a brother. We began the group session in the usual way, and then when we moved to the exercise, we wrote our sins down on a piece of paper and folded them. This time, we walked up to one by one, took a hammer, and nailed that sin to the cross. In mid-winter and freezing outside, one person removed all the notes and carried them into the parking lot, and we placed them in a bucket and burned them. This was against the rules of the church. Still, sometimes I had to go "outside of the authority" to accomplish what God wanted, not what the church necessarily wanted. I did this only a few times, and most in the counseling office, churches, and/or secular professionals would understand unless they experienced it.

Both exercises were symbolic of saying goodbye to that sin. We always shared repentance, but these symbolic acts were still compelling and sometimes with many tears shed.

These types of exercises were another means of bringing the brothers closer together. I was the counselor pastor, but we became brothers because of Christ, and their becoming to know Him. Peer to peer, and not lording it over another.

I might add here, again, that it goes against "tradition." We began at 7 p.m., broke at approximately 8:15 with our group, and then had small groups with a leader who had experienced freedom or further down the highway. Those groups, individually and independently, went to different lengths. Some went for an hour, some 3 hours, depending on the needs of that group. Connectivity took place with vulnerability and transparency, but "tradition" and professional thoughts go against this. So what? Truthfully, God worked in these groups and is undoubtedly THE ONE whose son BROKE TRADITION AND SHATTERED IT! This was rich at times, and God blessed my leaders (who were volunteers)!

When a group has love, acceptance, connectivity, and vulnerability and the time is founded on God's Word as the foundation, with books and subject matters I educated the men on, God honors that time. As we left, the meetings went in a different direction, at times, than planned, and we all wondered if this went differently than planned, but it became deep. We all knew God took over!

STORY #5

A man came to counseling, and I told him about Battle Lines in our session. He came from a background where he did not measure up to his father. This brother was Black, and his heart was beautiful and sensitive. He had become entangled in porn, masturbation, and prostitution and was on the verge of divorce. The community knew him well, and he had to carefully monitor and take medicine for his physical illness. He deduced that the embarrassment of being found out soon by the community would have to resign from his position, or so he thought. So, with that, he decided not to take his medication. Eventually, he slipped into a coma, and someone discovered him in his bed. He died three times and had to be revived on his way to the hospital. There were no heartbeats. He found that his community reputation and the organization extended much grace, and they gave him a leave of absence. In due course, he did deep work in counseling from childhood to now in counseling and Battle Lines. God started healing him. He learned that he had believed lies about himself for a very long time since his youth, and God had set him free from them. His marriage was healed, and his paintings take your breath away as an artist. His marriage, I might add, was touch and go for a while, but then his wife saw the evidence of change, and she extended grace to her loving husband.

When this man speaks, he thinks before he speaks and has a magnificent voice. Men listen when he speaks because they know he has something special to say.

As with almost all men that I have had the privilege to be involved in their personal lives and have had secrets shared with me, I sometimes was challenging, yet sensitive, pushing, and demanding in Battle Lines and counseling. This brother was no different. He rose to the challenge, read every book, did every assignment, and attended Battle Lines faithfully. What a brother he was and is!

Again, as shared about the other men, this brother challenged me in my faith walk!

STORY #6

This brother, what a story, and with that said, his journey became uncomfortable as the newspapers and TV exposed his secrets, leading his wife and children to hear and read about them. This is another story of faith in Christ, and I got to be a participant. Actually, in all the stories, in counseling and Battle Lines, when there is the transforming power of God changing lives, I am a spectator. I have the privilege of having front-row seats most of the time. He does it; I certainly do not.

He got caught in a sting operation by the police while soliciting a prostitute, and they took him to jail. His employer dismissed him from his job when they found out. His wife refused him his home. Thus, he stayed at his parents' house, where he grew up, and slept in the same bed as a child. He took jobs he never had before to support his family to provide monies. His children were furious at him, embarrassed, and did not extend any grace to him at all.

I must speak to it here. His wife divorced him. He wanted to have that marriage back, but brothers, it was hell and victory over four years of space, and he was in no-man's-land.

I do not know the timeline from his getting caught to his coming to Battle Lines and counseling, but he dove all in once he started. His wife was beyond traumatized, and it freaked her out what she knew, and at that time and for a season, she did not know all. He dove into God's Word and prayer and was allowed to spend a little time with his youngest daughter so he could read stories to her and tuck her in with prayers late in the evening.

He hated his work because it was not what he was skilled to do. However, that was his only option, and he took on another job to bring some additional money into the household. His wife had gainful employment, but during this time, the economy turned down, and her career job did not produce as it once did.

He developed accountably with the men in Battle Lines and was faithful in attending that and counseling. He could eventually move back into the home, but not the bedroom. Yet, not married. His teenage daughter kept her distance from him. In contrast, his oldest daughter, who he had out of a previous relationship with and was in her late twenties, kept her connection with her dad.

Two years passed, and there was a movement to a relationship between the client and his wife. His wife was also receiving counseling, and as mentioned, the journey was arduous for her, even after two years or more. The wife also had a confident mentor, a Christian leader, who she often visited outside the counseling center. She wanted to know all the truths and wanted it done. If I remember correctly, four years later, we had what Dr. Patrick Carnes called FULL DISCLOSURE, which she insisted upon before any movement took. Full disclosure sessions can be harsh on the spouse's hearing, and time unrushed must be the order of the day in these sensitive hours. She also wanted a polygraph test of her husband after the full disclosure to ensure that he was speaking the truth. Her trust level was almost zero. She walked in deep pain, and it is important to note men, that wives experience trauma from betrayal. Women just "do not get over it right away!" So, men, never say to your wife, "Why can't you just get over it?" That is a slap in the face to your wife and shows no empathy on your part whatsoever!

The couple's relationship improved, and there came a time when the client asked his wife to remarry him. Even though her pain continued, flashbacks came about at times, and she consented. The worship place, where the pastor mentored the wife, is where they were to be remarried in the chapel, which included families and some personal friends in attendance. I will never forget that during the ceremony, the pastor, knowing all about the couple, many times just stopped and said, "This is impossible;" again, "This is impossible;" still, "This is impossible." There was only a minimal reception at the couple's home, and the father and mother of the male client did not know me, but they knew my name. I asked the father, "What do you think about all of this?" I will never forget his answer; looking up at him, as he is very tall, he said, ***"This is the second miracle I*** *have ever seen!"* I asked him what the first miracle was, and he told me that he had been kept from the campus of The University of Texas during the Texas Tower shooting of 1966. Charles Whitman, a student and an ex-Marine, fired down from the clock tower on the University of Texas campus, killing fourteen people and wounding thirty-one others. The father was to be near where the victims ended up being shot. Still, circumstances kept him from being there as a student. He felt God had protected him.

This client and the previous ones mentioned continued their meetings in Battle Lines and counseling with me. Trust building is essential, as it speaks to the heart of the mate, as the time of healing differs for each spouse. A wife is looking for what a man is "doing," not what he is "saying!"

The last time I saw them was at a wedding reception for another couple, where this brother was the best man. What beauty we beheld with the daughter, wife, and this man (husband and father)!

Right here, I will share that this man's previous job rehired him, and this has never happened before. God does excellent things in his time!

STORY #7

A Hispanic brother came to counseling and the group. Many find this story hard to believe, but it is oh so real! It is another God story, who in all these stories is the healer and in setting the captive free! Oh, how I love this brother and what a mindset he developed. The Word of God became his absolute foundation, and nothing else. He did not waver, and he persevered. The following is his story.

He grew up in another war-torn country. His mom beat him with a whip that had knots on the end. His sister became a prostitute and still is to this day, according to the last reports I received. He had to choose between the military or being in the rebels at a very young age. At thirteen, his family kicked him out of his home, and he lived above a bakery. At seventeen, he traveled to the United States across Central America and Mexico.

It became explosive in an entire disclosure session that the client and I worked on in detail, having him rewrite it and think more when that session came. One of them walked out, and that is when the wife did not allow him back, and he spent his first night in his vehicle. A man offered a place to stay, but there was no bath, water, heat, or air conditioning other than just a small area to sleep. Remaining faithful to the work process, he continued for nearly a year. He did not complain; he had a smile that lit up any room he walked into.

What did this brother also do? He got before the Lord, read the Word, digested it, prayed, and went to counseling and Battle Lines. He created a strict schedule for himself that allowed no deviation. At 3 a.m., he got up and prayed for one hour. Whether for gas or anything else, he never carried more than a few dollars in his pocket daily and always got receipts for his expenses. Thus, he was accountable to his wife, even though he could not be near the home. He wanted his wife to know the truth if they could get back together. He came to counseling regularly and had significant accountability from Battle Lines.

The Word of God became his authority and foundation, and in the group, that was what he challenged the men with. His wife wanted to meet with him in time, and when she did, she met a different man (this transformed man, her husband). They went to counseling somewhere else as a couple and talked about getting back together. He continued his work with me and stated he would not go back home unless he could be "the head of the home," the biblical head of the household! The wife was a professional and brought more money in than him. She agreed to this request, and wow, a marriage healed, a family healed, his daughter graduating from college, and finding a job that was beyond superb.

This man used to wrap himself up in soccer and watch it on TV besides playing it. One day, he was shooting baskets in the driveway with his son, looking through the window and watching an international soccer game. His son prompted him to stop and give his attention, and he complied, never returning to this distraction practice while with his wife or children. Soccer became a "secondary" sport with him, with his son being the #1 focus in his participation in developing a relationship. He always had a smile on his face and just beamed, as I mentioned. Who can do that? You cannot make yourself do that; the Lord living through him did that.

Again, as with the others and so many more, I was a spectator in what God did, with men putting "feet to action" and doing all the work required to be healed and set free! It was and is just a wow! God works in mysterious ways, "if we but WILL!"

STORY #8

This man came to me and was married and had two children. He was acting out with other men sexually. As a child, a man who worked for his father molested him several times. The child kept it a secret throughout his life. His parents also divorced, and his father was more interested in other women, building his career instead of nurturing his children, particularly this young man. This client felt significantly depressed and had thoughts of suicide. I convinced him to go to a psychiatrist for treatment. He weekly came to counseling, became a member of Battle Lines, and did his homework. This man had and has a beautiful heart for others, and God started working in his life as he spent time with Him, learning the Word and prayer. He worked on forgiveness and repentance.

On his own, he goes out of state to spend time in a camp, in the wilderness, going up by a four-wheeler when he gets to his destination and forgiving and repenting. This was a three-day process, and that time was a transformational and healing moment for him. On his way back into the state of Texas, he initiated a call to his brother, whom he had been distanced from for many years, and spent the night in the city where his brother lived, reconnecting with each other. His marriage is healthy, his children are doing great, and his business and relationship with the Lord are ever-expanding.

He shared his testimony from the platform at a church, before thousands and gave all the glory to God!

God does nothing without us doing first. He does what we cannot do — a repeated theme throughout this book. Freedom and transformation are there for you, but you must do the work. The work required is different for every individual, which is why we are all different and come from various backgrounds, etc.

In Battle Lines, I began calling the men "brothers," which is true; they became, even as the leader, counselor, and pastor to many. Also, they called each other brother! That connectivity is an absolute must in a group. Only God can do this type of thing.

STORY #9

As a young boy, he was walking out of his house via the kitchen, opening up the screen door, and in doing so, his father was walking back into the house. The next thing he (the son) heard was a shot. His father committed suicide.

This man had been married several times, alcohol and porn addiction was part of his life, and in his last marriage, he had a son. This man, together with two other men, initiated Battle Lines and wholeheartedly dedicated himself to the work. Furthermore, he experienced healing in his present marriage, eliminated alcohol and porn from his life, and emerged as one of my leaders.

Men, nothing happens by "osmosis." It all requires the work God requires us to do, and then HE will do, depending upon the heart.

Once more, nobody is looking at me for any of this. I was just a conductor; the men were in the orchestra, and played the role that was particular to them. If the men would not do the work, I would not see them. If they were unwilling to read, I would not see them. And I would not work with procrastinators. Either they got serious, or I said goodbye and referred them out.

These stories are all true, and let me say here, as with AA and

SA, that the percentage of healing is hard to determine, but it is tiny — four to five percent in attendance over time and the same with Battle Lines. It could be the same; it could be a little higher. But it is also hard to do statistics on those who come and go.

With men in Battle Lines, I would never allow them to say, "Hi, my name is so and so, and I am a sex addict!" I stopped them in our circle in Battle Lines and said, "You are speaking lies to yourself." That is what you do, not "WHO YOU ARE!" As they surrendered their lives to the Lord, they became Believers who used to be addicts, but now are "sons of the King, who had an issue called sexual addiction." Men's issues do not define them. Know that! A man may define and judge you, but those are men, not the Lord. So stop telling yourself a lie because, soon enough, you'll live out the lie!

HOMEWORK

1. As you process the above, what do you gather from them as it pertains to you?

2. Can you imagine yourself, and if you are married, having a transformation and being healed for yourself and your beautiful wife?

3. What do you think it will take for the above to happen?

4. Do you want to get well?

CHAPTER 11
Group

Groups come in all types of shapes and sizes and are conducted differently by therapists, churches, independent individuals, and/or organizations.

Let me tell you about Battle Lines, which I began in May 2004 and ended my last group at the end of June 2019, with 28,432 men who attended on Tuesday nights and also, at times, an additional class on Saturday mornings.

When I began in my office with four men, I never wanted the group to be where, if a man had not read ahead or done the work required, he would not come. Since we were a Christian Group under the umbrella of our church and counseling center, I wanted to make sure we began and ended in prayer each time. We started using books to process and also the Bible for reference with Scripture, as my goal was several-fold, to eventually have the man set free from his addiction. However, foremost was his having a real relationship with the Lord.

I also had rules where we were not to argue or debate a subject matter, whether the material being discussed or our religious background and beliefs. We were to honor each man where he was. No pressure from any standpoint to "perform," if you will, to someone else's standards and have guilt trips. Throughout the years, we were not perfect here, but we were in the overall scheme of things. I also wanted to have that new man who came to feel "at home" right off the bat. Hugs and handshakes were the standards, and ninety-nine percent of the men wanted brotherly hugs, which brought out connectivity.

From day one, on our knees in prayer, we always began, with me leading or selecting someone. We then welcomed the new man by their first name only. Then we shared what the group was about, the confidentiality within our church or beyond it, and that confidentiality was uppermost. Over time, as word got out, men from other churches or a counselor somewhere in the city heard about our group and referred their clients to us. We did not have much publicity throughout the years, yet a desire of mine was to have Battle Lines grow due to sex addiction being such a big issue in Houston and beyond. We had, in the many years of the group, pastors coming who had an addiction, affair issues, etc., and they felt perfectly safe with us.

Battle Lines was like an embryo, growing and taking different shapes as the years progressed. Some great ideas came from men we incorporated, and some we tried and used for a while that I tossed away. One superb idea was at the end, and we circled, which grew in time to where we had seventy-plus, with arms over each other's shoulders or waist. We ended in prayer, again with me leading it or a man I selected to pray. We ended up calling that The Circle of Fire Prayer. What a powerful way to end.

As we grew, we began to do the following:

1. Began at 7 p.m.

2. Ended at 8:15 p.m.

3. Broke into small groups with a leader at 8:15 p.m.

4. Those groups began to be so powerful in connecting; many times, they did not end at 9 p.m. or later; some even went past midnight because something powerful was happening in the group, for one man or another type of situation.

At first, we ended around 8:15 p.m. and had no small groups. As we grew, and there were men whose lives began changing or being set free, those men, as I approached them, became our small group leaders, and that is where telephone numbers began being exchanged for accountability during the week. Those connections became precious over time.

At the end of this book, I will reference books for reading, of which I have read on the issues of sex addiction, trauma, brain development, marriage repair, etc., some that we processed in Battle Lines over the many years. A few we processed two or three times because we had new men, and some of the leaders felt it necessary to do so.

It was made known that there was only one leader, and that was me, and I operated under the umbrella of our church and counseling center. I had to honor my leadership, and if the men did not understand that they had to attend, it was a necessary rule that I had to uphold.

One of the brothers who God transformed prepared a handout in the latter years that we gave to the new men, which I include at the end of this chapter. At the end of this chapter, I also include newsletters I sent out each week to connect with the men and challenge them simultaneously. I felt it necessary to do that; thus, I did so. We always sent it out bcc (blind carbon copy with email addresses hidden), with the man agreeing before sending it out. If we had a major rainstorm or something else where we could not meet, bcc was the only way to communicate.

I allowed for discussion and crosstalk in the right way, in a challenging and endearing way, not in conflict or disagreement. If it moved to that, I stopped it and refocused us. Most men, with few exceptions, cherished this, as they learned each week, and I did too. Many groups allow only the leader to lead and discuss without input from those attending. Many groups will not allow a man to attend if he does not do the homework, buy the book or workbook, bring his Bible, etc. That I did not do. It is to be noted that, as the years progressed, the cell phone or iPad began to be a source for the book we were discussing and the Bible. For many, the very source of their issues, the electronic devices, where Satan and others meant for harm, became good by the Lord.

Battle Lines was free to attend, and you did not have to be a member of our church to attend. You did not have to be a Baptist; Muslims, Jews, Catholics, Mormons, and others attended, even with some having no belief in our Lord. As I noted earlier, a Muslim brother came to the Lord; his whole life changed, and he was set free and became one of my leaders. I did not do this; God did the supernatural work via Battle Lines.

We met every Tuesday night, and when we began Saturday morning meetings for those men who could not attend during the week, the lives of two men were dramatically changed. They led the group, with me doing follow-up at times. On Tuesday nights, we began at 7 p.m., as mentioned. On Saturdays, we started at 6:30 a.m. to 8 a.m.

Love became a common denominator in our group for each other, regardless of skin color. We became brothers, and we called ourselves brothers. We shared tears, joy, laughter (that was common, and it was right — it's good for the soul), etc. If I sensed special needs, I asked the man to sit in a chair in the center of the room, and we prayed for him, which was decisive. Several times, men developed a terminal disease, and we prayed for them.

I felt that love, the love of the Lord, was the theme that must be. Love invited men back, not condemnation. A man could say nothing and be accepted in the group. I wanted to make sure that each man felt safe and comfortable.

Some professionals in counseling charge $75.00 or more for each group session attended per man; some limit their groups to six or so men. I did not want that. I trusted that God could take care of it, regardless of size. When we met for a season, as we grew at a specific location on campus, we grew to over seventy men and had ten small groups, which was powerful! Men do not like change, and people with an addiction like to be safe and come to the same place each time. The church moved us to a different campus location, where we had to take an elevator. In our prior location, the men simply got out of their cars, walked through the doors, and came to the group meeting room without notice. We dropped to sixteen men when that change occurred, and it took years for me to rebuild the group. I was only able to build the numbers back to forty-five or so.

We broke for holidays, and several times shut down during December to give me a break and my volunteers. I depended upon qualified volunteers I vetted before asking them to pray about leading a small group.

Volunteers are to be praised and thanked a million times; however, since they are not paid and are volunteers, not all could be counted upon. The negatives were that there was no notice of their not showing up at times, and the small group attendees were confused as to what to do after we broke from our big group into a small group. I sought to have a second small group leader, but finding volunteers was not all that easy. Over the years, this became a toil on me.

I was set that the central leader had to be a man of integrity, free from the addiction or addictions (which many men had), and with a strong relationship with the Lord if married, a beautiful and family life. I was also set that this leader also must know God's Word as the absolute foundation of his faith: our God and His Son, Jesus Christ of Nazareth.

I will stop and pause here as I want YOU to understand Battle Lines. Battle Lines was established on a firm foundation: God, His Son Jesus Christ of Nazareth, His Word (The Holy Bible), and that alone!

Battle Lines was also established on this TRUTH; in the Bible, Luke 4:18 states*, "The Spirit of the Lord is upon me because he has anointed me to proclaim good news to the poor. He has sent me to proclaim liberty to the captives and recovering of sight to the blind, to set at liberty those who are oppressed."* Another translation states, *"The Spirit of the Lord is upon me; he has anointed me to tell the good news to the poor. He has sent me to announce release to the prisoners and recovery of sight to the blind, to set oppressed people free."* Note the words "to set oppressed people free" and "to set at liberty those who are oppressed."

This does not mean that we won't have temptations; we will

continue until the day we die. Still, it does mean that God can set us free and not be *"in recovery,"* as so many in the Christian community or secular community in counseling, state we will be! That is a lie! Know it, as I have seen the TRUTH visibility over a long period with men. I am not in any shape, form, or statement-making that it is about me; I am making the statement it is about God and His power; however, it does not come easily. It requires work and perseverance. God desires for us to be "overcomers!"

God's Word states in John 8:32, "And ye shall know the truth, and the truth shall make you free." In Ephesians 6:11 we read, "Put on the whole armor of God, that ye may be able to stand against the wiles of the devil." James 1:12 says, "Blessed [is] the man that endureth temptation: for when he is tried, he shall receive the crown of life, which the Lord hath promised to them that love him."

God's Word states in John 14:18–20:

> *I will not leave you as orphans; I will come to you. 19 Yet a little while, the world will see me no more, but you will see me. Because I live, you also will live. 20 In that day, you will know that I am in my Father, me, and you in me.*

Please note that Jesus is talking about the Holy Spirit and states, "I am in My Father." "You are in Me." "I in you." Let's look at this from a drawing to seek to understand, perhaps better, because it is hard to wrap your mind around it.

Take four Envelopes.

First Envelope — Place Christ in you. Seal each Envelope as you go.

1. Your name here

2. Christ's name here — you place the second envelope into the first envelope, Jesus, in you

3. Put Christ's name on this envelope

4. Put God's name on this fourth envelope and put the third envelope in it

As stated in a previous chapter, when we truly accept Christ and all that He is about and repent of our sins and forgive (God can only forgive us if we forgive others, the Word says), the Holy Spirit comes to dwell in us! It is through Him that He gives us the power to overcome temptations. However, it is by our choice, through our knowing Him, having a real relationship with Him, surrendering to Him daily, dying to our desires, knowing His Word, and prayer. We do not have to do this on our strength, even though our free will is involved. He gives us something that cannot be explained in human words. He IS He, and He is without definition because He is beyond that. He is God of the creation from eternity.

Battle Lines was founded on this foundation. You cannot beat this addiction or any other addiction without the power of Christ. You can overcome it with your strength, but that is limited, and most succumb back to their issues because your strength is temporary at best.

There was not a night that went back or a Saturday morning later that Christ was not glorified and shared.

God's Word speaks of this, which is not to repeat but to do so in a different way, and this is, Romans 8, "There is therefore now no condemnation for those who are in Christ Jesus. 2 For the law of the Spirit of life has set you free in Christ Jesus from the law of sin and death. 3 For God has done what the law, weakened by the flesh, could not do. By sending his own Son in the likeness of sinful flesh and for sin, he condemned sin in the flesh, 4 so that the righteous requirement of the law might be fulfilled in us, who walk not according to the flesh. Still, according to the Spirit. 5 For those who live according to the flesh set their minds on the things of the flesh. Still, those who live according to the Spirit set their minds on the things of the Spirit. 6 For to set the mind on the flesh is death, but to set the mind on the Spirit is life and peace. 7 For the mind that is set on the flesh is hostile to God, for it does not submit to God's law; indeed, it cannot. 8 Those who are in the flesh cannot please God. 9 You, however, are not in the flesh but in the Spirit, if in fact, the Spirit of God dwells in you. Anyone who does not have the Spirit of Christ does not belong to him. 10 But if Christ is in you, although the body is dead because of sin, the Spirit is life because of righteousness. 11 If the Spirit of him who raised Jesus from the dead dwells in you, he who raised Christ Jesus from the dead will also give life to your mortal bodies through his Spirit who dwells in you."

I wanted the men in the group, whether Christians or not, never to be condemned so that the Holy Spirit Himself or through a brother would draw them to Christ and surrender to Him. Thus, I allowed no condemnation, no matter what.

In Battle Lines, at times, I brought in an exceptional speaker, and on three different occasions, I had a couple of the lady counselors present to them, not to put a guilt trip on them in any fashion, but to educate them on the betrayed spouses' feelings. Our wonderful Dr. Milton Magness came on several occasions and was a hit, as was Jonathan Daugherty. Both were received in large numbers and with much attentiveness and questions afterward. Once, I had a couple come and share their transformed marriage, and it was well attended again.

Sometimes, I was moved to throw a curveball and do something different that needed to be addressed. I was enormously impressed to do this, educate, warn, and not take their wives for granted, etc.

Since we were biblically based, at times, I handed out identity Scriptures that I shared about earlier in this book, for men to claim a Scripture when they shared their first name in each session. Handouts were common in group meetings, and at times I asked one of the leaders to lead, and they always did a marvelous job. I could never have done Battle Lines without them.

As I have throughout the book, I want to repeat here that you can be free with hard work, individual counseling, group, accountability, boundaries, doing homework, reading God's Word and meditating on it, prayer, and seeking to walk His Ways daily. And that is a promise. Again, to repeat differently, perhaps, this is not a quick-fix type of thing; it takes discipline, courage, and perseverance, and God's timing is not ours. So many men want a quick fix. That quick fix has been and is a part of your issues. It's an immediate relief that you go to, with thoughts that flood your brain with chemicals, and you go into a chemical zone and find yourself doing the very thing you said you would not do again: acting out.

Some men even stated that Battle Lines was their church because they could be transparent in the meetings and could not be honest in a church or Bible Study because of Christian condemnation. They often talk about the artificial atmosphere in churches, where you are hurt but cannot share. I never wanted that and spoke about it frequently. Now, if they had an alcohol issue and not a sex addiction issue, they could communicate more freely and not be condemned. What is terrific about the purity of God and His Word is that transparency is there before us, but not in our modern-day churches. What effect would our modern-day churches have if they extended arms of love and acceptance? What numbers would flood in because of the Truth and Reality of Love that comes from the Body of Believers in that particular place of worship if this was so? Imagine a church that could not deter the flood of people flocking to an atmosphere of praise and worship that was real, not a show, not a performance, but simply the WORD taught. This was Battle Lines! The Holy Spirit was the programmer, and we participated with Him because I certainly was not adequate to bring it about. However, He was!

1. Are you in a group?

2. If not, why not?

3. What are you receiving from the group if you are in a group?

  a. Accountability?

  b. Connectivity?

  c. Education on the issues?

  d. Biblical truths being received?

  e. Walking out the biblical truths?

4. Are you doing homework that is processed in the group?

5. How faithful are you in attendance?

6. What do you do to contribute to the group?

7. Do you want to get well?

CHAPTER 12
Brain on Fire

Of all the subject matter in this book, this is one of the most important outside of developing a proper relationship with the Lord.

I will begin here with THE CHURCH and its significant lack of misunderstanding of the issues of sexual compulsivity/addiction. Churches and their leaders often shame and guilt individuals, which in turn perpetuates the secrets of addicts. The church shows more compassion for alcohol and drugs than this issue. Why is this IGNORANCE? In their IGNORANCE, they think it is a "choice" when it is and is not. They have no clue as to the brain, the patterns of the cause, the traumas in the background, low self-esteem, family of origin, etc. I am not making excuses for the person with an addiction, but I have extreme compassion for them. They need to know that freedom, healing, and transformation can take place with hard work, working with the right educated counselor, having strong accountability, and going to the group over a long period. Again, to repeat, short-term counseling, group, rehab, etc., will not work. Why is that? Years of patterns being set, which are the neuropathways in the brain and the chemicals in the brain, demand that its needs get met.

I believe in simplicity, black and white. Thus, when I get a counselee in, their issues are this: They feel that condemnation or something will take place with revealing, so I do the next thing. One counselee told his wife about "Benno's stick drawings." I have always accepted them where they are and sought to get in touch immediately and develop connectivity. Sometimes, the most simplistic of things seem to connect and affirm. Again, I never did "textbook" counseling, but "relational counseling," where trust occurs. Yes, I can be "tougher than toenails" if need be, but I found that the approach mentioned earlier is better.

They shared, and I got a sheet of paper and drew a brain first, and then them as little boys or teenagers, etc. I asked when they were first exposed. I asked about curiosity, magazines, masturbation, porn, or acting out with others, and I got affirmatives. Then I asked if they returned to it out of curiosity, and they answered in the affirmative. Then I wondered if the very thought caused excitement in the brain to act out, and they affirmed. I share with them that the chemicals and neuropathways demand more, and when this is the case, they feel out of control. And they again declared that they had no control over it. I also asked if it met a need, and they stated that they felt affirmed, more relaxed, and the escape made them feel good, etc.

Then I moved to the here and now and asked them if this is true. I again drew a stick man, and that man had thoughts of acting out but said, "I will not act out." Suddenly, they were at a place of acting out, as if an aura took over, where they actually had no control and were acting out in masturbation, pornography, massage parlors, prostitutes, affairs, etc. And they affirmed their particular issues. The very thing they said they would not do, they were doing. And again, I placed no shame or guilt, but I sought to get to an understanding of what was taking place in the men with addictions.

As a child or young adult, exposed to porn, molested, etc., by curiosity, he goes to porn, acts out, and it meets a need, develops a high. Later he goes back to it. The chemicals start demanding their needs to be met, and neuropathways are created, like Interstate 10, getting entrenched and demanding their needs are met. Thus, the very "thought" creates the chemical, and then you act out. Right? Answer,is "Yes!"

Thought hits, and you say, "I am not going to act out." Yet you entertain it. You have no escape plans (i.e. calling someone, etc.) All of a sudden, you find yourself acting out with the "magnet" (chemicals and neuropathways taking over.) And guess what? You retrenched it in your brain. Acting out is doing the very thing you said you would not do! And this will happen again.

When triggered, you will be tested, and with a long history of acting out, change does not take place for a long time.

One of the best examples of the sexual addiction cycle is by Dr. Patrick Carnes, below:

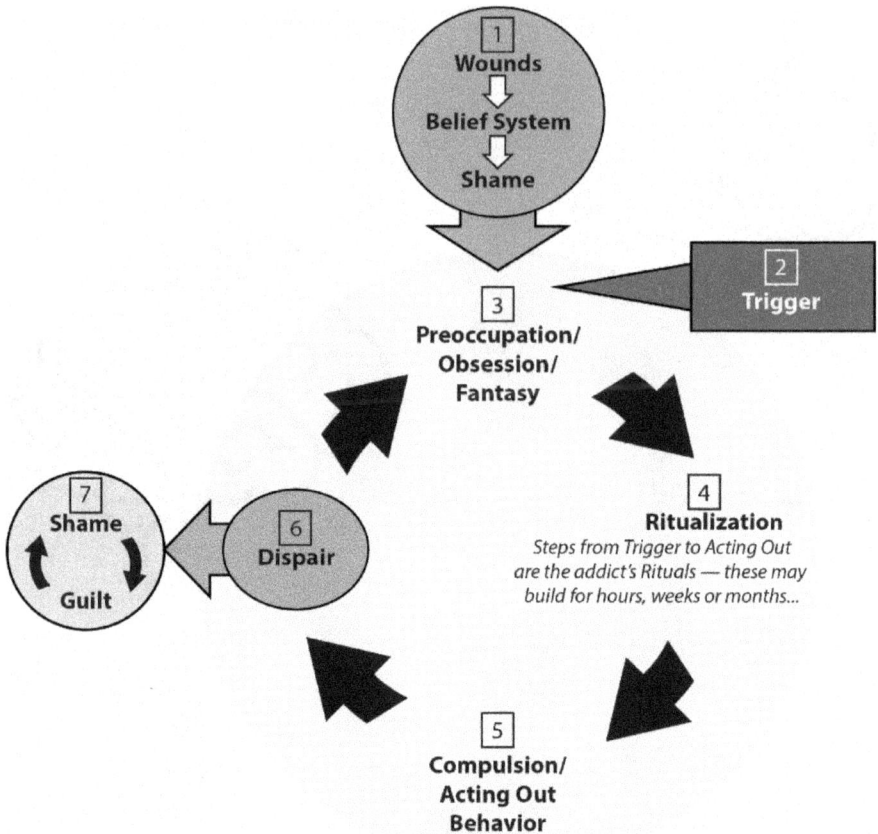

Cycle of Addiction

Notice #1 identifies "wounds and belief system/sham" as root issues that the person with an addiction must address to experience healing, freedom, and transformation.

Wounds:

- Childhood attachment injuries

- Emotional, physical, sexual abuse and neglect

Core **Beliefs** of an Addict:

1. I am a bad, unworthy person. (**Shame**)

2. No one would love me as I am.

3. No one will meet my needs/nurture me.

4. Sex (or an intense relationship) is my most important need/way I feel loved.

5. *God isn't good enough, doesn't love me enough, won't or isn't powerful enough to meet my needs.*

Notice #2 is triggers. Unless one has escape plans and understands his triggers, #1 engulfs him.

Triggers:

- Emotions — **B L A H S T O**
  - **B**ored
  - **L**onely
  - **A**ngry
  - **H**ungry
  - **S**tressed
  - **T**ired
  - **O**verwhelmed
- Stressors/problems
- Fight with partner
- Music/particular song
- Specific person
- Hair/body parts
- Memory
- Criticism
- Smells

- Movie/TV show
- Location/place
- Disappointment
- Money anxiety

Notice #3 Preoccupation / Obsession / Fantasy (almost instantly this happens) that drives the for one to act out, and that opens the door to #4.

Notice #4 Ritualization — pre-planning, thinking ahead, excuses, etc. which leads to #5.

Rituals:

- Clothing/apparel
- Makeup
- Grooming
- Shoes
- Perfume
- Laughter
- Texting
- Personal/intimate conversation
- Eye contact/smiling
- Fantasizing
- Taking off wedding ring
- Flirting/innuendos
- Touching
- Driving
- Drinking

- Dancing

- Being/acting needy/helpless

- Being/acting independent

Notice #5 Compulsion / Acting out Behavior (this can happen almost instantly and/or build up to acting out soon because he cannot get it out of his thoughts, which leads to #6.

Notice #6 Despair that he acted out and then the circle of #7.

Notice #7 Shame and Guilt (pain), which drives the addict to cover the pain. As a result, the addict repeats the cycle, and the chemicals of the brain demand satisfaction, strengthening the neuropathways with each instance of acting out. I call this "deep rut behavioral patterns." Do you recognize yourself in one of the two above diagrams?

ESCAPE

I want to insert right here that you must have a means of escaping your sexually acting out behavior for a change to take place in your life. You MUST practice your escape plans and know your triggers.

Almost all men who have sex addiction issues have a low sense of self-worth. There is always a root cause of the problems. It is the counselor's job, along with the counselee, to explore a family of origin and other areas of development as a child into adulthood where those roots may be.

I might add here that an adult who has sexual addiction issues may come from a healthy family of origin, and the problems of sex addiction did not show until later teens and/or adulthood. Let me give an example. Say, a fifteen-year-old accidentally sees a porn site, and once he's seen erotic images, he can't un-see it. "They can't get it out of their heads," states Clinical Psychotherapist Frances Duncan. "This stuff (porn) not only changes the brain chemistry but the structure in the brain, and these are young, developing little brains. It is the same addiction as to an opiate."

I have counseled teenagers who during internet searches accidentally found a porn site, and stated to me, ever since then, that they could not stop looking at porn and masturbating. It causes anxiety and sleep disturbances. It is traumatic and brings about shame. They are "haunted" by what they have seen and/or done but cannot stop. Seeing porn is trauma to the brain, and it is like a magnetic impact on the brain. You might recall that Dr. Patrick Carnes calls this the Trauma Template. Why is that? It is because:

When one is viewing pornography, mirror neurons fire in the brain. These neurons can lead to a state of arousal, which results in a person taking action to ease that state. When the person commits this act, to achieve relief, s/he is bound to the image that they were viewing, and for porn addicts, it's usually a pornographic image.

When you view pornography, dopamine is the primary chemical that is responsible for the aroused state and its release. The problem with this is that over time, the explicit images release more dopamine than looking at a partner. And frequently, this can lead the porn addict to lose interest in their romantic partner and rely more and more on pornography to achieve arousal. That person often develops a disconnect in their relationship, causing the wife to feel rejected and blame herself for not being attractive enough all the time. However, she is unaware that her husband is indulging in pornography, possible prostitution, massage parlors, and masturbation.

When a porn addict's brain gets used to the release of specific amounts of dopamine, the effect will be desensitization to that type of image. To increase the release of dopamine, the person with an addiction will seek more evocative images. And this is precisely why porn addicts seek more extreme types of pornography. The addiction requires higher and higher stimulation, thus capturing the person with an addiction to where risk-taking can even become dangerous, where they may get caught up in a sting operation when prostitution is involved. I called this an "aura," where it takes a life; it's all alone. With masturbation and orgasm, sexual acts with orgasm, etc. occur, the power of those chemicals goes away.

Repeating the sequence of watching pornography and reaching a state of arousal often causes it to become a preferred method of achieving satisfaction. When your brain prefers this oft-tread path, it becomes challenging for porn addicts to focus on actual relationships.

The facts about brain chemistry should be able to tell you about the psychological impact pornography addiction can have on a teen. And if nobody treats it for a long time. In that case, it can become the cause of debilitating sexual behavior issues in the teenage years and into adulthood.

You did this in secret if you began as a child, and as an adult, you did the same. By keeping it a secret, you integrated this secretive lifestyle into your life, extending to other aspects of keeping secrets. Just a question right here, where else do you "lie" in your life: in your marriage, your work, your relationships, etc. What else does your wife not know about? In marriage, your spouse will eventually discover your secrets, and they will ultimately erode your relationship. When she finds out about your porn, affairs, massage parlors, etc. Divorce may be right around the corner.

Parents of a teen, of a child under 10, DO NOT WANT TO face the fact that porn has this effect on their precious son and/or daughter, but it does. Parents must monitor the Internet appropriately before a child can access any computer, iPad, cell phone, etc.

The underlying defect, reduced to its most straightforward description, is damage to the "braking system" of the brain. It causes the brain to stun development as God designed it to be. In 2007, a VBM study out of Germany looked specifically at pedophilia. It showed almost identical findings to the cocaine, methamphetamine, and obesity studies. It concludes for the first time that a sexual compulsion can cause a physical, anatomic change in the brain, the hallmark of brain addiction. A preliminary study showed frontal dysfunction, specifically in patients unable to control their sexual behavior. This study used diffusion MRI to evaluate the function of nerve transmission through white matter. It showed abnormality in the superior frontal region, which was associated with compulsivity. The question here is, are you getting to understand the seriousness of porn? I'm just asking!

Researchers found that hours spent watching porn as negatively correlated with the amount of gray matter in a subcortical region near the front of the brain — the right striatum — that is involved in the processing of rewards (as well as lots of other things). In other words, men who said they spent more time watching porn had a smaller amount of gray matter in this part of their brain. Also, the more avid porn viewers showed less activation in their left striatum when they looked at racy images, and they appeared to have reduced connectivity between their right striatum and their left dorsolateral prefrontal cortex. The question here is, are you getting to understand the seriousness of porn? I am just asking!

Recent research has shown that non-drug addictions, such as gambling, binge eating, and sexual activities, affect brain function in ways similar to alcohol and drug addiction. Many addiction studies focus on what is referred to as the pleasure/reward circuitry and their corresponding neurotransmitters — chemicals that are responsible for the communication between neurons. One neurotransmitter frequently identified as central to addiction is dopamine. A behavior or drug that produces pleasure induces a rush of dopamine that ultimately "reinforces" that behavior, making it more likely to occur. The amygdala, basal ganglia, and other reward centers play a role in the activity's reinforcement that produces pleasure. The question here is, are you getting to understand the seriousness of porn? I am just asking!

"Plasticity" is the term used to refer to changes in the brain's neural pathways, as noted previously. Your brain has the ability, with your choices, to recognize itself by forming new neural connections "throughout life," unless there is something physically wrong with your brain, you can rewire your brain up to the time you pass on, like some you see on TV news, 106 and enjoying life in all kinds of ways! You can do the same!

Research substantiates the idea that porn addiction can alter brain plasticity. *However, you can also rewire, repeat, repeat, you can rewire your brain! Your* addiction is not irreversible. I just want you to know you can become free! Jesus came to free the captive, heal, and transform. In Jeremiah 29:11–14:

> *"For I know the plans I have for you," declares the Lord, "plans for welfare and not for evil, to give you a future and a hope. 12 Then you will call upon me and come and pray to me, and I will hear you. 13 You will seek me and find me, when you seek me with all your heart. 14 I will be found by you," declares the Lord, "and I will restore your fortunes and gather you from all the nations and all the places where I have driven you," declares the Lord, "and I will bring you back to the place from which I sent you into exile."*

What does the above say? Seek God with all your heart! With this, you take additional steps to honor God's Word and make healthy choices based upon HIS Word. You make your MIND. Scripture speaks of this in Colossians 3:2, "Set your mind on things above, not on things on the earth." You choose to set your mind on new things! Later in another chapter, I will give you tools that I have given clients and in Battle Lines over the years. Choose to act upon them with those suggestions.

Non-drug addictions, like the internet and pornography use, may lead to changes similar to those reported with long-term drug use. But these issues are not irreversible!

Increased pornography use is associated with increased striatum. The researchers found that the striatum, a region that processes rewards, had a smaller volume and less activity. However, it is not yet clear if this is because of more considerable time spent viewing porn or if people with reduced striatum volume will watch more porn.

These individuals also have less connectivity between the striatum and areas of the prefrontal cortex, showing reduced judgment, decision-making, or control over impulsive behaviors.

We are amid a massive social experiment that is having a seismic impact on the sexual templates, behaviors, emotional well-being, and attitudes of youth. Never have we brought up a generation of boys who are a click away from viewing free hardcore mainstream pornography or girls who are growing up in this pornified culture. The domestication of the internet, which began around the year 2000, made pornography affordable, accessible, and anonymous, the three key factors to increase demand and consumption. Porn sites get more visitors each month than Netflix, Amazon, and Twitter combined, with Pornhub alone receiving 22.8 billion visits in 2024. Studies show that nearly forty-nine percent of college males first encounter pornography before age fourteen. Given this early age of access, it is essential to investigate what type of internet sites these children see and their effects on them. According to the most respected and cited study on mainstream pornography content, the researchers found physical aggression, such as spanking, open-handed slapping, and gagging, in over eighty-eight percent of scenes, while verbal aggression was expressed less frequently. The study found that the porn sites viewed included calling women names such as "bitch" or "slut" in forty-eight percent of the cases. When both physical and verbal aggression were combined, the researchers found that at least one aggressive act was present in ninety percent of scenes.

Checking out what we've learned about teens and porn in the past twenty years, adolescents who used pornography more frequently were male, at a more advanced pubertal stage, sensation seekers, and weak or troubled relations within the family.

Jochen Peter stated in "Adolescents and Pornography: A Review of 20 Years of Research" that "People who used pornography had more permissive sexual attitudes and stronger gender-stereotypical sexual beliefs. It also seemed to be related to the occurrence of sexual intercourse, more significant experience with casual sex behavior, and more sexual aggression, both in terms of perpetration and victimization."

The Internet has become an integral part of the modern lives of adolescents. This allows youth to easily access information and topics of inters online, including sexually explicit material or pornography. Adolescent pornography use has expeditiously increased over time, and the age of first exposure to sexually explicit materials has also been getting younger. I have had cases where men were first exposed to porn at around the age of eight. It is essential to mention that errors are common when collecting statistics on secrets because the issue remains hidden, and individuals often experience guilt and shame. However, I believe the problem is much darker than any parent or researcher can bring forth. And the reason I shared that, with all the clients, plus men in Battle Lines, and doing the client's history, I have found that it began at five in one instance. The age of eight was not uncommon for first-time exposure. I might also add that the child cannot handle these exposures emotionally, as their young brains are far from wholly developed. Still, when they go back to it via curiosity, it does not take long for the child to be captured via my drawing previously shown in this chapter.

The estimate of prevalence rates has varied, but nationally representative surveys of adolescents in the USA have found that sixty-eight percent reported exposure to online pornography. Another study in the USA found that forty-two percent of youth between the ages of ten and seventeen reported viewing online pornography. Other prior studies show that nineteen to thirty-seven percent of teens reported intentional use. Comparatively, the range of unintentional pornography use in adolescents is from thirty-five to sixty-six percent. Again, I might add that I think these percentages are way low because how can you do true statistics on secrets when shame and guilt are also part of that secret?

Both deliberate and accidental use of pornography has increased in frequency with the age of sexual development. Social and environmental changes can also have an effect. Reported pornography use increased even more in the setting of the COVID-19 pandemic, lockdowns, and social distancing. Isolation is a critical factor in this issue of the use of pornography. A child has access to the internet via his room (isolation); the child has social problems with others (isolation); the parent must know of the child's internet use, and closed doors cannot be the home policy. If there is negativity in the home, a child may "escape to his room" to soothe himself and then find internet porn. If the child has access via a cell phone or computer, that moves from accidental finding to intentional use. Soothing becomes a neuropathway (pattern) created in the brain, with many chemicals of the brain being enacted.

I might add here how foolish parents are in letting their children have free rein over technology. They are foolish in thinking, *My child would never do that!* Foolish is as foolish is!

Adolescents may expect what they observe in pornography to be like real-world experiences. It may influence them to perceive sex as primarily physical and casual versus emotional and relational. God desires intimacy between a husband and a wife. Abandonment to each other emotionally and physically, and when porn has been in the addict's background, then, most times, they cannot connect to their mate in the manner that God desires.

As this issue of porn increases, the adolescent becomes more preoccupied sexually on the Internet, with sexually permissive attitudes. These attitudes may include the belief that women are sex objects rather than relations or partners. Adolescent males, especially those exposed to sexually violent media, reported more accepting attitudes towards teen dating violence and sexual violence.

People may use pornography to seek sensation and show characteristics related to impulsivity. These individuals with higher levels of sensation-seeking behaviors may report a greater frequency of pornography use and a higher risk of developing problematic pornography issues.

It is a suggestion for all parents/caregivers to gain insight into the adolescents' psychosocial needs. Common traits in adolescents who have higher rates of pornography use include more advanced pubertal development, minimal caregiver supervision, emotional connection, family conflict, and behavioral problems. Individuals with attachment (connectivity in relationships — especially parental) may engage in pornography use to seek relational or sexual connectedness and/or comfort in "any emotional commitment," reducing fears of rejection or abandonment. Another study found that youth may seek pornography to increase their sense of belongingness and increase loneliness. Lastly, individuals may consume pornography to manage emotional stress or discomfort.

Screening youth for pornography viewing should be a routine part of adolescent health care by the parents. I might add here that today's children, with computer knowledge, can get around firewalls, filters, etc. *Thus, parental involvement is a must.* And it is a must in a relationship, and I will get into this later in the book. Children seek relations with their parents, yet parents today are so busy in their own lives. With technology being a part of that, they *MUST* get involved in all aspects of their children's lives, *as they should and must do.*

To understand is to gain knowledge and help with your health and choices. You can rewire your brain, and if you have been caught up in addictive behaviors, it will take some time. *However, research has noted that the brain exhibits plasticity.* It is a gift from God that HE has gifted us with. Still, your choices can entrench your neuropathways in addition, or it can rewire over time and move you away from your addiction.

The journey (pathway) to overcome porn addiction (also included in this definition is prostitution, massage parlors, masturbation to thoughts and images). Like rewiring an old house from aluminum to copper wiring, overcoming porn addiction (which also includes prostitution, massage parlors, and masturbation to thoughts and images) requires a lot of work, such as tearing out sheetrock, running new wiring, installing new electrical panels, switches, fixtures, etc. Still, eventually, you have a brand-new operating system. Same with your brain, but it takes a lot of work on YOUR PART! Your brain is remarkable, as created by God, and it can change! Your brain can change and adapt!

YOU MUST CHOOSE to not act out! It would be best if YOU had the following in place for you to change, I might call this a BATTLE PLAN:

1. A plan

2. Have accountability with two men who are strong and can hold your feet to the fire.

3. ly plan out escape plans (you have to practice your escape plans ahead of time) so that when you are triggered (and you will be), you have mechanisms ready for escape.

4. Ensure that your accountability men have telephone numbers readily available.

5. Ensure you have filters on your computer, cell phone, iPad, and other devices.

6. Regarding your street patterns, it is important to establish boundaries when it comes to activities such as massage parlors and prostitutes. You cannot travel streets that you once acted out in regard to establishments of sexual activity.

7. It is necessary for you to attend counseling once a week.

8. You must be going to a group once a week.

9. Reading books on addiction is a must.

10. To experience real healing and transformation, it is essential to surrender your life to the Lord and seek a proper relationship with HIM. Outside of HIM, then you are only working with human effort, and human effort always breaks down! Guaranteed.

11. You must be on a journey of continual education on this subject of addiction!

Your well-being, marriage (if married), employment, friends, etc., are at stake here for you and before you! Take it all for granted, and you will end up losing! Guaranteed! The cost will be tremendous and can cause your life to be ruined, to where all you regret will go for naught because you thought you were more intelligent and more significant than the addiction issues that have captured you.

You have a great brain with the plasticity to reorganize itself; you are the car's driver who can bring that about. *No one else can do it for you.* You are the decision-maker here. *Oh, by the way, the car you are in is in for a long trip because it took a long time to create your addiction.* Thus, it will take a long time for change to take place. If you get lackadaisical, plan for no results, and you'll slip backward quickly!

In the realm of porn addiction, the cornerstone of change is your choices, with your brain connecting to these alternative choices. Little by little, rewiring takes place. Whenever you choose not to act out, you slowly rewire your brain. Every time you act out, you entrench your addiction. It is not permissible to go back and forth; You will make some mistakes, but with eighty-five alternative choices over ten percent bad choices you'll slowly build new patterns.

What a wonderful thing it is for your brain to slowly start healing and forming healthier connections. You disrupt bad choices for sound choices, and you will feel better within yourself! Bet on it, you will feel "free," and that is priceless!

Research has shown that prolonged porn consumption can have a stunting effect on cognitive development. It can lead to altered neural pathways that impair your cognitive functions, such as decision-making, problem-solving, and emotional regulation, which refers to the processes individuals use to manage and respond to their emotional experiences appropriately and adaptively. It encompasses strategies to amplify, maintain, or decrease emotional responses. The good news is that these effects are not irreversible! *With this news is that once an addict, not always an addict! I want you to know this is truth. It takes work to get here, but God is in the business of setting you free, when you choose to do things HIS way, which is "the way!" Establishing a relationship with HIM brings about a partnership that eventually brings healing for you.*

Let me stop right here for a moment. Whether you are in a group, counseling, etc. I do not want you to say to yourself and/or to others when you are introducing yourself, "Hi, my name is XXX, and I am a sex addict." Your issue does not define you. When you become a Christian, your name is xxx, and you are a child of the King and have a problem called sex addiction. Later, *your name is xxx, and you are a child of the King.* Guess what? Your work, your title on the door or your business card do not define you either. God wants to show you that *YOUR IDENTITY comes from HIM! HIM and HIM alone!* In my men's group and/or in counseling, I would always stop them if they identified themselves as a sex addict. *You tell yourself that enough, and that is who you are!* Those are lies! Don't lie to yourself, and don't allow any group, S.A., or whatever, to define you! That is a period!

Fear of permanent brain damage is common among men fighting sex addiction! Not so! Neuroscientific evidence does not support this fear! *I want you to know YOU CAN MAKE A FULL, not "recovery," but "healing!"* Recovery means you are always in recovery! **Healing means you have healed!** Day by day, your brain is constantly reshaping itself with all the new daily information! Men, take 1 day at a time and do not get ahead of yourself for change.

This new journey that awaits you can only be possible by making the right choices (steps)! You must begin not only quitting porn but the other adverse decisions that have gotten you into the mess you are in! Over time, your hyperactive brain will settle down. Don't you want this for yourself?

Rewiring the brain goes by overcoming the habit; it's about enhancing overall mental and emotional health! Don't you want your relationships to have much improvement? That is what will happen if you make the right choices. The choice is one step at a time, one day at a time, one week at a time, one month at a time, one year at a time. Take your time, make your right choices today, and don't get ahead of yourself; time will take care of that. This is a repeat. Repetition is my theme in sharing information. If you do not get it once, perhaps the second or third time you will.

What do you think about establishing new habits? What about exercise, a new hobby, new books to read, enjoying your relationships, reading God's Word, the Bible, and prayer, and relaxing and listening to good music! YOU can do it! *It just requires alternative choices!* You cannot do it all at once, so take your time. Just like eating a delicious meal, chew your food and savor it.

In today's world, whether it is watching TV, walking through a mall, grocery shopping, driving your car, going to church, going to the movies, etc., you cannot avoid SEX! It is everywhere. *You do have a choice, whether you entertain it!*

Suppose a sexual behavior or fantasy provides you with pleasure or relief from pain (escape). In that case, the body learns how to attach to that. This behavior tends to occur more frequently, and repeated behaviors become a habit! You know that! This is called conditioning. Your behavior becomes attached to repeated choices in conditioning. Breaking the conditioning is complicated and extremely powerful, as you know by now!

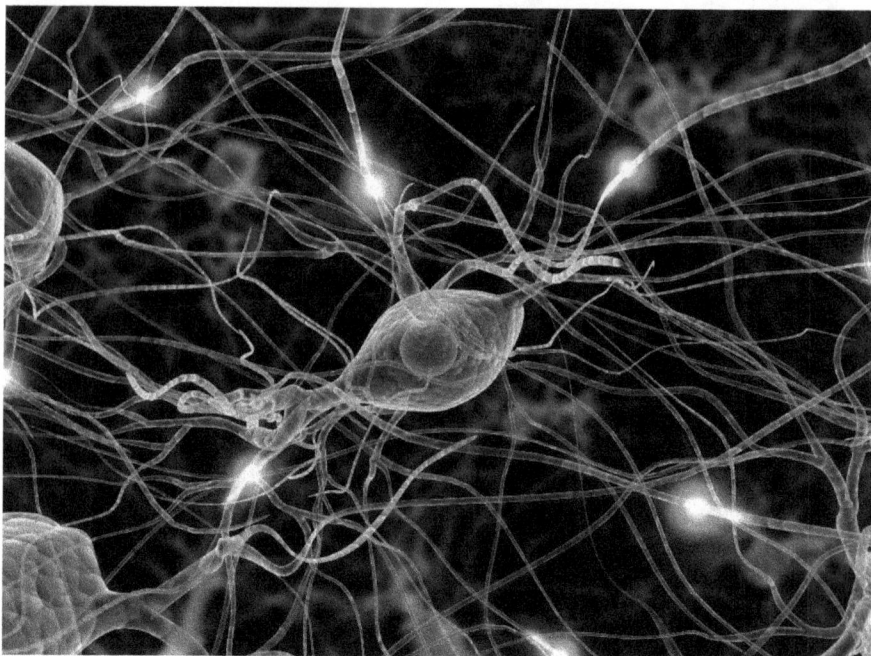

Neurochemisty: the study of neurochemicals, including neurotransmitters and other molecules, such as psychopharmaceuticals and neuropeptides, that influence the function of neurons. This field within neuroscience examines how neurochemicals influence the operation of neurons, synapses and neural networks.

Just imagine your brain's multifaceted aspect, seen by science and the medical arena, and all that is yet to be discovered. Your brain is ever experiencing and changing; you can change your old habits and ways with new ways. What appears above to capture you can be uncaptured with your choices called sex addiction, to new patterns and habits that bring about health to you, that once was called unhealthy! YOU can do it, men!

Mood-altering chemicals that stimulate the body maintain sexual addiction. Sexual addicts become tolerant to the chemicals that sex produces, such as adrenaline, serotonin, and dopamine. For sex addicts, sexual behavior or fantasies become the primary way to condition their brains to meet their neurological needs. ***The very thought of porn or sexual they cause the chemicals to automatically release and draw you to act out.*** The brain craves more and more and demands more and more via the substances and the neural pathways. Addicts will seek other means to get their sexual chemical needs met. The adage, "whatever it takes," is the theme for the person with a substance use disorder to get their needs met. And risk is part of that equation. They take risks with no hesitation!

The intense focus on sexual fantasies causes distress and problems for the person with a substance use disorder, affecting their health, job, relationships, and all parts of their life that they can't control. Regardless of the name, it can significantly impact their self-esteem, and they often end up unemployed because they act recklessly.

As noted, this chapter is called Brain On Fire — and on fire it is! The risk factors are that sexual content is readily available, it is private, and it is free. *However, it Is not free; it costs you everything, as you have choices to have this as a drug of your choice over the years.*

The significant question is, when did your issues begin.? How did they start, and how quickly did curiosity turn into addiction? Have you had the following complications because of this issue called sexual compulsivity?

1. To soothe emotional pain?

2. To escape from your issues?

3. Has it cost you in your work — have you lost days of work because of the addiction?

4. Has it cost you in your relationship with your wife and family?

5. Has it cost you to lose focus?

6. Has it cost you financially over the years? How much have you spent on this issue? Fill in the blank: $_____

7. Have you received and/or has this addiction in the past affected you with a sexually transmitted disease?

8. Do you have other addictive behaviors, like drugs, alcohol

or gambling?

9. Have the authorities arrested you because of this addiction?

10. Have you harmed yourself physically, with your sexual organ, because of obsessive masturbation?

11. Do you have other issues, such as depression?

12. Is there any history of physical or sexual abuse caused to you in early childhood?

13. Have you been engaged in gaming? Gaming mirrors the same neuropathways as sex addiction differently, but it captures you, and you lose track of time. Agreed?

14. Has chatting on sex sites been an avenue for you? Or have your sex chat on your phone with others?

Did you know that your sexual addiction MIRRORS that of drug addiction? However, during the early days of my training, I heard in different symposiums and workshops that it is the most challenging addiction to break, harder than crack cocaine! I have found this to be true via counseling men and in Battle Lines.

This addiction carries a significant liability of being covered in shame and guilt because of its secrecy. It has been a secret in most addicts' lives since inception. This secret carries forth in your behaviors to other secrets, such as spending, lying, half-truths, embellishments of stories, etc. The very nature of the issue being a secret, which has shame attached, is one trigger that causes you to act out repeatedly.

Have you lost track of time in your addiction to porn, masturbation, etc. But as soon as you experience an orgasm, that issue evaporates, and the demand instantly goes away. The brain chemicals evaporate, satisfying the demand instantly. Have you experienced this time and time again? Are you tired of the cycle and ready for change?

When exposed to porn at an early age, the brain is still developing, and when parents are not doing due diligence in monitoring their children's electronic devices, the parents, in effect, give permission for these children to venture into websites they should never go into. **Many parents "assume" their innocent child would do nothing like this. The assumption is totally incorrect and makes a significant statement about the lack of excellent parenting.** Church attendee parents and their children are mostly passive, and this opens the door for their children to get hooked on porn. It's a naivete that can be costly! Parents should educate their children to age appropriateness. It is necessary that parents create healthy relationships with their children, and in this openness, trust develops. Children are going to be exposed at school. It is essential that your child communicates with you about what is going on in school, and the parents thank them for their honesty and do not place guilt or shame on the child.

What is sad, again in the "church system," this subject seems to be taboo, instead of being open and sharing the truth about the issues. My daughter received early education, and we developed trust and shared openness. I so valued that with my daughter, as my wife did the same.

Sexual addiction, from a behavioral psychology viewpoint, focuses on objectively observable behavior, learning, and habit information. If a sexual behavior or fantasy provides people with pleasure or relief from pain, then the body learns how the attachments occur. This behavior then tends to occur more frequently, and repeated behaviors become a habit. Repeated experiences of association between sexual behaviors and attachments form learning, known as conditioning. The learning process is so deep and automatic at the physical level that the conditioning is challenging to break and extremely powerful. You do not want your child to enter this issue, as you more than likely have by reading a book like this.

The addiction area commonly uses the term "brain hijacking!"

It can literally blow your mind! Your brain takes over your choices with the chemicals and entrenched neuropathways you have created. Just a "thought" can bring about massive chemical releases that capture you into your addiction, doing what you said you would never do.

How The Brain Gets Hooked

The brain is a puzzle with sections, structures, and connections. The brain has three distinct areas: the forebrain, which is the innermost part. Each section comprises structures that are responsible for many functions. We'll focus on the forebrain and the midbrain.

Within the midbrain, you'll find tiny structures — substantia nigra and ventral tegmental area — that release the neurotransmitter dopamine. To summarize, neurotransmitters are chemical messengers that help carry information through the brain cells or neurons to other neurons. (There are other neurotransmitters, too, like serotonin.) Each neurotransmitter has receptors that accept its "message." Dopamine has five of these receptors in the central nervous system, and the most abundant helps regulate the reward system, motor activity, memory, and learning receptors.

What Reward Does to Your Brain

When we experience a reward or pleasure, the ventral tegmental area sends dopamine into the basal ganglia. This structure is responsible for many things such as executive functions, behaviors, and emotions. And it is this release that tells us that whatever we just experienced was wonderful and to please do it again. This chain of events helps us change behavior, provide motivation, and affect our mood. All in all, it makes us feel good. And this is where substance use steps in.

"All addictive substances work on the same common reward pathway," said Anna Lembke, MD, medical director of addiction medicine at the School of Medicine at Stanford University. "Different substances will release different amounts of dopamine, but they all release dopamine in a reward pathway, and that's what relates to their addictive potential. When your brain is flooded or hijacked, it gets flooded with chemicals, namely dopamine. Mood-altering chemicals which stimulate the body to maintain sexual addiction. Sexual addicts become neurochemically tolerant to the chemicals that sex produces, such as adrenaline, serotonin, and dopamine."

Men, it is essential to be educated on this vital organ in your body, the brain. It is the secret of your addiction; in addition, it is the secret to building new neuropathways, breaking old neuropathways, reducing the chemicals in your brain, and making alternative choices in your brain to become healthy.

You know that by now, your brain has its reward centers, and it captures you in your addiction. This issue has pleasure, excitement, control, and, most important, from the standpoint of addiction, distraction. It is a soothing and temporary escape for you, and *you regret it after acting out.* Sometimes, the distraction is more relaxing than the pleasure for you.

As you read this book, you will come across the same information multiple times in different ways, and you must understand and be knowledgeable about this information. Thus again, repeat, repeat.

God gave you a beautiful body and desires multiple pleasures for us: food, fellowship in relationships, exercise, and the outdoors. However, you can hijack the pleasure centers by flooding it with unusually high levels of dopamine, anywhere from two to ten times the amount provided by regular pleasurable activity. Is it any wonder that your body wants more and more! You have moved into new highs, where your body wants more because that last pleasure did not meet your needs. Do you see the futility in all of this? Are you not tired of the ever-increasing empty demands your body seeks to be met. Do you not see the emptiness of it all? Are you not tired?

STOP FEEDING THE BEAST

You can stop feeding the beast, lose your "friend" (sex addiction), and become lonely. In the loneliness, you can grow and mature, along with finding your support structure in accountability men, groups, and in counseling. YOU ARE GOING TO CHOOSE to cut out every negative thing in your life, including friends, and start building a NEW LIFE with good people, what you look at and do!

In a later chapter, I will include tools you can use to bring forth freedom by setting boundaries in your life, escaping avenues when triggered, etc. Tools are only worthwhile if you use them. Your choice!

It is essential to grab hold of what porn does to the brain and the psychological well-being of the addict. The excessive use of pornography can lead to various physical effects, which are all about rewiring the brain; when I use the word pornography here, I am also inclusive of massage parlors, prostitutes, and repeated affairs.

So often, as you know, depression, anxiety, and self-worth issues intertwined with this addiction, along with a great deal of shame and guilt.

If married, your addiction will and does interfere in your personal relationships, emotionally, sexually, relationships, and in all kinds of different ways. Your wife will feel your distance but does not know what is happening. You may compartmentalize for a season, but that compartmentalization will eventually come apart, and your relationship with your wife will be severely strained. There is a "secret," and that "secret" men keep you from your wife. You can't give all yourself to her because you have another "mistress (addiction)."

Like General Patton, knowing Rommel's war tactics to win battles, for you to seek to win battles, requires understanding the brain's neuroplasticity. Your brain can change and adapt, but it is up to you, with this addiction, to get it to change into a New Interstate Highway. And it can be done. This process is crucial for you to understand 1st: the choice brings negativity and reinforcements to your addiction, and the 2nd choice brings forth new patterns and, eventually, freedom from your addiction. What choice do you want to make?

In other words, hopefully, you will seek to build NEW HABITS! And over time, these new HABITS will build new neuropathways. They can eventually become deeply ingrained in the same manner your addictive patterns have become so deeply ingrained that you see no possibility of helping. But that is a lie. But the truth is, you have to work hard to build new patterns.

Your repetitive behaviors create your addiction; in the same manner, *repetitive behaviors can break it.* You have to develop a mindset to build a new. Up to now, your brain has been driven by chemicals, sex, and deeply ingrained neurochemical patterns that demand more and more of your acting out.

As we've discussed, YOUR BRAIN CAN BE REWIRED. However, even with total commitment, I have seen no one do it quickly. They will sometimes slip along the way of change, but those slips can come further apart by refocusing. By fighting not to act out sexually, the you become desensitized, so to speak. Slowly, new chemical reactions and patterns are set as your brain rewires.

Dopamine, as mentioned earlier, has a significant role in the brain's reward system and gets released during pleasurable activities, such as engaging in porn, visiting massage parlors, hiring prostitutes, and more. After a while, the more one acts out, the tolerance for dopamine reaches the level where the person with an addiction needs intense stimuli to achieve the same level of pleasure. Have you realized that, and with that, you risk more to accomplish that need? A vicious cycle.

You can rewire your brain, which has been out of control, but it takes a lot of focus and discipline, which is discussed elsewhere.

All of your negative behaviors formed over time, making it difficult to change. almost automatically so. Our God (yours and mine) gave us a gift for change; our brains have plasticity. *There is a saying, "What fires together, stays together." And that is true with your addiction.*

Dan Siegel, MD, in his book, *The Developing Brain*, states: "If a pattern has been stimulated in the past, the probability of activating a similar profile in the future is enhanced. If this pattern is fired repeatedly, the likelihood of further activation increases at the end."

For example, suppose we become stressed, agitated, angry, or upset and take a drink of alcohol or view pornography. In that case, physiological changes, such as feeling euphoria or sexual stimulation, can reduce anxiety and stress. After this happens repeatedly, the cells wire together so that when we experience the stressor again, the BRAIN will naturally fire on the PATHWAY toward drinking or viewing pornography. The more it occurs, the stronger the synaptic connections in the BRAIN. I keep spelling out the BRAIN. Your brain is being WIRED! These connections can become so strongly linked that it takes very little to get them firing (slightest of triggers — slightest of thoughts).

"Cellular-memory groups can be activated without seeing or hearing something from the outside world. Once a person has used Internet pornography to heighten their sexual fantasies, all they need to do is call up these same feelings and images is express the desire or intention. Once this intention or desire is expressed, a whole network of cellular-memory groups is activated at the end." The *DRUG OF THE NEW MILLENNIUM* by Mark B. Kastleman is one of many books Battle Lines used to process this information in great detail.

You must "get it in your BRAIN." That is where the problem is! Over long periods, this negative wiring is why it is so tough to change. Again, the good news is the plasticity of the brain. Please repeat that again! Our God, our Creator, gave us a gift for change. You must want, I would pray, a wholesale remapping of our "real estate" — YOUR BRAIN!

God's truth will set you free, but you have to walk out — step-by-step — in a mindset that you are going to establish a new pathway and make new choices each day. In addition, this includes your *"thoughts,"* and you will take captive those thoughts and switch them to God's Word and new thoughts*!* ***Push away the old; walk in the NEW!***

Also, your false beliefs about yourself must be thrown out with the wash; you will get rinsed in a large tub of fresh water! You will also choose to walk in the new LIGHT because you seek to walk according to HIS WORD, and the only way you can do that is to KNOW HIS WORD. Please fight for these alternative choices that will bring you LIFE, which is new and refreshing in time.

I want you to look in a mirror in the morning and at night, look yourself in the eyes, and say *"I love you!"* Every morning and every night. It is important, no it is essential that you love yourself, not in an egotistical way, but via what God's Word says about you. You are a child of the King, so ***stop saying negativity about yourself.***

It is essential to understand that YOU must "stand back" and know that "your thoughts" are not your thoughts; you ARE NOT your BEHAVIORS or your FEELINGS! You have to fight to get into the new car's driver's seat and visualize (figuratively speaking, it's a Porsche), and you'll enjoy this new car. You deserve to drive, and you need to seek to enjoy your thoughts, your feelings, and your behaviors in it, in this body that Christ developed when you were first formed in your mother's womb.

Dr. Jeffrey Schwartz calls this choice your WILL, your INTELLIGENCE, you the OBSERV ER. We can observe our thoughts, actions, emotions, and physiological state. If you think about a blue sky and I tell you to know, think about a yellow car can do that. You can change your thoughts. Therefore, we are not our thoughts! A part of us is not addicted or compulsive but can observe the addiction or compulsion.

You observe your thoughts and feelings as passing, but they are NOT YOU! You begin to realize them as events in your brain; they pass through the mind.

This is essential in your journey that you view thoughts and emotions, and behaviors, and beliefs that can cripple you. Still, when you state they are not you, they are not your identity, they are not reflective of you as a person, and you reset your mind on new things and thoughts, start controlling your brain, and set new neuropathways.

Previously, in the chapter on your relationship with Christ, a few Scriptures speak to who you are. You have Christ in you if you have indeed received Him. He is in you, you are in Him, and He is in the Father (John 14). Your old beliefs, you are not going to walk in them! It is a choice. You are going to do it.

Most men are lazy and want a quick fix. Thus, they stay in a rut. These rules become more profound and in-depth as you have chosen the same thing repeatedly over time. Get this. YOUR BELIEFS can cripple you. God wants to set you free, transform you, and heal you. God can accompany you as you do deep work necessary for you; the old root habits have to go so that God can build new roots (in HIM) and grow you into a new being, so to speak. The old is no more, and the latest is forever more!

Your healing journey involves practicing, practicing, practicing new ways, and not repeating the old patterns. In time, your new patterns will be fixed, and the old will diminish. The brain on fire redevelops because you have made the choices. Just think, YOU made new choices!

In your TOTAL NEW BEHAVIOR, you are DOING and taking control of your body. With your thinking, you are thinking new and positive thoughts. With your feelings, you are going to deny the negative and receive and anchor into the positive, knowing your feelings are not you! As a result of your thoughts, actions, and feelings, the brain releases neurochemicals and hormones that cause a physical response on the body. This body response is pleasurable at the rate moment. The chemicals they release are enjoyable; this euphoria sends a message throughout the body. The body's response can then drive more of the behavior as the body builds up tolerance and sets in a new way. *Remember, you are the captain of your ship*, and you are building anew.

You are going to change your actions. You will not give in to your urges but fight to do your new actions. The only way for the brain to change is to pay attention to the new behaviors. With all the force of will and mind power that is available. YOU can do it! The more you choose the right thing to do, the more you fire neurons on the new pathways, and the weaker the old ones become. *You will CHOOSE to have SELECTIVE THINKING* and not make excuses for not going all out. You're going all out with new patterns; the old becomes faded as they set. *You are in the driver's seat of YOU.*

You have to refocus, refocus, refocus on this journey of change. Willfully directed attention can filter out unwanted information; another example of how directed mental force, a proper mindset, you can literally direct your brain to filter out the suppressive effects of distracting signals. This is another example of nudging the brain with one signal, not another and one circuit nudge over another. Positive choice vs. negative choice. Directed mental force, generated by the effort of directed attention, can modulate neuronal function, per Jeffrey M. Schwartz, MD

You know it takes real effort to maintain the appropriate focus, so it takes a lot of concentration to get into the proper exit lane at a complicated freeway interchange. However, once you muster the appropriate focus, you can direct your brain to filter out the suppressive effects of distracting signals.

Brothers, there is a split-second between a thought or urge and the resulting action. It would be best if you became a *fighter with a mindset* to the highest degree. Mental force must come into being. If you're being serious about changing your brain, *results come*. But it comes with absolute focus. This will be your mindset from when you wake up to when you go to bed at night. You fight for the new ways and give yourself grace as you make a wrong decision. Those become less over time because you are a focused man!

As mentioned elsewhere, you must practice ahead of time for escape. Similarly, with any thoughts and feelings in a safe place, you practice via select behavior what your choices will be in the day when you are busy and about. So, when you are out and about, you select the good behavior and focus all your attention and willpower on it. You become totally immersed in the sensations and emotions of the alternative experience. Remember, you are not your thoughts.

Previous patterns die when they are not stimulated. What fires together stays together. What doesn't fire dies.

What fires together stays together / thus reshaping your brain / therefore walking towards healing, setting the captive free, and true transformation by the Lord!

1. What have you learned about the brain?

2. What have you learned about an alternative choice?

3. What have you learned about a new mindset?

4. What have you learned about the repetition of good choices?

5. What have you learned about your old patterns?

6. What new choices are you going to make for the future?

7. Do you want to get well?

CHAPTER 13
Your Brain Can Change

God says in His Word, Ecclesiastes 3:11, "He has made everything beautiful in its time." He has planted eternity into the human heart, if you read the Scripture further. God wants you to know that you are beautiful!

You are a creation of the Creator, and when YOU can understand and grab hold of the fact that within you, your will can bring forth change, and when you have that relationship with the Lord, He enables you to comprehend, in some sense, the miracle of your brain, and that it can change. God wants you to worship Him, the Creator! God wants YOU to find your potential, that He has a plan for you, and your past does not have to determine your future.

By utilizing your ability to think, feel, and choose, your brain and body collaborate to construct your mind. Your mind controls your brain. Your focused choices create patterns in your brain that can store new thoughts and wire the brain differently. You are fearfully and wonderfully made, and you are Perfect in His Sight because He formed you and developed you in your mother's womb. When you have received Christ, as we talked about before, you have the perfection of Christ in you, you in Him, and He is in the Father. This is the core of who YOU ARE! It is not how you feel, it is what God's Word says, and you are to choose to accept it, as fact! Your brain is UNIQUE to YOU; it is like a fingerprint; there has never been, nor will there ever been another like you. We are all different. That is an excellent thing because we are UNIQUE, I repeat!

Did you know that via research from Binghamton University, your brain wave responses can identify you! In a PUBLIC RELEASE: 18-APR-2016 — Researchers can identify you by your brain waves with 100 percent accuracy. BINGHAMTON,

NY — Your responses to certain stimuli — foods, celebrities, words — might seem trivial, but they say a lot about you. In fact (with the proper clearance), these responses could gain access to restricted Pentagon areas. The article states the following:

A team of researchers at Binghamton University, led by Assistant Professor of Psychology Sarah Laszlo and Assistant Professor of Electrical and Computer Engineering Zhanpeng Jin, recorded the brain activity of 50 people wearing an electroencephalogram headset while they looked at a series of 500 images designed specifically to elicit unique responses from person to person -- e.g., a slice of pizza, a boat, Anne Hathaway, the word "conundrum." They found that participants' brains reacted differently to each image, enough that a computer system was able to identify each volunteer's "brainprint" with 100 percent accuracy.

"When you take hundreds of these images, where every person is going to feel differently about each individual one, then you can be really accurate in identifying which person it was who looked at them just by their brain activity," said Laszlo.

In their original study, titled "Brainprint," published in 2015 in Neurocomputing, *the research team was able to identify one person out of a group of thirty-two by that person's responses, with only ninety-seven percent accuracy, and that study only incorporated words, not images.*

"It's a big deal going from 97 to 100 percent because we imagine the applications for this technology being for high-security situations, like ensuring the person going into the Pentagon or the nuclear launch bay is the right person," said Laszlo. "You don't want to be 97 percent accurate for that, you want to be 100 percent accurate."

"If someone's fingerprint is stolen, that person can't just grow a new finger to replace the compromised fingerprint — the fingerprint for that person is compromised forever. Fingerprints are 'non-cancelable.' Brainprints, on the other hand, are potentially cancelable. So, in the unlikely event that attackers could actually steal a brainprint from an authorized user, the authorized user could then 'reset' their brainprint," Laszlo said.

On your journey of healing, changing, and transformation, you have to understand your thinking, feeling, and choosing and how that brings about, via your choice, new patterns. You do not have to be stuck with the old. God wants you to know you can come out with "the new you!" In Scripture, 2 Timothy 1:7 states, "For God gave us a spirit not of fear but of power and love and self-control." In our relationship with Him, He enables us, as we surrender to Him, and develop that relationship with Him. He does something we cannot do over time with our bodies (the brain). Scripture points out in Acts 17:28, "For in him we live and move and have our being as even some of your own poets have said, 'For we are indeed his offspring.'"

You, from the time you get up in the morning, until you go to bed at night, have the option to choose right or wrong. Each time a choice is made, it *affects the wiring of your brain.* I can recall so many times men saying they acted out (masturbated) before they got out of bed in the mornings. That was their choice because they did not fight hard enough just to get up, not act out, and resist the temptation (desire). They had the opportunity (test by God) to see what they would choose, as James speaks of in Chapter 1:12–18:

12 Blessed is the man who remains steadfast under trial, for when he has stood the test he will receive the crown of life, which God has promised to those who love him. 13 Let no one say when he is tempted, "I am being tempted by God," for God cannot be tempted with evil, and he himself tempts no one. 14 But each person is tempted when he is lured and enticed by his own desire. 15 Then desire when it has conceived gives birth to sin, and sin when it is fully grown brings forth death. 16 Do not be deceived, my beloved brothers. 17 Every good gift and every perfect gift is from above, coming down from the Father of lights, with whom there is no variation or shadow due to change. 18 Of his own will he brought us forth by the word of truth, that we should be a kind of first fruits of his creatures.

Do you want to be responsible, or do you want to continue to make excuses? You alone are responsible for how your life flows, and your future is ahead of you, good or bad, based on your choice. Handing forth freedom is such a gift of love and, in truth, trust. I have extended that gift of trust to my twenty-five-year-old daughter, and over time, she honors it. She honors not only me and her mom but also her God, our Lord and Savior Jesus Christ of Nazareth. We were created to reflect Him and His glory, and when she honors God, she is given back to Him, in truth, "praises!" This does not infer that all things go well in life, but with healthy choices, there is a feeling of peace within a person that one cannot explain. Wrong choices bring forth turmoil and churn inside that eats like cancer. Patterns set by an unhealthy brain can destroy you. You can also set wiring in your brain, bringing you life and enjoyment.

Your free will is a gift from God to make healthy or unhealthy choices. He also desired that you not be a robot and be oriented towards worshiping Him. He wanted that to be YOUR CHOICE! You have unlimited possibilities for good in your life if you choose to set your mind like flint and not deter. It is unfathomable how God uses science today, in its ever-new discoveries, to reveal Himself to us through this gift of freedom.

Our Father and others play a significant role in fostering our relationships as we grow and develop. This is also about how you find the uniqueness in yourself and even in others.

We can love or fear. God's perfect love drives out fear according to what I John 4:18 states, "There is no fear in love, but perfect love casts out fear. Fear is related to punishment, and those who fear have not yet attained perfection in love." That perfect love is Christ. Christ loves us and does not want us to walk in fear. Dr. Waguth William IsHak, a professor of psychiatry at Cedars-Sinai, states the following:

> *The warm feeling of wellbeing that washes over you when you've done something kind isn't just in your head. It's in your brain chemicals, too.*
>
> *Acts of kindness can release hormones that contribute to your mood and overall well-being. The practice is so effective it's being formally incorporated into some types of psychotherapy.*
>
> *The trick you need to know: Acts of kindness have to be repeated. Biochemically, you can't live on the 3-to-4-minute oxytocin boost from a single act.*
>
> *We all seek a path to happiness. Practicing kindness toward others is one we know works.*

Kindness is Chemical

Most research on the science behind why kindness makes us feel better has centered around oxytocin. Sometimes called "the love hormone," oxytocin plays a role in forming social bonds and trusting other people. It's the hormone mothers produce when they breastfeed, cementing their bond with their babies.

Physical intimacy triggers the release of oxytocin in our bodies. It's tied to making us more trusting, generous, and friendlier while lowering our blood pressure.

Research suggests that acts of kindness can also boost our love hormone levels.

"We're building better selves and better communities at the

same time," said Dr. IsHak. He also says studies have also linked random acts of kindness to releasing dopamine, a chemical messenger in the brain that can give us a feeling of euphoria. This feel-good brain chemical is credited with causing what's known as a "helper's high."

In addition to boosting oxytocin and dopamine, being kind can also increase serotonin, a neurotransmitter that helps regulate mood.

Using Kindness as a Treatment Can Help with Pain, Depression, and Anxiety

What we know about the science behind acts of kindness is influencing how we treat certain health conditions, according to Dr. IsHak.

Studies are investigating if oxytocin can be beneficial in treating some conditions. The hormone is a protein and cannot simply be taken as a pill. It's being studied in injection and nasal spray forms.

Mindfulness-based therapy is becoming increasingly popular for treating depression, anxiety, and other mental health conditions. The therapy is built on mindfulness meditation, documenting your gratitude, and acts of kindness. People being treated in a mindfulness-based therapy program incorporate acts of kindness into their daily routines.

According to Dr. IsHak, helping others is also believed to increase levels of an endorphin-like chemical in the body called substance P, which can relieve pain.

Put Kindness on Repeat

The good news is that a simple act of kindness can reward our bodies and minds with feel-good chemical substances.

However, the effect isn't lasting. A single act of kindness isn't going to carry you through several days — or even hours.

"The trick you need to know: Acts of kindness have to be

repeated," Dr IsHak says. "Biochemically, you can't live on the 3-to-4-minute oxytocin boost that comes from a single act."

That's why kindness is most beneficial as a practice — something we work into our daily routine, whether in the form of volunteer work, dropping coins into an expired parking meter, bringing a snack to share with your office mates, or holding the elevator for someone.

"The rewards of acts of kindness are many," says Dr. IsHak. "They help us feel better, and they help those who receive them. We're building better selves and better communities at the same time."

HOMEWORK

Look up KINDNESS in:

1. Merriam-Webster

2. Dictionary.com

3. Cambridge Dictionary

Define INTENTIONAL and write it out for each resource mentioned above.

1. Which road are you going to travel? Explain both for yourself and others and why you will do so.

2. The world's ways (secular)

3. God's way

4. How are you going to walk this new way? Assuming you are going to walk God's Way.

5. Explain:

6. Who are you going to have around in your life?

7. How are you going to study and read God's Word?

8. What books, and you should know some by now, as you process this book, and what other resources will you read?

9. What church body will you be a part of?

10. Not just in attending, but what Bible studies, groups, etc., will you be a part of?

11. Share about how you will seek the Lord in prayer.

12. How will you set your mind in a new way when the old way "pops up?" And men, it will!

13. Explain this sentence: "YOU ARE WHAT YOU THINK."

14. Do you believe this statement?

15. What are you going to do to walk according to walk according to what God thinks of you?

16. Write out five Scriptures from the Bible that speak of who you really are, and do you believe it? If so, why?

17. Do you really believe that your mind can change? Do you really?

18. Do you want to get well?

CHAPTER 14
Renewing the Mind

YOU ARE WHAT YOU THINK! YOUR MIND CAN BE RENEWED!

YOU CAN HAVE A TRANSFORMED MIND! THIS IS A PROCESS OF CLEANSING AND THE PUTTING NEW IN FOR YOU!

UNLESS YOU ARE INTENTIONAL, DO NOT EXPECT CHANGE.

Romans 12:2 states: **"Do not conform to the pattern of this world, but be transformed be renewing your mind. Then you will be able to test and approve what God's will is — his good, pleasing and perfect will."**

My brothers, this is the key passage for you and me. Romans 8 speaks of this.

> *5 Those who live according to the flesh have their minds set on what the flesh desires; but those who live in accordance with the Spirit have their minds set on what the Spirit desires. 6 The mind governed by the flesh is death, but the mind governed by the Spirit is life and peace. 7 The mind governed by the flesh is hostile to God; it does not submit to God's law, nor can it do so. 8 Those who are in the realm of the flesh cannot please God.*

There are two options before you this day. Live according to the ways of the Lord, or live according to the ways of this world. One brings forth renewal, and the other brings forth a cesspool of living. One is LIFE, and the other is DEATH. One is LIGHT, and the other is DARKNESS. Your CHOICE!

This is one of the most critical chapters of this book. I hope to convey and challenge you that without Christ in

your life, your efforts are all self-effort, and self-effort always fades, tires out, and often fails.

Men, there is no NEUTRAL here. There is no IN-BETWEEN here. You can make one up and mix it up, but God's Word holds no NEUTRAL. Mixing up is futile! Mixing it up is like mortar holding a brick wall up; it will crumble and fall! It will not hold up! Cutting corners never ever works and in truth, you know it!

What, then, will restore the sexually addicted soul? The truth? Ever-increasing intimacy with the Lord. These are simple but powerful words. Any approach that falls short of this goal is deficient in a genuine Christian relationship and sound biblical teaching.

You must have a focused oneness with Christ, a relationship that moves into deep intimacy, which is necessary for Christ to do His work within your soul, which needs to be closed from the depth of your being.

It is great to memorize Scripture and biblical truths, but that is not enough, men. Acquisition of facts is not sufficient either. God desires to break you free from guilt and shame — that emotional bondage and baggage that engulfs many of you. Once you repent at the cross, Christ dies for your sins, and you must receive that forgiveness. If you do not, you make yourself bigger than God. In other words, by rejecting God's transformative love, you are relying on your own ineptness. You are relying solely on yourself. How's that working out for you?

It's imperative to know before you begin this authentic journey of renewing the mind, leading to transformation, that Satan wants to hold you in bondage. Satan, the enemy, wants you to fail. But Christ wants you to walk in freedom, forgiven and unbound from sex addiction! Christ, when you receive Him, refuses to look at those sins repented! If He refuses to bring up your forgiven sins, then you shouldn't bring them up either. Those sins are in your past, not in your present or future.

I might also add that behavior modification is a no-go here

with Christ. He wants you to develop intimacy with Him so He can be the true healer from inside your person so you can be a reflection of Him. Behavioral modification is self-effort, which breaks down eventually. Healing from within by Him is renewing the mind and transforming.

I think you are ready to begin that journey of intimacy, aren't you? I pray that the following speaks to your person in the way intended. I pray the Lord's Truth breaks through, and as you do your due diligence in reading the Bible, praying, meditation, and other material in this journey, God will continually speak His Truth to you.

I think the following Scripture should speak to you here, and I hope it will: Psalm 139:23–24 says, **"Search me, O God, and know my heart! Try me and know my thoughts! And see if there be any grievous way in me and lead me in the way of everlasting."**

As you journey on the pathway for change, your mind can be renewed by setting your mind on the Lord each day and reading His Word as you seek to walk His ways. This, again, is CHOICE. God wants to clean your mind so that your choice of health, which is His Word, and your relationship with Him, He does something to cleanse your mind as you participate with Him. He wants to free you up in your thinking on this sanctification journey.

What you CHOOSE to THINK ABOUT and dwell on in this life will make or break you! That is a fact! And for the addict, it has almost broken you, but there is an answer, and that is Him, our Father.

God expects YOU to play a part in this transformation process. The choice is involved. In truth, it must be with a fight, going against what you have developed in yourself and in your addiction. Nothing happens without choice, as you so well know by now.

Let's stop here for a second. DO YOU WANT TO

CHANGE? DO YOU WANT TO BE SET FREE? DO YOU WANT YOUR MIND RENEWED? DO YOU WANT TO BE TRANSFORMED? If you do, the next step is to seek these things! You have to put away the old and seek the new.

The secret of this new journey of a good and new mental life is, "For as he thinks in his heart, so is he" (Proverbs 23:7). The key Word in this verse is "thoughts." The word "thoughts" tells you that God is targeting your thought process — what you think about daily. Another way to look at this is, YOU ARE WHAT YOU THINK!

This principle is easily seen in our world today. You can tell who is operating on this principle in the way the Lord intended for us to operate with it and who is not.

The people who always seem to be more upbeat, happier, and more fulfilled with their lives are the people who are always thinking about and dwelling on the more positive things in this life. And this is one of the keys to your healing from sexual compulsivity. With their own free will, they choose to dwell on the positive side of life.

The people who are unhappy, unsatisfied, pessimistic, half-depressed, and have negative attitudes towards anybody and anything are all choosing to think about and dwell on the negative side of life. Porn, prostitutes, massage parlors, affairs, masturbation, etc., is the dark and negative side of life. Why would you want to continually put yourself here? There is LIGHT, Christ and His ways, with His Word, and there is fellowship with like-minded men and fellowship in a Bible-believing church. Get yourself in this atmosphere and away from the darkness of this world.

Yes, we are in a world in which we live that has a mixture of life and death in it. There is light, and there is darkness. Jesus Himself said we would all have various trials and tribulations that we would have to go through occasionally. Just walking through a mall presents the darkness of how a woman dresses; the window displays almost nudity from women's wear stores. It is time for training, where you look, and what you think. It is a place of testing, as is a grocery store. You are to set your mind on things on high and not of this world. You are no different than others who are faced with trials as a part of life, and no one gets by not having to go through various storm clouds from time to time; you may be defined as "different," but nevertheless, you are responsible for your thinking and your actions.

However, we have many good and positive things going on in the world, and you are responsible for placing yourself in those places. As you develop your walk with the Lord, He is on your side to take the storm clouds away. His Word is that pathway that shows you each step you should take.

Those who are always positive, happy, and upbeat have chosen to look on the bright side. Note the word "chosen." And in the worst of circumstances, they have "chosen" to look on that bright side. Guess what, YOU can too! With their free will, they choose to dwell on the positive side of life. I know This is sometimes a fight, but you seek to focus, think, imagine, and walk it out — live it out. It will be a part of your life, in time, as you fight the battle, no matter what. You say, "Hell no" to the negatives, the impossibles, and say, "HELL YES" too good. And you fix your mind on that. You are to immerse yourself into HIS Word and bring those Scriptures in Proverbs and Psalms into your life. One Scripture at a time. Let that Scripture be a dinner for you as you feast on it, reread it, and then decide, *I will walk in this way*.

I know that in much of your life, as an addict, you think wrongly about the things that can happen. You think wrongly about what can go wrong.

When you have chosen to think and dwell on all of the bad things that can happen or what can go wrong, those thoughts wrap its arms around an addict. And then, for many, that negativity feeds to drive you to your addiction to feel better for a moment in time. However, afterward, you walk in shame and guilt. The negative type of person has chosen to think and dwell on all the bad things that can happen or go wrong in life. No matter what good may come their way, they will always have a comment that something better could have come their way. Is that you?

Nothing makes them happy or content because nothing is ever good enough for them. Is that you, the addict? Inventory time, my brother, to ask about your inner being and your mindset because, if the previous is the case, that is stinky thinking. Don't you want your mind and heart transformed? It can be!

YOU CONTROL YOUR THINKING; it does not control you. Negative thinking can be broken. For many, it has become an actual stronghold (addiction is a stronghold); in the same manner, negative thinking can become a "mental stronghold" because your mind has become mired down in negative thinking for such a long period.

You are directly responsible for choosing what you think about and dwell on. Your mind can lock into negative thinking, or you can lock into Godly thinking, which is God's Word! Those Scriptures are included throughout this book. The power lies with us. It is called "choice." You cannot blame anyone else — including God Himself — if you have chosen with your own free will to constantly dwell on the negative and "darker" side of this life.

Are you not tired of the negative mindset? The bottom line is that we all must learn to develop the correct thinking process. Our part is to do the best, the very best, and not give up on the things that God wants us to concentrate and focus on. You know, as many know, that you only have a certain amount of mental and psychological strength in this area.

This is where the Holy Spirit comes in to help our thinking process straighten out and be grounded in the Lord in the way He wants us to be. This is all part of the sanctification journey that God wants us to start within each of us. This is a journey, not a sprint. It involves footsteps, one foot in front of the other, also called a process.

For years, the medical field has operated under the assumption that the brain cannot heal itself; however, more research and experience have shown this is not the case. The brain has a tremendous ability to improve and restore itself. But here, for the addict, you don't want to be repaired; you hopefully want to be transformed.

As stated above, the apostle Paul tells us in Romans 12:2 to be "transformed by the renewing of your mind." Most people assume this verse refers to a spiritual renewal, and it does. Still, spiritual renewal profoundly impacts your physical state of mind. Proverbs tells us that the Words of God are "life to those who find them and health to a man's whole body" (Romans 4:22). Brain scans show that prayer and positive thinking have a tremendous effect on a previously troubled brain.

Philippians 4:8 states: "Whatever is true, whatever is noble, whatever is right, whatever is pure, whatever is lovely, whatever is admirable — if anything is excellent or praiseworthy, think about such things."

Note the word "think" and set your mind on excellent things, Him #1, and the Word #2, and in time, in HIS time, HE works out all things. As you honor HIM, HE honors you!

I know that while you are on the journey of healing, being set free, and transforming, God is concerned with your spiritual, mental, and physical health. And one of the reasons for some of the preceding is that your brain is involved in everything you do, and HE cares about YOU and YOUR CHOICES. Your positive choices will evolve into positive work within you as YOU CHOOSE to set your mind on things on high, HE and HIS WORD (repeat, repeat). When your brain works right, YOU WORK RIGHT! And note that your brain can change, as has been mentioned before, because it has plasticity. You can literally change your brain through your choices and thinking. Yep! God designed a brain that can be "reprogrammed and rebooted!"

Here are some ways to help your brain:

1. Protect your brain. In this world of bikes, hiking, jogging, and the like, your brain needs protection in some sports activities. Be wise and do so!

2. Do away with digesting (intake) of toxins. Junk — caffeine, nicotine, drugs, **preservatives**, sugar, salt, and the like are to be not taken in and cause detriment to the brain. Minimize as much as possible and bring healthiness in. Eliminating them will be a massive step in restoration.

3. Get enough sleep. Your body requires at least seven good hours of sleep a night.

4. This will boost your blood flow, which significantly aids healing; plus, the brain releases endorphins.

5. Pick up new things to do, hobbies, outings, and interests; this is a great way to bring healing to your brain. Your brain will bring forth new connections.

6. Again, watch what you eat!

7. Take multiple vitamins with extra E and C vitamins. Supplemental care has been proven to help prevent several diseases.

8. Pray — individual prayer time, praying aloud, sitting in a chair, on your knees and conversing with our awesome God. Let your heart be open to HIM with transparency and vulnerability. In time, when HE determines, HE reveals HIMSELF to you, and you feel HIM. This is a must, must, must.

9. Read God's Word — meditate on it. Please don't rush through it. Let it soak in. Sometimes, one Scripture can stop you, and you reread it, think upon it, and process it, and it brings forth a challenge to you and your inner being. This is the TRUE FOOD that you must digest.

10. Again, repeat, repeat, set your MIND ON THINGS ABOVE. Fight to switch your mind from negative to positive.

11. Determine who you will be around. Negativity breeds negativity, and positivity breeds positivity. This is a must. Cut out all negative people, places, and things out of your life! You are not responsible for what they think of you when you do. Surround yourself with positive people, people who love the Lord, and healthy couples.

You have a job to do, and that is to choose, by your own free will, to work and cooperate with our Lord via His Word in those areas of changes He wants you to make. He will not FORCE anything on you; you have to choose to put in your person what He wants and, likewise, for Him to take out of your person what He wants.

If you choose to walk with Him on making changes in your life that are through Him and His Word, then in time, the Father will allow supernatural power to come into your life via the Holy Spirit to truly begin to sanctify you in the way and manner that is most pleasing to Him! He does something we cannot do. It's something only He can do.

Men, let's just be honest here, man to man. Do you want your thoughts to change? Do you want your life to change? Do you want your behaviors to change? You can be a "man" or be like a "young boy." Scripture speaks of this in I Corinthians 13:11: *"When I was a child, I spoke like a child, I thought like a child, I reasoned like a child. When I became a man, I gave up childish ways."* Are you ready to pull up your britches, tighten your belt, stick your chest out, and say, "I am going to become a man, and stop thinking of childish, negative, and sexual ways?"

Renewing your mind aligns God's Truths of His Word and your brain by learning to recognize the lies of the enemy that seeks to destroy you. God's Word states in 2 Corinthians 10:5: "We destroy arguments, and every lofty opinion raised against the knowledge of God, and take every thought captive to obey Christ." Will you destroy negative thinking or entertain it and let it become a part of you? Are you not tired of that being a part of your life for an extended period? Do you desire to walk forward like you have been, or are you sick and tired of being sick and tired? Do you enjoy your way of life, or are you sick of it? You are not ready for the new unless you are sick of the old! The old is comfortable, and God wants you to peel off that old stinky shirt that is messed up with tears, stitched, patched, worn out, and put on a new one! You can do it, my friend!

You can take negative thoughts captive, push them aside, choose good and positive thoughts, and add to those ACTIONS! ACTIONS are what YOU DO! **NOTE:** ACTIONS ARE CHOICES THAT YOU MAKE!

I want to speak to non-Christians, who I pray someday become Christians. I desire for you to be set free from your addiction. I desire for you to have a change of life that is positive and healthy. You can choose to stay with what you know about lifestyle and relationships or change that.

First of all, you must change from being isolated; you have to engage in the community, and in the community, I mean positive and healthy relationships that set excellent moral examples of conduct. Men, YOU BECOME WHO YOU ARE AROUND! This is the beginning. You have to, again, get rid of the negative and put in the positive. You have to rid yourself of all negative influences. Walking in new, healthy relationships might feel uncomfortable, that you do not belong, that it is different, etc. Yes, that is true, but newness is just that, walking in newness.

What's after this? Seeking out a solid Bible-believing church. A church with great community and connectivity in your age group is essential. Try it out, men, and I know it may mean it feels like sticking your feet into the water to see if it's cold. It's okay to do so. This will be all new. I am telling you straight talk that without Christ, without a relationship with Him, the chances of backsliding and going back into your addiction are high.

Let's stop here for a second. You will read many books and literature about statistics — don't believe them on addictions. Addictions are in secret. Thus, gathering accurate stats on secrets is impossible. I will not tell you that twenty percent / fifteen percent / ten percent / etc. were set free in Battle Lines, as I do not know. Nor does SA or AA see the truth about their groups, of so many men coming in and out, as was Battle Lines. Still, the fact is that the percentages are minimal; however, when men do the hard work, it pays off, like the runner who prepares via a schedule to run a marathon. The marathoner runs and finishes because they put in the hard work.

You can be that marathon runner, running at your pace but finishing. And guess what? With all that is required, you will find that your thinking changes because you engage with the Lord, and He changes you. I used to run, and one day, I was running at Memorial Park in Houston, Texas, a three-mile loop, and I just kept running and running and was euphoric. I ran twelve miles and could have run more. That was totally unexpected, but it was because I ran many three-, six-, and nine-mile stretches over many months. God wants you to experience Him on this journey, and in experiencing, He works on your inner being as you seek to connect with Him in a relationship.

One of your responsibilities is to have that renewed mind and pray for it. The Holy Spirit can do what you cannot, but you must believe He can! If you don't trust Him to the degree that you ought to, it means you're not really trusting God to do what He promised He would do. If you do not ask God for what He told you to ask Him for, you have not because you ask not. James 4:3 states: "You ask and do not receive, because you ask wrongly, to spend it on your passions."

He is our Father, and we must ask Him to renew our minds. And He does that by the Holy Spirit, who is in you if you have surrendered your life to Him. Again, repeat, reading His Word, meditating on it, and praying out loud conversationally to the

Lord means that in time, your mind is filled with the Word and pushes out the negative. When you are walking His ways and doing His ways, it will naturally, but truly supernaturally, cause a change to take place in your mind.

Studying the Word of God is a need for you, and your need to be around joyous fellowship is part of the Godly mystery of regenerating a man's mind. To truly worship regularly in a church that is not rigid in ceremony but open in worship is where you need to be, with the Word of God being unapologetically taught, not preached, but taught Word for Word. This is where God desires for you and me to be. Move away from the performance of professional church to fellowship with like Believers; in worship is where the Holy Spirit works and does what you cannot do, but others see you changed in time. You know your mind is being cleansed as you "think differently!"

In the past, you stayed in isolation primarily because of your addiction, but now, you cannot isolate; you must have a community like Believers. You grow in a community face-to-face, studying together, laughing together, worshiping together, and connecting outside the church. In time, that brings forth healthy relationships, but not perfect, as there is no such thing as perfect in church or outside.

I also want you to know that the addiction that you are moving away from and healing from, being transformed from, and being set free from is not a "disease," as the professional community might claim. Here is the definition of a disease according to merriam-webster.com: "a condition of the living animal or plant body or of one of its parts that impairs normal functioning and is typically manifested by distinguishing signs and symptoms: sickness, malady, infectious diseases, a rare genetic disease, heart disease." Sexual compulsivity/addiction is not a disease; it is an issue of compulsivity that affects the brain via chemicals and neuropathways, but it is not an infection. It is an engrained habit that was developed by choice and continues by choice, even though the chemicals and neuropathways demand their needs be met. You have to fight against the chemicals and neuropathways that you have developed. Choice develops the issue, and choice settles the problem of being set free. That choice is to be fought for. As one's mind is renewed, that choice is not desirous; another choice is the relationship with the Lord.

I never want to hear you say you are a sex addict or have a disease. No, that is what you do, not who you are. In Scripture, it speaks of who you are "in Christ" if you have received Him. You have an issue, but the issue does not define you. Don't let yourself or the professional arena of counselors define you. Another way to renew your mind is to destroy the lies you have believed about yourself and/or allowed others to place on you. That does not mean you are removed from responsibility to work on your issues and make new choices not to act out. No, you have the added responsibility to make new choices. Still, suppose you think of yourself as a child of the King who has an issue with sexual compulsivity. In that case, I believe this encourages you to think more positively of yourself.

Embrace Christ as your Savior, and choose to walk His ways, "the Way!" Yes, you have an issue, but you can be free from it in time. Yes, you can become healed. Immerse yourself in God's Word and think upon those things in His Word that encourage you and challenge you. Run the race to win the prize and beat your body, and you will be a victor. With you, set your mind upon Christ, and He will slowly clean your mind. A new mind! Oh, by the way, it does not happen overnight! Again and again, I encourage and remind you that this is a journey and a process!

Being RENEWED is an essential pathway to TRANSFORMATION. Renewal and transformation are not things you can do in and of yourself; they have to come by the power of the Holy Spirit, and that, again, men, is through a relationship with Him! Not a knowledge of Him, but an intimate relationship with Him.

Romans 12:2 states, "Do not be conformed to this world, but be transformed by the renewal of your mind." You must be ready to remove yourself from being confirmed to the world if you desire to be transformed from the INSIDE! You have to seek to understand that your mind is "fallen," as the pronouncement came upon Adam after he sinned. From then on, we were born "sinners." Our minds, in effect, are fallen, and we have a mindset at odds with God Himself. By nature, we are lost, and God gave us up to a debased mind, as it speaks of in Romans 1:28. If you are truly honest about who and what you are, you know that your mind is opposed to the things of God. It takes effort, men, to seek Him, but it is so priceless to get to know Him and Him changing you and having you desire the things of God versus the things of this world. But it takes time for all of this to occur.

Paul speaks of the deceitful desires in Ephesians 4:22: "You were taught, with regard to your former way of life, to put off your old self, which is being corrupted by its deceitful desires." These are self-operating, and they get their power from the deceit of our minds. Only through the renewal of our minds can we be liberated from our minds' deceit and power. We must not walk according to the world but only through walking according to the Word of God. Walking and choosing His Ways brings us into an awakening of the supremacy of Christ Himself.

When Christ renews your mind, you are like that white sheet, flapping in the wind from a clothesline in the bright sun, looking so pure and clean. You are clean; you need to keep choosing His Word to stay that way. It is an everyday choice as you wake up each day. You should choose each day to pray before you begin your day by putting on the Full Amor of God, as it speaks of Ephesians 6:10–18:

> *10 Finally, be strong in the Lord and in his mighty power. 11 Put on the full armor of God, so that you can take your stand against the devil's schemes. 12 For our struggle is not against flesh and blood, but against the rulers, against the authorities, against the powers of this dark world and against the spiritual forces of evil in the heavenly realms. 13 Therefore put on the full armor of God, so that when the*

day of evil comes, you may be able to stand your ground, and after you have done everything, to stand. 14 Stand firm then, with the belt of truth buckled around your waist, with the breastplate of righteousness in place, 15 and with your feet fitted with the readiness that comes from the gospel of peace. 16 In addition to all this, take up the shield of faith, with which you can extinguish all the flaming arrows of the evil one. 17 Take the helmet of salvation and the sword of the Spirit, which is the Word of God. 18 And pray in the Spirit on all occasions with all kinds of prayers and requests. With this in mind, be alert and always pray for all the Lord's people.

Choose to develop your own words in time. As you begin each day this way, you are honoring God, seeking to implant Him into your day, and speaking to the evil one that today is God's, and YOU ARE GOD'S MAN!

As the caterpillar metamorphoses into a beautiful butterfly, you can you have that metamorphic Holy Spirit journey into you with a renewed mind and then be transformed into a man of God. You will be a testimony just by how you live; you don't have to say anything other than live. And guess what? If married, your wife will see this beautifulness before you realize it within yourself. And guess what? You did not do this; God did. Another powerful example is in John 15, as Jesus is the Vine, and you are a branch if you have Christ in you. As the branch gets its life source from the Vine, as you focus on Him (abide in Him, trust in Him, depend on Him, surrender to Him, and other words like that), He is the one that brings forth fruit in your life (Galatians 5:22). You cannot produce that fruit, only Jesus can!

Remember, sanctification is gradual and progressive and not a sprint. So, with that, be patient, as it speaks of in James 5:7: *"Be patient, therefore, brothers, until the coming of the Lord. See how the farmer waits for the precious fruit of the earth, being patient about it, until it receives the early and the late rains."* God will set the pace, not you! He will test you, as it speaks of in His Word, and Satan and your flesh will tempt you on this journey. In one sense, this can be a painful journey in the beginning, as it is all new, and your flesh, your being, wants instant change, and that cannot happen. Another great verse is 1 Corinthians 9:24–27:

> *24 Do you not know that in a race all the runners run, but only one receives the prize? So run that you may obtain it. 25 Every athlete exercises self-control in all things. They do it to receive a perishable wreath, but we are imperishable. 26 So I do not run aimlessly; I do not box as one beating the air. 27 **But I discipline my body** and keep it under control, lest after preaching to others I myself should be disqualified.*

NOTE: I made in **bold, "discipline my body."** That is what you must do; you must fight your body and discipline it. There is a prize worth winning, but it takes time. Do not get ahead of yourself.

It is going to take the supernatural power of the Holy Spirit to help you break free from sexual compulsivity / sexual addiction and your behavior and negative thinking. In most cases, the addiction begins with one single choice. Your mind grabs hold of you, and your brain (chemicals) is heightened, eventually taking over your life. Now, the journey of a renewed mind and being transformed takes place similarly. However, you are now bringing God into the picture.

You need to let God help. Through His Word, let Him instill the correct thinking in your mind.

The Bible tells us that the measure we use will be the measure measured back to us. In other words, if we want God's best, then we have to give Him our best. When it comes to the sanctification process, we have to give Him our best by reading and studying the Word of God. He wants to make the changes with us, in us, and through us! We must attempt to put on, to decide, to choose these Godly qualities He wants us to have!

When we give God our best, then He will give us His best and then begin to transmit His Godly qualities and attributes right into the middle of our persons via the Holy Spirit!

Oh, guess what? As we have shared, this sanctification process is not an overnight thing! Again, this process and journey, as shared throughout the above, will occur over the rest of your existence on this earth! Again, "if" you are willing to work with God in this process, He will work with you. He will do it gradually and progressively to transform and satisfy you to make you the kind of person that He wants you to be! Remember, you are unique, and His plans for you are different from those He has for me. Instead of comparing yourself to others, compare yourself to His Son Jesus! You will have joy within you and be a joy to be around others in these wonderful pathways that He has just for you! You will no longer be caught up in the miry clay, but God will place you upon the solid rock! Know this! Believe this! Receive this!

Finally, self-control is saying no to sinful desires, even when it hurts! However, the Christian way of self-control is not to "just say no!" The problem is with the word "just." You don't say no; you say no in a certain way. You say no by faith in the superior power and pleasure of Christ! The "NO" is just as ruthless and maybe just as painful. But the difference between worldly self-control and godly self-control is crucial. Who will get glory for victory? That the issue! Will we get the glory? Or will Christ get the glory? Only He can get the glory because it is with Him, by Him, and through Him that change has taken place with you!

LIFE is not a resort but a bumpy pathway that leads to conformity to Christ. We can face the bumps with genuine joy, knowing that a loving and caring Father for our redemptive good placed every bumpy road in our path to GROW! Grow in and through HIM! He did not cause your issues in life. However, He allowed them. Lamentations 3:37 states, "Who has spoken and it came to pass, unless the Lord has commanded it?"

We have covered a lot here, including many challenges,

straight talk, and God's Word. I pray that the message of having a renewed mind and being transformed has been understandable. I know this is all possibly new, but if you are patient, consistent, and focused with great intention, He will do the rest.

There is an excellent song I like by the Maranatha Singers titled In His Time. If you have a chance, look it up on YouTube and enjoy

MEN

In His time, in His time
He makes all things beautiful
In His time

Believe It!

If you seek to be intentional in your training, your mind to stay on the Triune God and His timeless Word, you will be on this journey of renewing your mind. But as you do so, your confidence in Him will grow. You will, in time, realize the Lord is unmovable, unsinkable, unassailable Rock. As you seek Him, He will seek you and do what you cannot do in renewing your mind as you meditate on His Word and seek to diligently walk in His ways. You trust in Him, and He gives you peace that you cannot explain, other than that it is Him. He seeks to provide you with His peace! Perfect peace!

The truth of God's Word is greater than the flesh, the news of this world, and the anxieties of life. He is more significant than your addiction. He is about your freedom, healing, and transformation, but again, please note you must be intentional in your diligence of focus and walk. Walking according to His Word out of love for Him!

HOMEWORK:

1. In your own words, write in detail how your mind can be renewed. Don't write it down to give an answer; write it

down as this is what you are going to do.

2. What Resources do you need to have at your disposal to renew your mind:

3. How are you going to use these resources?

4. What are you truly going to commit to and why?

5. DO YOU WANT TO GET WELL?

CHAPTER 15
No Two Are the Same

Psalm 139 speaks of your being unique, fearfully, and wonderfully made. Your fingerprint is unique to you; no two are ever alike. In the same manner, your treatment for sexual addiction may be different than another because of your background is entirely different.

One thing that is the same is that **YOU MUST ADMIT YOU ARE OUT OF CONTROL** and need help, as well as your willingness to do anything necessary for your freedom. Until you are at this place of desperation, in seeking healing, you are wasting your time, your family's time, and those seeking to help you.

One of the places to possibly process is *The 30 Tasks Model* **by Dr. Patrick Carnes**, only with your counselor. You can go online to print it out. You should establish a 3-ring notebook to have those things you process, not only here but also with all exercises, counseling exercises, notes from books, etc. Not all exercises may apply to you but be diligent in seeking everything you can to get well and work with your counselor to process them! Do not leave a stone unturned! This notebook is written as "evidence of your work," and you can go back to it repeatedly as you sear things in your brain about what it takes to walk in freedom. Be a *General George S. Patton.* Doing it alone does not allow guidance from someone equipped to do so. Let's process it only in scanning, with *my comments*, which are the following:

1. **Break Through Denial** — you cannot even begin your healing journey unless you get here. No one can bring you to this place, ONLY YOU!

2. **Understand the Nature of Addictive Illness** — unless you are willing to read, go to counseling, or come to a group, you are going to be walking in blindness. You must

educate yourself in those appropriate skills, such as being a counselor!

3. **Sexual Addiction Component** — Understanding sexually compulsive patterns, as shown in the Carnes model, is a must. See Arousal Template by Dr. Patrick Carnes via the internet — "the total constellation of thoughts, images, behaviors, sounds, smells, sights, fantasies, and objects that arouse us sexually."

4. **Surrender to the Process** — this is where you accept what the addictive life is about and, hopefully, know your limitations and understand the difference between what you can control and what you cannot. There is a lot of personal work that you must do here to come to an understanding of what your addiction is about. The PERFORMABLES of Carnes' tasks are a must!

   I've added more reading recommendations in the back of the book to assist in educating yourself on the personal issues that apply to you. Hopefully, your counselor is skilled in assigning those books. You are to educate yourself about the problems, which include the brain, trauma, the addiction itself and the power it has on you, and how you can be set free. Again, be a General Patton and know your enemy!

5. **Limit Damage from Behavior** — You limit what you can and cannot do. The performances are excellent. Here we will make a shift, and it is not A HIGHER POWER that you write a letter to, to turn things over to; it can only be JESUS CHRIST OF Nazareth and not a belief, but a relationship with HIM, otherwise you are doing all in YOUR OWN POWER. It will not work, and no matter the 12 Steps and HIGHER POWER, this will be an offense to our Lord, so tread lightly here. I might get heat here, but I must stay faithful to biblical truths.

6. **Establish Sobriety** — You have to stop (emphasis on

STOP) acting out with sexual compulsivity! You must have boundaries and accountability in place, plus escape plans!

7. **Ensure Physical Integrity** — You have to understand — no, you don't! Only if you want to break free from your addiction, you must, as it states, understand the physical aspects of the addiction (brain) and the neuropathways (brain) and identify your arousal (trigger) patterns. Just note that nothing is forced upon you; you must take the initiative for yourself, and passivity will be your downfall if you do not understand. Make choices!

8. **Participate in a Culture of Support**

   a. You must be in a support group that you attend each week that is "educational," not just going in a circle stating you have an addiction. You have not acted out in 7 days...

   b. You must have accountability.

   c. You must have a competent counselor who you see each and every week.

9. **Understand Multiple Addictions and Sobriety**

   a. Understand that there is usually a strong possibility of having another addiction, along with sexual compulsivity.

   b. Have a relapse prevention plan written out and practiced for escape plans, etc. It is one thing to talk about it, another to write about it, and another to truly practice it in escaping. When the triggers do occur, and they will, you will immediately know how to respond to prevent you from acting out.

10. **Acknowledge Cycles of Abuse**

    a. The trauma egg is a tremendous guide to helping identify abuse — and with a counselor, you have a

lot to process, depending upon your background
— and you may be someone who has no trauma.
You started watching porn and became addicted at
age 14. Guess what? That was trauma to your
undeveloped brain. That is why you became
"hooked."

b. This is a time to prepare, not do, but prepare a list
of all those who have offended you, to prepare for
the day for forgiveness from your heart.

c. It is also, again, with your counselor to recognize
shame and guilt and the falsity of that so that they
are not triggers of your acting out. When you
accepted Christ, God took care of all offenses,
shame, guilt, etc., at the Cross, so HE set you free.
So, if He set you free, who are you not to walk in
it, as you are not greater than HE! The great I AM!

11. Reduce Shame

a. An outstanding book to process *is HEALING
THE SHAME THAT BINDS YOU* by John
Bradshaw, a close friend of Dr. Patrick Carnes.
John passed away some years ago, but his wisdom
is still current.

b. God wants to heal you, and you must know that
Christ took care of this again at the Cross, so walk
in freedom!

12. Restructure Relationship with Self

a. Start enjoying yourself, find new hobbies, make
new friends, extend yourself to others, and dare to
experience new things.

b. Each pace differs from others on the performable
but continual attendance with Group and
counseling.

13. **Grieve Losses**

a. There is grieving of losses that you did not get to experience due to your addiction. Those losses can never be replaced. However, you can grieve those and get in touch by allowing the pain that is deep inside to come out. Cleansing deep within is healing.

b. In addition, if you have lost a parent, sibling, or friend and have never grieved those losses, this is a perfect time to experience that. The best way is to get with your therapist and appropriately process things.

14. **Bring Closure and Resolution Taking Responsibility for Self**

a. If your counselor and spouse's counselor deem it appropriate, then couples counseling is the next for you. Seek to continue counseling as an individual, as considered relevant by your therapist, but keep current with the homework and your couples counseling. You be the leader here, as your wife watches to see if you will lead. She is not seeking to hear what you are "doing," she wants to SEE IT!

b. Continue working on issues that have not been dealt with per your therapist via homework. You are also to be a self-initiative man, reading books on your own and discussing issues. Your wife is watching again; what are you doing in running the extra miles. You build trust by doing, not talking about it.

15. **Restore Financial Viability**

a. Many times, finances have been devastated by the addict's behavior and secret spending. This needs to be examined thoroughly with your spouse, and significant decisions perhaps need to be made to restore and build a new financial security.

b. It is often wise to take everything to an accomplished financial advisor to help restore your financial house.

c. Absolute honesty, transparency, and vulnerability are a must here, as well as not having any secrets withheld.

d. It is best to have someone again, like a financial advisor, with all income and expenses on the table and a third party looking at all objectively to help you rebuild your financial house and security. Again, men speak to the wife, being humble and contrite and seeking help beyond yourself!

e. Your wife and men seek financial security. They need to know they are safe in the economic area, and your initiative here speaks to them in great measure.

16. Restore Meaningful Work

a. Suppose your addiction has interrupted your career. In that case, this is another area of security that speaks to your wife. It would help if you restored your work ethic and established your career path with passion and focus.

b. It is imperative, if at all possible, depending upon our economic well-being and where your wife is, that you ensure that you ENJOY your work! Suppose it is possible, depending upon our economic well-being and where your wife is. In that case, you must sit down with her and have a plan for redirection, seeking advice from your financial advisor and others.

17. **Create a Lifestyle Balance**

   a. I will say here that you must have well-being at home, at work, in your own enjoyment, and the same for your wife and then your family.

   b. If life is out of balance, stress can lead to backsliding. Seek to achieve balance for your teammate — your wife — and for yourself and your family.

   c. Be wise to eliminate and be wise to add those things to you and your family that have less stress plus added enjoyment plus relaxation.

18. **Build Supportive Personal Relationships**

   a. One of the big things for men is that they tend to be "loners," which is not a healthy place to be.

   b. YOU MUST REACH OUT and initiate. Men will not come and knock on your door in most cases.

   c. I want you to go beyond your Group to healthy men who have healthy relationships with their wives and healthy, not perfect families. If you feel uncomfortable with an approach, say "hell with it" and dare to go beyond your comfort level. Dare to believe in yourself and that you deserve healthy relationships / if it is golfing, fishing, hunting, photography, or whatever, seek to advance YOUR NEW TERRITORY. Men are looking for connections, and so are you! So please do it!

   d. Do not do this with any man in your Group. They are processing their addiction plus, more than likely, issues in their family. YOU DO NOT NEED THAT, which is called a boundary, and your wife must know that you are surrounding yourself with positive relationships. Period!

   e. You must maintain your accountability men —

you should have two strong accountability men who are not part of any addiction group! YOU must nourish these two men in your life — you reach out to them and let them see that you are serious about change in your life. You seek breakfast with one no less than once every two weeks. And telephone calls are important too! NO TEXTING, as that is a hidden disguise that hinders relationships!

19. **Establish Healthy Exercise and Nutrition Patterns**

a. This is a significant area of your life. It would be best if you got OUT OF THE HOUSE and exercised.

b. Gyms and memberships (no for at least two years) — temptations are too great and only when your wife gives permission to do so after two years and your two accountability partners

c. You have parks and other places to run, walk, etc.

WHAT EXERCISE AND A HEALTHY DIET DOES FOR YOU

According to Kenneth H. Cooper, MD, MPH, Founder and Chairman of Cooper Aerobics Health & Wellness, we should exercise a collective thirty minutes a day most days of the week through moderate physical activity. Moderate intensity should elevate your heart rate to where you can talk but are winded. There are many types of cardiovascular exercise: taking a brisk walk or jogging, kicking the soccer ball with the kids, playing a game of touch football, swimming laps, jump roping, and hopping on an elliptical machine. Whatever you choose, just get moving!

A collective thirty minutes a day — here's the good news. You don't have to exercise for thirty minutes if your schedule doesn't work, or those bad knees won't last. You can do three spurts of activity for ten minutes each or break it into two fifteen-minute intervals. It all adds up, and it all counts! A total of thirty minutes is a realistic amount of time to fit into your schedule. Put it on your calendar like an appointment, and stick to it.

Five days a week — This is important because if you do thirty minutes of moderately intense cardio over five days, you will have logged one hundred fifty minutes of exercise. This is the magic number to reap heart health benefits, prevent diabetes, cancer, and other diseases, and improve quality and quantity of life.

Make healthy food choices most of the time — We like to say it's about moderation, not deprivation. Or eat healthy eighty percent of the time and have that cookie the other twenty percent of the time.

That may be a big bite, so what's the first step to building healthy nutrition habits? We'd say eat more fruits and vegetables daily. An adage is, "Five is fine, but nine is divine." That's talking about servings (one serving is half a cup) of fruits and veggies daily. If you're not getting five servings daily, start there, then work your way to nine.

Research shows by doing this, you can lower your blood pressure and cholesterol and are at a lower risk of stroke, heart failure, osteoporosis and kidney stones.

Maintain a healthy weight — If you have a lot of visceral fat, the worst type of fat, which usually accounts for the "pot belly," your waist circumference is the best measurement. Men's waist measurement should be less than forty inches, and women are less than thirty-five inches.

Maintaining a healthy weight is one of the most important things you can do to prevent illness and disease, enjoy a higher quality of life, and live longer. We know it takes a combination of good nutrition and consistent exercise to do this!

Take the right supplements for you — Supplements are just that; they are supplements and not replacements. You have to start with a balanced diet; vitamins and supplements can help bridge the gaps to achieve optimal overall health.

No matter how hard we try, most people are not getting the proper amounts of vitamins and minerals their body needs through diet alone. Generally, we just don't eat very well. Less than a third of Americans get at least five servings of fruits or vegetables daily. Our diets are incomplete.

So, start with a good multivitamin taken with meals. This will cover most of your basic supplement needs.

Then, check your blood levels to determine if you are deficient and need additional supplementation. Research shows the majority of people are vitamin D deficient, which has been linked to diseases such as hypertension, depression, diabetes, certain cancers, and arthritis, to name a few. Studies have also shown the benefits of omega-3 in blood pressure, triglycerides, cholesterol, metabolic syndrome, and cognitive health.

Get a regular, comprehensive physical exam.

Manage stress and prioritize sleep — We all get "stressed out" at some point. It's part of life. Yet you may not realize how dangerous it can be to your physical and emotional health.

Stress can raise blood pressure and resting heart rate, leading to weight gain. It can also lead to anxiety and worry, which may impair your ability to fall or stay asleep. On the other hand, not getting an adequate quantity and quality of sleep certainly raises stress levels. If stress and sleep problems go untreated long-term, they can cause physical and mental health problems.

We spend nearly a third of our lives sleeping, so it's important to prioritize and protect sleep at all stages of life. Most adults need seven to eight hours daily. Develop a bedtime routine and get on a schedule of going to bed and getting up at the same time daily. Be sure caffeine and alcohol intake aren't interfering with your sleep.

Exercise is an effective way to manage stress. Physical activity reduces anxiety and improves health in so many different ways. It can boost the mood, improve energy, and significantly improve both the quality and quantity of sleep. In fact, a study by The Cooper Institute showed that doses of physical activity were as effective as taking prescription drugs for mild to moderate depression.

Taking time to de-stress and relax is not a luxury! Finding something that works for you and helps you balance your life is essential.

Do not use tobacco. We all know smoking is "bad" for you and a leading cause of lung cancer. But all tobacco products, not just cigarettes, can threaten your health.

Tobacco is associated with a number of different types of cancers, including esophageal, cervical, stomach, kidney, pancreatic, and more. On top of that, tobacco is the number one treatable cause of cardiovascular disease, which is the leading cause of death in America.

It's never too late to quit using tobacco. And the sooner you quit, the better your long-term prognosis.

Control alcohol — This one is always a mixed bag. There are both benefits and drawbacks to consider when it comes to alcohol.

Among other things, excessive alcohol can cause weight gain, damage your liver and your heart and increase the risk of developing some types of cancer. Yet, for some people, moderate alcohol intake may also have a benefit for the heart.

Alcohol, as you know, maximizes our vulnerability, and you know that vulnerability exposes you to issues such as affairs, porn, massage parlors, etc. So, no bars, no hanging out in restaurants where there is major drinking of alcohol, and a major boundary is no friends you drink excessively. Choose new friends and develop a healthy lifestyle with friendships that honor their drinking habits!

1. **Involve Family Members in Therapy**

   a. At the appropriate time, as determined by your therapist and hopefully the therapist, your wife, has, determines your counseling.

   b. Keep the circle small; hopefully, your wife knows, and other family members do not need to know. If there is one or two, yes, at the appropriate time, seek to include them in counseling and healing. But only in the proper time.

   c. I strongly recommend that your children are not to be included, too much information taints, and as best as you can, if possible, maintain purity for them and your relationship.

   d. If you do not have a healthy relationship with your children, now is the time to start on an INDIVIDUAL basis and determine their interests so they can enjoy them from their perspective, not yours.

   e. Men, this is a primary exercise and lifestyle for you and your children, and it is also imperative that you develop this relationship with your wife that God wants you to have.

2. **Commit to HEALING, SETTING THE CAPTIVE FREE, and TRANSFORMATION**

   a. I'm not too fond of the term **RECOVERY**. SAMHSA's working definition of recovery is a process of change through which individuals improve their health and wellness, live self-directed lives, and strive to reach their full potential. Recovery signals a dramatic shift in the expectation for positive outcomes for individuals who experience mental and substance use conditions or the co-occurring of the two.

b. Yes, if something has been wrong with a family member, and they are age-appropriate in bringing forth healing, keep the circle tight about who knows and who does not know.

3. Resolve Original Conflicts and Wounds

a. This is big, men, with your counseling. You must share everything with your counselor and seek to have them explore your childhood and adulthood for hurts, rejections, and traumas.

b. For many, this requires a lot of processing and work, but true healing can occur. Still, you have to be wholly vulnerable and transparent with your counselor so that he/she can do his/her job appropriately.

c. Transparency is a must in the Group, whether it is an educational group or a long-term group, because many can open up about their successes in their healing process and encourage you to do what it takes and do all it takes to be healed.

d. I will be straight here — true healing cannot occur without a real relationship with **Jesus Christ**. All effort for healing, without Christ, is in the "flesh" (self-effort), and it fails. Christ came to free the captive, heal, and transform.

e. You must work on forgiveness, as shared earlier in this book, and you must work on repentance, which is included in the attachments suggested for homework.

f. Here is another essential part of healing. **YOUR IDENTITY**! Your identity, worth, and value are not in your job, your titles, your possessions, your zip code, or what your body looks like; God wants you to know your identity comes from HIM, as

Christ is in you; if YOU have a relationship with HIM, and received HIM as your LORD and SAVIOR, and walk in HIS WAYS. Not walking in perfectness. I included Scriptures about your identity in Chapter 4. God wants you to look into the mirror and say, "I love YOU!" You are precious in HIS SIGHT, so walk in it! Live it out. And at some point, God does something in your life that you cannot explain, other than it is God HIMSELF, doing what you could never do!

4. Alter Dysfunctional Family Relationships

    a. Boundaries are essential to who you let into your life and who you do not let into your life.

    b. Suppose you have negative relationships that harm you and your family emotionally. In that case, boundaries are necessary and cannot be in your life. Unhealthiness with family and friends cannot be a part of your life. They are not required to understand why you have shut them out of your life. You do not argue or debate; you set it in stone and establish that your responsibility is your and your family's health. I had to do this with family members. It is not easy, but it is healthy. As I did, you can establish healthiness with healthy people around you that you find in church, Bible study, and through your children's friends (if you have been good and are making sure your children are associated with healthy friendships). Most of our friendships have taken place this way and have been precious and celebrated with grand celebration. You can do the same; you must choose where you put yourself, in healthy or harmful areas. BE WISE, PLEASE YOU are a GROWN MAN! Make a healthy choice today!

5. Resolve Issues with Children

Go to Number 19 for information shared.

6. Resolve Issues with Extended Family

Go to Number 19 again for information shared.

7. Work Through Differentiation

a. Healthy relationships are so meaningful, and you can learn how to communicate, handle conflict, etc., with the counselor's help and with excellent books sitting before you on choices and how to establish healthy family relationships, some of which are included in my suggestions in the bank of the book.

b. You and your wife can go to excellent weekend marriage intensives. Seek to find those out, and you will be the initiator. Let your wife seek you, going all out to be the best man you can be. God will bless you for it! You will learn things that perhaps your family of origin never exposed you to. Healthiness comes with work, and with newness, even more challenging work but you can do it, and in time, you will enjoy it all. Why? There is less conflict and more connectedness in relationships, and they feed off each other.

8. Succeed in Intimacy

a. The # 1 thing here is emotional intimacy. Your wife desires to be honored and valued, and you're seeking to meet her emotional needs. This is where healing occurs. Putting her #1 above you.

b. Again, weekend intensives and marriage retreats are before you; seek them out and see if your wife would like to do them! Again, you initiate!

9. Commit to Primary Relationships

a. Your # 1 priority relationship is to be with Jesus

Christ.

b. Your # 2 primary relationship is your spouse.

c. Your # 3 primary relationship is with your children.

10. Explore Coupleship HEALING

Again, men, marriage retreats, marriage intensives, counseling, and you are to be the initiator.

11. Restore Healthy Sexuality

God wants you to have emotional intimacy and connection to your ONENESS, your wife! This has to be established in dating, helping, finding out her needs and seeking to meet them, speaking in pleasant tones, etc. Without this, you are just pursuing "physical intimacy" without emotions! That lasts for a very short time, especially with your mate. She wants to be pursued, courted, loved, cherished, etc.

12. Develop a Spiritual Life

a. This is # 1 above all your work!

b. This is not about a "higher power!"

c. This is about Jesus Christ of Nazareth!

d. See Chapter 4 on this

13. Do the Work

a. Complete and true healing can take place by HIM, but you have to do the work described throughout this book and the books referenced and seek to have intimacy with our Lord.

b. He is the great I AM; without HIM, you can do nothing!

c. John 15:5 says, "I am the vine; you are the branches. If you remain in me and I in you, you will bear much fruit; apart from me you can do nothing." Nothing means nothing, men!

d. God desires to heal you from the inside out, not your behavior! Your behavior follows forth from what is inside of you. Either you have Christ in you, or you don't. In your own power, you cannot heal yourself from within; only Jesus can.

e. I shared true stories about men's lives being healed, changed, and transformed. They did the work required for them that was specific, and then they worked on developing that relationship with Christ, and then later down the highway, HE did something they could not do.

One thing I would like to point out is that there are no stages or steps to this issue, as there are none for grief. It is a process that ebbs and flows in different directions. Breaking free from any addiction is a process, and healing (as best you can from a personal death, such as a child), is a process. One day, you may find yourself in the heaviest of grief and be angry at God. It is only via God that healing can take place, and even these many years later, I can have tears flow sob on occasion. am I in a different place today when the tragedy occurred? Yes, but there is still, at times, sadness. I have gone through June, forgetting his date of death. This shows that there is a process of healing.

It would help if you did not think that you check the boxes off because someone said there are steps, stages, etc., to break free, and you don't, then you throw up your hands because you bought into this type of thinking. Just because someone "said" does not make it so. It is a *process*, and that is how growth takes place; that is how you grow and heal.

Many will be outspoken about this towards me, but believe me, I know, and I have seen it in all the years of counseling and doing a men's group. It is beautiful to see a man walking to the other side, and he did the work that was "particular and specific for him, and him alone, NOT YOU!" Get it? I hope so.

CHAPTER 16
Light Bulb Moments

You are a man; you don't need to be spoon-fed. Thus, the following is for you to process and integrate into a part of your being. You can pull up your pants (figuratively speaking) unless you are twelve years old and immature and seek to become a MAN in battle. There will be many wars to choose from, both practical and biblical. It's time for you to grow up! It's time for you to take responsibility! It's time to be healed, transformed, and set free. No one can do it for you, only God and your choices!

NOTE: In my counseling and in Battle Lines, I encouraged men to get a notebook, place their processed homework, and then have time each week to go over their completed work. Completing some of the attached is one thing, and IT IS A COMPLETE OTHER THING TO EMBRACE AND PUT INTO PRACTICE.

Homework is required for anyone who has ever counseled with me and/or came to Battle Lines. Books are to be read. And also, in due time, developing a genuine relationship with the Lord is the only secret to success. It is a secret to many because if they go to church, that is all they do, no genuine relationship, as they are walking unknowingly in thinking they have a relationship, but in truth they do not; it is a secret embedded in them, that they know not of. And it is a secret to those who don't know about the Lord; thus, they have come into new information. Whether it was in counseling and/or Battle Lines, I always ended sessions and groups in prayer.

Men, get a notebook to place some of the following into it, then purchase a Bible and prepare to read books, not just this one you are processing, but others, including those I recommend at the back of this book. It is time for you to become like a man like General George Patton! Know your enemy, which is called sex addiction! If you want to win the war that you are in, be a fighter who destroys his enemies, like George S. Patton! You have an enemy, and it wants to destroy you!

OVERCONFIDENCE

Overconfidence is a significant threat to healing and transformation. This is the belief the person with an addiction has in their own abilities to handle situations without respect for the insidiousness of addiction. Signs of overconfidence are:

- Calling your own shots

- Inability to hear what others are saying

- Contempt before investigation

- Wanting immediate results and having unrealistic expectations

The **first sign** of overconfidence is calling your own shots. When the person with an addiction first enters into healing, they often attend many meetings, establish a relationship with their accountability partner, and build a support system. As time in healing progresses, the person with an addiction often begins to feel better about him and life in transformation. Once they feel better, rejecting what they are suggesting is easy. In fact, it is almost human nature to do so. The person with an addiction replays those old tapes, "I know what is really best for me" or "I can do it by myself; I have for all these years, and I am still alive." There is a saying in Twelve-Step Groups:

- "I am not like those people."

- "I am not dead yet."

- "I have not lost my wife yet."

- "I have not lost my job yet."

The above are the "yes, buts" — yes, but...yes, but...yes, but...

The person with an addiction is ready to take back total control of their life. This shows the power of the addictive process and grandiose thinking that people with an addiction regularly engage in. To paraphrase an AA saying, "My best thinking kept me drinking, drugging, gambling, etc." The person with a substance use disorder forgets what they learned in the first step of any Twelve Step healing program, "We admitted we were powerless over our addictive behaviors and that our lives had become unmanageable."

The **second sign** of overconfidence is the inability to hear what others are saying. The person with an addiction is in a self-help group meeting and discounts what others are saying because they know themselves best. The person with a substance use disorder is so well practiced at listening to their own voice of denial and justification that they cannot absorb input from outside resources. Again, the person with a substance use disorder says, "My situation is different. I was sober for about two years. Then, my old friends invited me to a birthday party. I called my accountability man, who told me to attend a meeting and avoid the party. I went anyway because I had confidence in my healing program. When I got there, everybody was using it, and I thought to myself, *Maybe this time*...and that was when I relapsed."

Contempt before the investigation is the **third sign** of overconfidence. Here, the addict attempts to discount methods of healing. Someone suggests that they go to a group or a Twelve Step meeting. After the first fifteen minutes of the meeting, the addict decides this meeting is not for them. I have seen this happen time and time again. No one here has anything to offer them. Or the addict does not even bother to try the meeting out. They reject the idea with no investigation. "I wasn't like those people around me. I hadn't lost everything in my addiction, ended up divorced, and lost my hour or anything like that. I left Twelve-Step meetings because I couldn't identify with how sick those people really were!"

Wanting immediate results and having unrealistic expectations are the **fourth and final signs** of overconfidence. People want results right away in this world in which we live. This is especially true for the addict whose pattern has been one of instant gratification. The person with an addiction addict says to himself, "After all, I've been sober for six months, and my employer still hasn't given me back all the responsibility I once had," or "My wife does not fully trust me around other women even though I was only unfaithful when I was using." An aside — "I only used for the last fourteen years."

The addict's thinking here is, *I expect that because I have stayed sober, the world will give me what I want and will give it to me right now; if it doesn't, then why should I put all the effort into my abstinence?* The person with a substance use disorder has the attitude that the rest of the world owes them. The person with an addiction may think, "I deserve something; everyone else owes it to me." Many people know the addict's thinking as "terminal uniqueness." The addict believes that their situation differs from everyone else and that they deserve preferential treatment.

For most people, life in healing does not get better, but it takes time and is not always in "our time frame." Remember, healing, transformation, and satisfaction is a process — NOT AN EVENT! Healing and eventual transformation is the ability to genuinely recognize that others have something of value to offer. None of us has all the answers!

TRUST

Trust is the glue that holds relationships together. It allows you to feel safe so that you can be vulnerable enough to emotionally connect with another person. In the early stages of relationships, individuals often extend trust early as part of an unspoken code of honor. People we engage with socially are generally considered trustworthy until proven otherwise. Over time, as we get to know someone, that trust grows and deepens. When we break this trust, it is not just with the other person but often with ourselves. You question what the other person did and how you let the betrayal happen. To move forward in a relationship after a betrayal, it is crucial to re-establish trust, not only with the other person but, possibly even more importantly, with yourself.

In marriage, secrets are as dangerous as lies. Your spouse should have a "master key" to every part of your life. Never have a conversation you wouldn't want them to hear, view a website you wouldn't want them to see, or go somewhere you wouldn't want them to know about. Complete transparency is vital to building complete trust. A great place to create transparency is on your knees every night with your spouse before the Lord, with YOU beginning in prayer, without sending "hidden signals," when you finish saying "amen," it is your wife's turn to pray also with transparency. This transparency will bring itself into your everyday life in time.

Forgiveness and trust are two different things. When you've been wronged, offer forgiveness instantly (which is "Grace"), but you should give your trust slowly (which is "common sense!"). You cannot earn forgiveness. We cannot give trust by nature. Carte blanche cannot grant it. Forgiveness has to come first, and grace can pave the way for trust. It will take time for your wife to forgive you for the betrayal, so be patient and do not push her. Seek to build trust by not what you say but by what you do. You are to be an example; with that example, love is "patient!" If you have to be patient for one and a half years, you are to be so. You are to exemplify Christ to your wife on your journey of change as you surrender your life to the Lord. You are not to demand forgiveness. You are to demonstrate love and seek to have Christ live through you to your wife. Trust is earned, men. When trust is extended, then perhaps your wife can forgive you.

When someone breaks their arm, doctors have to put it in a cast to restrict its motion and allow it to heal. When you've broken trust, you must be willing to temporarily give up certain freedoms and accept certain restrictions to allow time for healing. This is usually the most uncomfortable part of the process, but it's vital. Do you understand you have to give up your demands and seek to allow the boundaries that your wife places upon you to build that trust? Do you love her? If so, prove it! Put your demands away and be a servant of the Lord, seeking to show that you will do whatever it is to build trust. You are the trust broker, to be the trust builder! You cannot do it, but Christ in you can if you surrender to HIM!

I heard a man say to a prisoner in a maximum-security prison, "I'm having a hard time extending forgiveness." You can't, but the Jesus in you can!

The Bible says, "Love covers a multitude of sins." I love that picture of love being strong enough to cover our imperfections and fill in the cracks of our broken hearts. Don't quit when it gets hard! Keep loving and allow God to use the power of love and grace to bring wholeness and healing to your relationship. You seek to focus on the vine and be a "fruit bearer" with Him, producing the fruit. You carry that fruit to your wife! The love that originates from Him can be expressed towards your wife in a way that you, in your flesh, could never love her as you did in the past.

Cheating is one of the most significant tests a relationship can face. It's difficult to build back the trust lost after someone is unfaithful, but some people manage it.

Some special notes concerning building trust:

- Being honest, truthful, and not seeking to make any excuses helps build trust over time. Cheating is one hundred percent a choice. It comes from a place of entitlement. Own it as such.

- Rebuilding trust is about selflessly doing everything possible to help your partner feel safe.

- Even if your partner is guilty of many mistakes of her own in your relationship, don't blame her for your cheating. Instead of cheating, you could have dealt with the issues in other, more honest ways. While discussing your partner's mistakes, avoid the implication that your cheating or lying was because of these mistakes. It wasn't.

- Don't expect sympathy. Your partner may have been unhappy or frustrated with the relationship but instead decided not to lie to you, cheat on you, or betray you.

- Avoid tired, bogus excuses, including "it just happened," temptation, seduction by someone else, confusion, not realizing that it was happening, not meaning to do it, it was only an emotional and not physical relationship, or falling prey to the influence of others. Unless someone coerced you, you made your own choice.

- Avoid being defensive. Defensiveness will inflame the situation and prevent you from dealing with your mistake. This is not a time when "the best defense is a good offense." This is the time to be regretful, empathetic, honest, and emotionally available.

- It is essential that "no details" are to be shared. More often than not, those details get into the spouses' heads and cause havoc. We highly recommend processing "full disclosure" through a professional counselor and setting aside time based on "who, what, when, and where."

  Be patient as your partner rebuilds trust. Suspicion and distrust are natural reactions when a person has been cheated on and lied to — after all, the evidence supports a belief that you aren't trustworthy. Trust can be rebuilt but does not come quickly, even for kind-hearted people.

- Anticipate that your partner will be on a roller coaster of emotions. Mood changes, sleep and appetite disruption, health declines, sudden tears, anger, or withdrawal are natural. They may have a good day today but will have another devastating day tomorrow. Be patient as they go through the process. It is a process that takes time.

- Do not dictate the length of time it should take your partner to be "over it," and don't ask them for a time frame. Instead, do all that you can and check in with them periodically to find out where they are.

- Your relationship with your partner during this time is not necessarily an indicator of how it will be from now on. Your partner's suspicion and distrust can eventually dissipate over time. With God, this can be an absolute so with the power of the Holy Spirit! Be around. Your partner needs the opportunity to work through things with you. At a minimum, you need to be emotionally available. However, physical presence can help further, as it will counteract your partner's feelings that you don't value.

- Be there to listen, even though you caused the pain. Otherwise, your partner will have lost one of the most influential people in their lives to whom they turn for support: you. Listen. LISTEN, NOT FIX!

- Be there to answer questions so your partner does not feel hopeless and to prevent suspicions that often develop when Cheating are absent.

- Be patient. Although it may be difficult to repeatedly answer questions and deal with her suspicions, doing so in the short run will prevent explosions.

- Understand that your partner may become suspicious when you spend time with other people for a while. Again, do not dismiss this sort of distrust as paranoia. Instead, work towards combating it with openness.

- If you can't be with your partner physically, keep your phone on whenever possible so they can access you. They may not even need to call or message you but knowing where you are and that you are available may help them see you in a more positive way. Send text messages of love and that you are thinking of him/her throughout the day.

- Proactively ask your partner if he or she is eating, sleeping, etc., and whether he or she is doing okay. This may seem basic, but if your spouse is in a traumatic state, he or she may not be functioning normally and may be too distraught to convey or even meet personal needs. It is, in part, your responsibility to try to predict and account for these needs.

- Be available at an appropriate distance even if your partner needs some time alone.

- Make your partner feel #1 again. Perhaps your spouse has never felt # 1, and it is a new learning curve for you to make her feel so. When you cheat, you give someone else attention and value you normally would reserve for your partner. As a result, this may make your partner feel that you don't value her, or that she lacks things you sought in the person you cheated with. It can also make your partner believe other people don't realize you value them. It is up to you to counteract these feelings and convince them that you will not betray them again.

- Ask yourself whether you are failing to appreciate your partner. It could be that the things you looked for outside the relationship were actually available all along inside the relationship — and that you just failed to realize that or make it happen.

- Make a list of things that are special about your partner. Seek to appreciate them within your own mind and heart. Tell and show appreciation, too. Compliments can help a bruised ego and wounded heart. Better still, give clear, action-based assurance that your partner is valuable to you. Sprinkle those comments to her over time, letting her know this truth!

- Show them you love them. Your actions may have caused

them to question your love for them. Dedication to this goal is significant immediately following the incident.

- Show and tell other people that your partner is essential to you. This will not only help you show your partner that you value them but also help your partner overcome any feelings of humiliation. It may help you feel better about yourself, too.

- Be ATTENTIVE to her needs. Watch her from a distance. "Honey, can I do this for you?" and "Will it help you if I do this for you?"

THE HALF SECOND RULE

The Half Second Rule (1/2 Second Rule) is simple and, when applied, can save the sex addict from collecting more data about someone else than he should. If you look at someone inappropriately and then "turn away," DO NOT LOOK BACK; you capture that moment in your mind. Practice the "blink" for half a second and focus elsewhere. This works in any environment, but it is a choice and discipline you incorporate into your life. In a way, it is to have a FIRE ESCAPE, having planned what you will do in certain situations with your eyeballs!

The "no turning back" is the hardest part. If you stick with this, it is easier for fantasies to subside, and it reduces the cruising around "for a better look" and/or connecting to that person. You know exactly what I am talking about! In a way, this is "rubbernecking" in reverse. Instead of stretching to see what or who you are looking at, **YOU JUST BLINK, WHICH IS A 1/2 OF A SECOND! And your eyeballs at moving away from the temptation to another look elsewhere**. You control your eyeballs. If you do a three-second look, that is forever. In those three seconds, that image locks into your mind! So stop it! This is a much safer journey of transformation as you seek to get "in control" of your person! With this PRACTICE, you are literally building new neuropathways in your brain. You're setting your mind on something else. Bring Scripture into your mind as you do this! Think of things above and not on this earth!

Remember this **GOLDEN RULE OF THUMB** as you transform, and you will begin the journey of staying clean for the rest of your life!

"WHATEVER YOUR ADDICT TELLS YOU TO DO, YOU DO THE OPPOSITE!"

You must choose to do the opposite immediately!

Let me share an example from a man who was at a noted grocery store with his wife. Activity concerning shopping can be exciting for an addict even if you buy nothing. This man noticed a woman, a second glance caught her eyes, and HE KNEW THAT HE HAD TO LEAVE THE STORE; RIGHT THEN, HE CHANGED DIRECTION. HE "RUBBERNECKED IN REVERSE" AND DID, IN EFFECT, WHAT SCRIPTURES SAY: "RUN FROM TEMPATION." Now, with this, he honored God, he honored himself, he celebrated his wife, and he honored the other woman!

If you are driving and you see a woman on the sidewalk, your addict (the voice in your head) says to speed up to get a better look and then slow down. DO THE OPPOSITE AND STAY CLEAN!

Do you have a battle plan for all situations regarding your issue? One thing General Patton always did (and I have said this in this book, but it bears repeating) was to have not only a battle plan but be a student of his enemies! And that is why he defeated Rommel in the desert of Africa and caused 1,500,000 casualties in Europe afterward. Patton was a student of war; Rommel was not! Oh, do we have a leader like that today in our world? And it is sad; we do not. Do not be like Rommel, be like Patton! Patton laid strategic plans, whereas Rommel was impulsive and made decisions in seconds. Being caught up in the attempt to overthrow Hitler, he ended his life that way. He was given a choice between a treason trial and suicide, with no repercussions to his family, and a state funeral.

Please read up on General George S. Patton and see where he was right; politicians and generals were wrong almost one hundred percent of the time. He was a man of study and a student of his enemies. He was out to destroy his enemies. ARE YOU?

I pray that you are a student of your issues and that you have plans in place for all the triggers that can cause you to stumble! I hope that you have gained a deep understanding of what it takes to be on the journey of transformation so that you can walk into victory, as General George S. Patton did!

Also, remember here, as I have in other places in this book: No one can babysit you! MAKE NEW CHOICES AND FIGHT FOR THEM YOURSELF!

FORGIVENESS AND GRIEVING ASSIGNMENT

READ THE FOLLOWING FORGIVENESS SCRIPTURES:

- John 20:23
- Matthew 18:16–35
- Matthew 6:14–15

BLESSING SCRIPTURES:

- Romans 12:14–21
- 1 Peter 3:8–9

HEART SCRIPTURES:

- 1 Corinthians 4:4–5
- Psalm 139:23–24
- Romans 1:18
- Hebrews 3:13
- Matthew 15:8

- Proverbs 27:19

- Romans 8:5–8

- Psalm 51:6

- Daniel 2:22

- Psalm 7:9

- Jeremiah 17:5, 9:10

Find a very private and secluded place to go through this assignment, as your mind needs to be focused and your heart ready to engage in the process. Have prayer and invite the Lord to plow your heart and mind. Invite Him to be with you as you go through this process. Just have a quiet time of prayer and fellowship before you begin. Your Heart must be totally engaged in this.

It cannot be looked upon as "an assignment" or something just "to do." I suggest you dedicate at least two or three days to this at a place out of town, such as a cabin somewhere. Forgiveness and grieving are two of the major keys to healing the inner soul. Your life cannot move forward in a healthy way until you walk through this.

Get in touch (embrace, remember, feel, visualize) with your hurts, pains, rejections, abandonment, etc.

Step 1:

1. Write down your most recent hurt and who did it to you, no matter how big or small.

2. Write down how you reacted to that hurt, externally (outward behavior) and internally.

3. SPEAK OUT: Repent of your reactions (be specific) and receive GOD'S forgiveness.

4. SPEAK OUT: Forgive the person and/or person that offended you, and Bless them in the name of Jesus Christ

of Nazareth. You may also have to Forgive yourself.

5. Be quiet before the Lord.

Step 2:

Repeat STEP 1, asking the Lord to reveal to you what is next (Psalm 139:23–24) and keep doing this back to the time you drop out of your mother's womb. Take your time to cover each and every hurt, and work your way, day-by-day, week-by-week, month-by-month, and year-by-year. Embrace the moment and visualize yourself there. Grieve those times in which the emotional and/or physical trauma was really deep. Stay in the moment. You may have to be here for a while.

You also need to forgive and grieve what you did not get from your family of origin that you should have received in a well-adjusted and mature home.

FORGIVENESS is putting everything in the "filing drawer," locking it and never opening it again. When you can be in the presence of one who has hurt you, and that hurt and pain don't come up, then you know that true forgiveness has taken place.

When the time is right, take all that paper, page after page of a major work having been done, and roll it up, tie a string around it, and go to a party store to get the appropriate number of balloons. Then go to an open field, tie the paper to the balloons, and "let it go." Watch it disappear into the sky. It is a symbolic picture but a real one of "letting go."

FIRE DRILLS — RELAPSE PREVENTION

Identifying your relapse triggers and determining ways to avoid them is essential. In our society, certain things prepare us for the possibility (no matter how remote) of various problematic and dangerous situations that may arise. For example, fire drills prepare us to be ready in case a fire breaks out in public buildings or schools. Anyone on a cruise ship is familiar with lifeboat drills that teach the passengers what to do if the hip encounters trouble at sea. Indeed, no one believes that requiring people to participate in fire drills increases the probability of future fires. The aim is to minimize the extent of personal loss and damage should a fire happen. The same logic applies in the case of relapse prevention.

Include a "relapse drill" as part of your prevention strategy. Remember, this is about "practicing ahead of time!" learning precise prevention skills and related techniques is more helpful than relying on vague suggestions to "follow your program!" Think of situations that you know could trigger a relapse for you. Begin with scenarios that would be less likely to do so, then move on to ones that would place you at a higher risk until you finally list the situations that would be the most dangerous for you. For each of these situations, think of ways to react that would enable you to escape the "fire" without being burned! As the intensity and risk of relapse increase with each situation, you will need to better plan your escape plan. List at least six to ten relapse-threatening situations. Finally, choose three — one that is a pretty low risk, one that presents a more moderate risk, and a high-risk situation — and write your escape plan for each on an index card. Keep those three cards with you at all times, or install them on an app, possibly your cell phone. You may also find that referring to them occasionally will help remind you of your goals in being set free.

To make it secure, I suggest that you get each laminated and make it the size of a business car. You can place it in your billfold and/or on your persona at all times. Plus, your cell phone may have wonderful ways to double-duty this reminder.

ESCAPE

ESCAPE IS A SUBJECT that many talk about in Battle Lines yesterday and in counseling at the counseling center when I was there, and those practical plans that one must have "in place" ahead of time regarding not acting out to your addiction!

We discussed the above fire drills, and in Junior High and High School as a child, we had fire drills where we literally slid down the fire escape slides to practice those fire drills. We knew how to get out of the building in case of a fire, as we practiced it unannounced at different times throughout the years.

When traveling to a state like Colorado, you take Interstate 70 West of Denver and climb the mountains. Eventually, you reach Eisenhower Pass. It's a major east-west corridor for trucking and provides emergency escapes for 18-wheelers with failed brakes and other issues.

On the downward side of each mountain, the 18-wheelers have to down-shift and watch that they do not overheat their brakes. Because of years of history on the roads, the number of 18-wheeler crashes, and the loss of lives, the highway engineers devised an ESCAPE PLAN when brakes go out.

As you can see from the photo above, traveling down the interstate, if brakes go out, the truck and/or car can go "right" and the major inclines prepared to bring them to a stop; if their brakes go out and bring their vehicle to a major slow down. Truckers are keenly aware of this and have it in the back of their mind in case of brake emergency failures. This same idea is for ESCAPE PLANS, and I repeat, repeat, repeat throughout the book, the things you must know to walk into freedom, eventually!

Men, you are not smarter than your addiction, nor can you travel down a significant highway decline that goes of miles safely if your 18-wheeler brakes go out.

Similarly, a person who parachutes will have a backup parachute, as a pilot in a jet has an injection seat with a parachute. The trucker going downhill must have a safety plan to escape if his brakes go out. YOU MUST HAVE AN ESCAPE PLAN, MEN, ahead of time, set in place, and PRACTICED if you are serious about breaking free from your sexual compulsivity and/or any other addiction.

As one brother in Battle Lines shared, he had an escape plan. When his computer triggered him out of nowhere, he got up. He ran outside and sat in his front yard until the chemicals settled in his brain, and he was completely relaxed. He had practiced this beforehand, and what he did was almost automatic!

What are some things you can do in planning of time to escape:

1. Instant dialing of multiple men on your accountability list

2. We position ammonia capsules at a strategic spot and ensure they are readily accessible to snap under your nose, effectively breaking you out of the sexually addicting trance.

3. Pictures of your wife and family, in your billfold, on your cell phone, etc., and seeing the cost of your addiction if you keep acting out and losing them. And do not think for a moment that you will not lose them; you very well can!

4. Pictures of your job-boss-company and the possibility of losing your job if caught. Have them accessible on the cell phone or billfold to look at, to be reminded what you can lose. Do not think you won't for a moment because I have seen it often in Battle Lines and counseling!

5. The possibility of jail, prison, being on TV, etc. if you are caught up in the illegal activity of sexually acting out.

6. Have this all written and immediately available to you. What can it cost you if you continue to act out? Be very detailed and specific and in touch with reality. Even your parents, your siblings, etc. will be shocked if they are found out.

Now let us go to God's Word:

Proverbs 12:1

Whoever loves discipline loves knowledge, but he who hates reproof is stupid.

Romans 1:22

Claiming to be wise, they became fools

Jeremiah 4:22

For my people are foolish; they know me not; they are stupid children; they have no understanding. They are 'wise' — in doing evil! But how to do good they know not.

Proverbs 28:26

Whoever trusts in his own mind is a fool, but he who walks in wisdom will be delivered.

Folly is a joy to him who lacks sense, but a man of understanding walks straight ahead.

Men, you get the message. I pray, don't be STUPID!

FOUNDATIONS FOR LIFE — HOW TO DEVELOP EFFECTIVE ACCOUNTABILITY

Be Radical in Your Approach and Not Passive

Life is replete with Irony. One of the biggest ironies connected to personal health and safety is that the best time to develop personal accountability is when we don't need it. Unfortunately, when the need for accountability strikes, most people don't have any significant relationships on which to lean. We haven't invested consistency in deep friendships, and our isolation often increases in times of trouble.

The Christian men's movement has raised awareness of the need for accountability because it remains challenging to develop — especially for men. Various accountability programs are available, but nothing takes the place of intimacy between two or more transparent people who really care about each other. We had that in Battle Lines and our small groups, in which men hungered for every Tuesday from May 2004 to June 30, 2019. Most organizations inside and outside the church have no clue as to how this comes about, but it does. You cannot place a time restraint on it, to begin at a specific time and to end at a particular time, which does not ALLOW FOR:

- Transparency
- Vulnerability
- Trust

Our most basic need in life is a relationship with God and with others. Within the relationships, we can safely discover our blind spots and receive new input and teaching. Sadly, it's our nature to hide ourselves if we sense disapproval from others. It always takes time to build on trust and leadership in an enormous group, which was me and my volunteers with a small group. That time opens quickly when there is no judgment, no criticism, no placing of guilt or shame on a man based upon his addictive behavior. I allowed love and acceptance to be open to all, and men were attracted to that.

Some would say that their Tuesday evenings were "their church." These men came from all walks of life and from every corner of Houston, with no cost to go and no membership or attendance in our church, Second Baptist. It was open to all economic backgrounds, colors, and creeds.

Another factor is that Christians seek moral perfection. We focus more on our performance and base our standards on good behavior. Messing up is one thing, but admitting our imperfections is quite another. Many of us have seen what happens when a person within the Christian ranks stumbles. We shoot the wounded rather than grapple with the ongoing reality of sin in the camp and bring strong love and consequences into the picture. I call it all "performance-based Based Acceptance!" Men perform well "at church" but go beyond the parking lot, which is another story. How fake can you get? That is not how it was with Battle Lines; stories of transparency and vulnerability came about when there was no criticism, shame, or guilt. Men responded to the love and sought the higher ground or moral character via the Word, and what was being taught and shared in group and leadership displayed that truth of Christ; if only the pulpit could see how much they stink at times and how they push men away from the church instead of drawing men in!

QUALITIES WE NEED

This might not describe you currently, but the person who desires to be accountable to another Christian desires spiritual growth (this is a must and a key to success in change). This person recognizes his need. More than mere behavioral change, he hopes to experience an inner healing that is fostered relationally with another Christ-follower. We experienced that in Battle Lines. I had that every Thursday night in Battle Lines, where I alternated patios with a younger brother who was seventeen years my junior. We challenged one another through books we processed with open hearts and God's Word as our foundation. I was challenged to be a better man, and I prayed that this went on with Battle

Lines for most men all those years. You cannot please all men, but the Lord changed many lives, not me. And it came with transparency, vulnerability, and love! The readers may skip the rest of this because they "know" the one thing they do not need is more religion! I ask you to continue reading. The difference between Christian accountability relationships and those based on secular ideas is that Christians seek to transform and redeem the entire individual, not simply the harmful behavior.

Would you instead find a way to just stop DRINKING, SMOKING, MASTURBATING, WHORING, DRUGS, OR LOOKING AT PORNOGRAPHY, OR WOULD YOU PREFER YOUR INNER BEING HEALED OF ALL THE PAIN, ISOLATION, AND ANGER that often lies behind such behaviors? If you desire the latter, consider seeking our mature (**very important**) Christians to walk with you on the road to healing, not recovery. Recovery is always in recovery; never want that, and desire to heal, be transformed, and be set free! Stay away from recovery! That is like a continual journey to MD Anderson Hospital with the plan of never being healed! Get the picture!

In Christian **accountability** relationships, all parties appreciate and attempt to adhere to God's Word, contributing a teachable spirit and a willingness to change. I must add here that there is no such thing as perfection, and to demand that is not being Christ-like in acceptance. That is called judgment. Flee from any group or individual seeking to place judgment upon you! There must also be a discerning spirit; even a well-intentioned accountability partner can mislead you. Therefore, we measure all things against the Bible and the teaching of the HOLY SPIRIT.

Above all, we recognize that our first accountability is to God. In sharing our needs with another person, we hope that he will be an encourager who points us beyond judgment to the grace of God through Christ.

QUALITIES NEEDED IN AN ACCOUNTABILITY PARTNER

Truth be told, accountability partners are difficult to find! We need someone of the same gender who sees himself as our peer unless we are intentionally seeking a mentor. This person should be sensitive, kind, humble, and wise. His willingness to confess his shortcomings will measure your ability to trust him and your safety with him.

CONFIDENTIALITY IS CRUCIAL! We need to share with people who know how to keep our confidence and when to confront us about our unhealthy secrecy.

TWO DIMENSIONS OF ACCOUNTABILITY

Christian accountability has two dimensions: Internal and External. The Internal dimension with God is PRIMARY! Here, we invited HIM to examine our behaviors and our motives. We recognize that HE knows us better than we know ourselves. Like King David in the Old Testament, we surrender our deepest needs, hopes, and dreams to God; in that surrender, we find food for our souls.

The external dimension of accountability occurs in the community with other Christians. Having examined ourselves before God, we offer a few safe individuals what we have learned about ourselves, and they do the same. Here, we describe our experiences and invite their feedback. This process allows personal accountability and a time of encouragement for all!

Like everything in the Christian life, our accountability experience matures over time. Going to God first can be challenging. Our impatience may want a more immediate or audible answer that God will not provide. Waiting on God, however, grows our faith in HIM. Note the Word F A I T H! Then, having experienced intimacy with a healing examination before HIM, we are prepared to go to a few Christians and seek the external accountability that will encourage us to stay the course.

PRACTICAL CONSIDERATIONS

The selection of our accountability partners is CRITICAL! The Bible teaches that "bad company corrupts good character." Consistent with the ICEBERG, we need true friends who will encourage us to remain:

- BEHAVIORALLY FOCUSED — They don't tempt us with immoral activities.

- COGNITIVELY CLEAN — They don't pollute our minds with ungodly thoughts.

- EMOTIONALLY RELEVANT — They encourage us to be open and truthful.

- SPIRITUALLY RENEWED — They consistently invest themselves in our personal relationship with God.

STRENGTH IN NUMBERS

If the accountability process becomes too cumbersome or time-consuming, it will die a natural death. With this in mind, I encourage people to invite *three others to participate in the accountability relationships. If you cannot identify three mature people, start with one or two. Sadly, as shared previously, we in the church fall way short in doing this, as so many men are untrained, unwilling, caught up in their own self-interest, sports, and/or a variety of other things that keep them from truly serving our Lord in helping brothers.*

Sadly, few individuals possess the skills to be accountable partners. How can men disciple others when the church is not focused on discipleship? They cannot. Did I step on a few church toes here? If so, I am glad I did because you, the church, have failed to work with men in need in your community. You have not prepared men for battle; they eat milk toast and can barely help themselves, much less help others. My brothers are in need, and slim pickings are for you. On behalf of the Lord, I apologize to you for our churches failing YOU.

If you had three strong accountability men, I would have said, good-naturedly, "I can lie to one. I can confuse two. But with a third man, the three of them will catch up with me!" There is safety in many counselors, as the Bible speaks of. Oh Lord, only if men were available to help others! We need them!

THE GAME PLAN

The three-person accountability team has a built-in advantage. During the first three weeks of each month, you can meet with each person individually. All three can meet as a team in the fourth week of the month. You can openly share insights and concerns gained throughout the month and thanksgiving for how God is working in your and the team's lives.

We need to keep these meetings simple and choose a location where people can share their private thoughts. Meeting over breakfast or lunch may not be the best option, as food for the stomach competes with food for the soul!

TROUBLESHOOTING

Ongoing accountability is essential, but it can ensure if something goes wrong. Therefore, we need to know how to troubleshoot these unique relationships.

No relationship can bear the strain of a judgmental attitude. An accountability partner is not spiritually superior. If he is into religious legalism, this, too, can destroy trust and a willingness to be known.

Christian men can easily slip into the dynamic of a spiritual father-son relationship. We need to remember, however, that a new ACCOUNTABILITY relationship is fragile. Therefore, we want to be cautious about adding the parent-child dimension to an accountability relationship — especially were carrying unresolved wounds from family relationships. It is sufficient to celebrate we are BROTHERS AND SISTERS IN FAITH! My men in Battle Lines became "brothers." My men in counseling moved from counselees to "brothers." Connectivity moves to the heart when we see each other as brothers, for those who are like-minded in our Christian FAITH.

CLOSING THOUGHTS ON FAITH

Christian accountability is a gift we give ourselves and a sacrifice of time and priority offered to God. It is a means of discipleship in which we humble ourselves before God and others. Our transparency and respect for those who serve us build the community for which we hunger.

Realistically, we are accountable before God and others, whether we are faithful Christian practitioners or not. Consistent accountability is necessary because we need input and teaching to overcome our blind spots that hinder spiritual development and relationships.

Accountability requires a support network of a FEW SAFE INDIVIDUALS. We must prepare ourselves; however, these folks come and go. God has assigned us to each other for a season, but HE remains at our side throughout every season of life. My volunteers in Battle Lines came and went. It was okay for them to go on in life. It was sometimes challenging to find that new leader, but God eventually found someone to replace those who moved on. We comprehend that the individual moving on is not about REJECTION thus, you are not to receive it that way.

An example of accountability from Battle Lines in the past was...

One man in Battle Lines said he had three accountability partners but added a fourth, and that fourth comes from the group itself. Why? His comprehensive understanding of the issues and problems prevented him from being deceived and gave him the courage to ask questions others might shy away from or feel embarrassed to ask. So, with that said, on your journey of being RADICAL, IN THE APPROACH TO WALKING INTO FREEDOM, do also in being RACIAL IN

THE ACCOUNTABILITY side of this journey of being TRANSFORMED FROM YOUR ADDICTION!

NO MASTURBATION!

PERIOD!

STOP IT!

For the NEW MEN, and a remember to men of the past in groups, such as Battle Lines or in counseling: if married, no sex for **ninety days** since the last time you acted out. This is to settle the chemicals in your brain and establish new neuropathways. You guessed it, if you masturbate and/or fail during this ninety-day period sexually, you begin all over again. This is RADICAL but effective. Decide how seriously you are in changing your new pathway of life. One pathway brings freedom and healing; the other path brings failure. One can say, "Benno, you are too tough!" I would say, "Benno, you are not tough enough for those seeking freedom." Men, you are in a life-or-death struggle, and being complacent will bring failure! I love you too much to allow you to fail! If married, and your wife wants sex during these ninety days, the answer is NO!

You must be willing to chemically settle your brain down for ninety days!

Men, you cannot hold hands with God while masturbating! Think about about that!

You are on the journey of establishing new neuro pathways and let nothing keep you from doing that! Your DISCIPLINE will bring you victory, and the lack of DISCIPLINE will defeat you! It's your choice!

But more importantly, according to HIS WORD, it does not honor God. It is as simple as God says: As you think, so you do it! And God calls that "sin!" Acting out sexually is a S I N, in the same manner as anger and outbursts of anger. It separates us from God, and if you read the Old and New Testament, it speaks of a place WHERE you continue to do so, that... there is a possibility that God lets you go into your sin and into death itself. The choice is yours. That choice that God allows you to walk into is hell when you keep on doing your addiction your way! You may say, Benno, you are too hard on me! Not hard enough! Keep on in our addiction and see where it takes you. Put the penis in your hand and masturbate to your mindful images and see where it takes you! The Word says you will know them by their "fruits!" Without fruits, there is no Christ. Now, do you know you have "fruits?" No, Scripture says, "YOU (others) will know YOU by YOUR FRUITS!" If you can talk about your fruits, you don't have them. Others will see them in you first. Years of seeking HIM develop fruits, not in a week's time or sometimes not even a year. Get your eyes off yourself and put your eyes upon GOD and HIS SON, Jesus CHRIST! Get the PENIS out of your hand! That's enough!

Men, remember every time you masturbate or sexually act out, you are reinforcing your neuropathways and the chemicals in your brain, which demand their needs to be met. So do not leet anyone tell you that you can masturbate. No, you cannot. Your life depends upon your choices. Excellent choices bring victory; bad decisions bring defeat!

BOUNDARIES

Entertainment

Television and the computer can present some tough dilemmas for a sex addict. The current pop culture is HIGHLY SEXUAL. The increase of sexually explicit scenes, jokes, sexual innuendos, and the show of naked bodies and extramarital activities on television, movies, and the intranet can trigger a sex addict into a myriad of sexual thoughts and behaviors. This does not include the issue of commercials that are often erotic and objectifying. Television and movies are not safe places for anyone struggling with sexual addiction, especially in the early part of healing. Here are some BOUNDARIES that you or your spouse may not like, but these are a must:

1. No television or movies for ninety days since the last time you acted out

2. Later — after ninety days, pre-selected shows only, and this is done by your spouse if married

3. No channel surfing — the computer and the television are in an OFF mode!

4. No television dish or pay channels

5. No watching TV alone after ninety days since the last time you acted out

6. No television in the bedroom, period!

7. No television in the bathroom, period!

8. Only watch television with your partner, only after ninety days, or with your family

9. No television after ninety days at a certain time, agreed upon by your spouse, if married

10. No television, period, in the middle of the night

11. No cable television of any can within the first ninety days of recovery and this includes all sports channels

In other words, no television, no movies, no surfing your computer for ninety days since the last time you acted out. You may say, I cannot do so, or my family wants to watch; the answer is NO, NO, NO, and no excuse to violate this boundary.

In addition, you agree that for the first year, you will not see any movie within the first six months without obtaining your spouse's or accountability partner's approval.

Suppose you want to walk into healing, freedom, transformation and being set free. In that case, your DISCIPLINES or the lack thereof will determine your fate regarding success or failure.

You can exercise, read, pray, work on your issues, go to church, go to Bible Study, develop strong accountability

partners, and have breakfasts and lunches with men, all who encourage you. You have an opportunity here for a new way of life, but you must choose what you will let go of and what you get HOLD OF!

LOOKING THEM IN THE EYE

There is only one place to look at a woman, and that is her eyes! Men and sex addicts over the years condition themselves to the female figure often portrayed in pornographic sites, advertisements, movies, magazines, etc. Where can we find this "object" that conditions men to look at body proportions first?

Looking at a woman in an objectifying manner is a conditional response. Looking at the person directly in the eyes can keep you from thoroughly scanning them like an object you might purchase.

Every time you have your wife with you in a mall, a restaurant, etc., what do you think she is thinking when your eyeballs seek out? Please stop it. Don't search anymore; Once more, it's up to you to decide. One brings healthy habits, and the other reinforces your old ways and entrenches them to where it is most difficult, if not impossible, for change to take place, all because you could not grow up as a man and take proper responsibility for your actions, and in this case, it is your eyeballs.

The more you look them in the eyes, the more you keep from fantasizing. Looking your partner directly in the eyes during a sexual experience will also help you stay more in a relational pattern, and you will experience your partner as a person, which she truly desires. This keeps them from objectifying them, and believe you mean, your wife does not want to be an "object!"

Remember, EYES FIRST!

GOING TO MEETINGS

In going to a meeting, in AA, there is an old express that says, "There are three times when you should go to a meeting."

1. When you do not feel like going to a meeting,

2. When you do not feel like going to a meeting,

3. At eight o'clock

It is not how you feel about it; it is how you behave about it. Twelve-step meetings have a "ninety meetings in ninety days" rule. This rule is ideal for sexual compulsivity / sexual addiction individuals.

The meeting supports you and gives back to others what you have learned through your journey in your transformation. Being around other men who are on the journey of change and transformation as sex addicts is helpful. First, it is going to give you hope as you see other sex addicts have some sobriety. Second, you may believe that if they can do it, SO CAN YOU TOO. You can learn things from them they have learned through negative or positive experiences.

At this point, I would like to suggest that you hold as many meetings as possible for groups such as Battle Lines and any other groups that are out there in the community in which you live. Battle Lines was an active group working on the issues both from the addiction side and the spiritual side. One thing you must do is that the group you go to must be educational, and you are not to go to a group that is just "checking in" to see if you have done well or not in acting again. This type of group does not benefit you at all, so don't waste your time doing so. The group you go to must be one that you leave with something in your pocket, like a nugget, so to speak that has positive benefits every time you attend.

You can have maximized benefit in your thinking by going to individual counseling, doing your homework, going to groups, going to marriage counseling (if married), going to intensives, cutting out negative old friends and familiar, old places attendance must be cut out, and anything that causes you to stumble. You do this as long as it takes for your journey of healing, transformation, and being set free. You can maximize the thinking and/or do the minimum with the thinking process of "How little can I do? Can I possibly attend one meeting a week and still satisfy my wife or my conscience?" You are the one; I must remember you will suffer in the long run. If you decide "on your own" to heal, HIT IT HARD ON THE FRONT END FOR AN EXTENDED PERIOD.

This is the best way to do it. See what you can remove from your daily life that is not necessary. Three months out of a lifetime is a short period. Three months is not long enough for SA, AA, or any other group. That philosophy is harmful to you, and for sexual addiction, it will take several years. You can choose to experience true healing on your journey or opt for a temporary solution that will inevitably manifest itself again, most likely through your acting out sexually. You have to either totally commit and focus on whatever it takes and for as long as it takes or decide, "I love my addiction more than healing!" Your group is a key to your healing, that educational group, that accountability group, that support group that confronts you, all wrapped up in one great package.

I might add that you can "go to group," or YOU CAN GO TO GROUP! One is just attending, and the other is genuinely taking part. Do not waste your time attending; if you do not take part, you waste your time and the time of others who attend and take part. Commit totally and focus on doing whatever it takes. Did I say this before? Yes, repeat, repeat, repeat, like a drippy faucet, so that you to get the picture. Remember, it takes three to five years to walk into freedom. It takes 175 hours of group and 65 hours of counseling. Why? Because you've been in your addiction ten, fifteen, or twenty-five, so change does not happen without a significant commitment on your part to do whatever it takes for your brain to be rewired, your heart healed and transformed.

Are you a minimized thinker and/or a MAXIMIZED THINKER? Will you get serious about a group or minimize going to a group? Suppose you want to take your recovery seriously as a sex addict. In that case, prioritize attending a group for education and accountability, where transparency and vulnerability must occur for maximized benefit. Going to a group is just one thing you must do, not a single thing, as it won't benefit you if you do not do all the other necessary things that you must engage in. As God says in HIS WORD, do not be stupid!

TRIGGERS AND TRIGGER GROUPS

Men, you must identify your triggers in your sexual acting out. Triggers are where you go to immediately objectify and fantasize about, whether in reality or our fantasy world, that triggers you to act out. No matter your triggers, you must identify them in advance to be alerted that this is dangerous to you and your acting out. When you can identify your triggers, and later when you are triggered, you can have escape plans to break from that trigger and not act out. There is something powerful that takes place when you think, when you write it down, and when you see that writing has taken place. It is resonating within you, in the written Word. Please don't go to your computer to do this by hand; take your time doing so.

In other words, triggers are people, objects, feelings, and times that cause cravings. For example, if every Friday night you cash a paycheck, go out with friends, and use drugs, the triggers would be the following:

- Friday night
- After work
- Money
- Friends who use
- The bar or club

Your addicted brain associates the triggers with drug and alcohol use. As a result of constant triggering and using, **one trigger** can cause you to move toward drug or alcohol use.

The trigger thought craving use cycle feels overwhelming.

An important part of treatment involves stopping the craving process. The first and easiest way to do that is this:

1. IDENTIFY TRIGGERS

2. PREVENT EXPOSURE TO TRIGGERS WHENEVER POSSIBLE (for example, do not handle large amounts of cash).

3. DEAL WITH TRIGGERS IN A DIFFERENT WAY (for example, schedule exercise and an outside meeting for Friday nights).

Remember, triggers will affect your brain and cause cravings even though you have decided to stop using drugs and alcohol. Your intentions to stop must therefore translate into behavior changes, which steer you clear of possible triggers.

In the section below, write down what triggers you, being specific and focused on details.

1. What are some of the strongest triggers for you?

2. What particular triggers might be a problem in the near future?

IDENTIFYING TRIGGERS

1. Place a checkmark next to activities or situations in which you **frequently** used drugs or alcohol. Place a zero next to activities or situations in which you **never** have used drugs or alcohol.

_____ When home alone   _____ After work

_____ When home with friends   _____ When carrying money

_____ At a friend's home   _____ After going past
                                            dealer's residence

_____ At parties   _____ When with drug-using
                                            friends

_____ At sporting events   _____ After going past a
                                            liquor store

_____ At movies	_____ After payday
_____ At bars/clubs	_____ Before going out to dinner
_____ At the beach	_____ Before breakfast
_____ At concerts	_____ At lunch break
_____ At the park	_____ While at dinner
_____ When I gain weight	_____ After passing a particular freeway exit
_____ Before a date	_____ At school
_____ During a date	_____ While driving
_____ Before sexual activities	_____ In the neighborhood
_____ After sexual activities	_____ Before work

2. List any other settings or activities in which you frequently used drugs or alcohol. What were your patterns or triggers?

REROUTING

Defensive Driving

Many sex addicts have particular driving routes that feed their sexual addiction. These routes may include driving by a specific convenience store, a city park, a bookstore, an adult dance club, a massage parlor, an exercise gym, or simply your local coffeehouse. Many of these places become a regular part of their driving route. Before or after work or maybe on lunch break, the person with an addiction will go to one of several places to "get a look," but something that reinforces his addiction once again.

Conditioning yourself to these places is powerful. Driving by any of the above areas often triggers you into thoughts of acting out or even rationalizations such as "I've had a bad day, I deserve this!" Many sex addicts feel the rush their body receives just by driving by a place such as the above in your patterns of the past. Some people with addiction even have to REROUTE the way they drive to work and come back home because of billboards that objectify women.

To reroute your driving, carefully consider how you are around your geographical area. If you have a relapse because of your driving route, it is definitely an indication that rerouting has to happen. For personal healing, you can make rerouting a part of your accountability, such as not driving by the school, pool, college campus, or other relapse situations. Rerouting can help stop some rituals of our driving by the old familiars where you have acted out so many times.

Rerouting can also apply to those who work in offices where a particular female sex addict or victim is working, and people may have objectified her in the past. Find ways to reroute in the office, past their desk or office work area. Suppose it is a waitress in a restaurant. In that case, you can find another place to eat and no longer go to that restaurant. THE QUICKER YOU CAN REROUTE YOUR LIFE, THE BETTER FOR YOUR HEALING TO TAKE PLACE SOONER THAN LATER!

- The places I need to avoid:

- The men I will discuss this with and be accountable to are:

AVOID

Halt

On your journey to be set free, the acronym HALT has been used to stand for Halt, Angry, Lonely, and Tired. These are essential feelings to AVOID for the recovering sex addict. But keep eating regularly and correctly, and do not allow yourself to get too hungry, which may make you more susceptible to less logical thinking. Some researchers believe that eating a particular food can help you on your transformation journey.

Anger can sneak upon any of us in a New York minute and put us emotionally in incorrect thinking. For the addict, the thought may be, *I'll show her!* — and you can rationalize why it might be okay to act. Some sex addicts have a complete system arranged where they purposely start a fight with their mate, leave, act out, and come back later, justifying the acting out because they are ANGRY. Anger can be a vital part of managing our journey to freedom.

Lonely is a complex feeling for a sex addict to handle. Feeling alone can make the sex addict vulnerable to wanting to medicate by acting out. Having an action play or an "I will do" list available in our wallet, or in this modern age, your cell phone for when you get lonely, may be helpful. Some suggestions for lonely feelings are:

1. Go to a public place such as a mall, park, or restaurant.

2. Call someone in the group you attend and/or groups.

3. Plan AHEAD to avoid your alone time gaps, such as weekends or when your partner may be out of town.

4. Exercise (a great place to work on your body and to build in your brain chemical releases). If your knees can handle it, run to the park, build up your program, and watch what happens! You will build excellent self-esteem through your accomplishments. Still, your body will respond beautifully to your attention and watch how you feel about yourself.

5. Get your eyes off yourself and help someone else with a project and/or serve others in your community!

6. Go to a meeting (other groups), church, Bible Study, and/or other social gatherings. Even city events that have food, games, and booths to buy t things can be an excellent avenue of enjoyment. Your choice! Farmer's Markets are always fun to go to.

7. Pray.

8. Go fishing / go to the rifle range and practice shooting.

9. Ask others for suggestions to what to do!

Being tired in your busy, fast-paced life is a familiar feeling.

Tiredness can lower your resistance to the point of feeling, "Who cares?" To heal, to walk in freedom, and to be transformed, we need to stay **alert!** Your sex addiction desires to be fully activated whenever it finds an opportunity. To prevent tiredness, get regular sleep, and if you need to rest here or there, take it as you can and do not feel guilty for doing so.

LIST YOUR ACTION PLAN FOR THE FOLLOWING FEELINGS:

- **H**ungry

- **A**ngry

- **L**onely

- **T**ired

Prayer of Surrendering Your "Organ (Penis)" to the Lord

Lord, I invite you into my situation. You are my only hope. Come and do what only You can do. Set me free from watching pornography and masturbation.

Every feeling of loneliness and lack of fulfillment making me masturbate and/or act out in sexual addiction, let it break now, in the name of Jesus Christ.

Lord, I surrender my penis to you; I ask you to support me in not masturbating and/or being sexually impure in acting out against YOUR Word and to keep it only for Holy living, and that is only in marriage with the gift you gave me, will express love to my partner.

Every spirit is monitoring me and influencing me to masturbate or act out in sexual impurity; be broken in the name of Jesus Christ. The evil spirit fighting against my salvation now break in the name of Jesus Christ. I'm redeemed and set free.

I am the apple of God's eye, and God's jealousy is on me.
God, who does not sleep nor slumber, is watching over me.
I am an obedient child of God, in the name of Jesus Christ.

Amen

Matthew 5:28 — "But I say to you that whoever looks at a woman to lust for her has already committed adultery with her in his heart."

Men, are you getting tired as you process this chapter over time? Also, process it with your accountability partners and perhaps the group you attend. Processing it with your counselor would be excellent!

Oh, by the way, we have just begun! For your betterment as you continue to process this homework, contact the inside of your person and bring all of you into the light. There is no more darkness. The transformational hard work with many of these assignments and the use of tools to help in your healing make all the difference. The decision to participate or not is up to you.

WHAT MY ADDICTION GAVE ME

You have had a relationship with your addiction for a very long time, and your addiction became a "friend" to you because it met a need. Just reflect and count how long you have had this relationship. Regularly, you ran to your addiction to celebrate, to be encouraged, to feel wanted, to feel powerful, to think in control (although you, in fact, were out of control), to feel sexual and confident. In real terms, this has been your most committed relationship.

Your addiction has given many things to you, including but not limited to 1. A false world; 2. It keeps your secret; 3. False intimacy; 4. False identity; 5. Sense of success; 6. Being validated; 7. Acceptance; 8. And the list goes on.

Attempt to list as many of the things you can that you have RECEIVED by your sexual compulsivity. Once again, take your time. This is not about shame or guilt to be placed upon you, but to identify the lies you believed of your being the addict was receiving. With pen and paper, write and connect to each lie you received. This can be a powerful time of exposure to help you walk into freedom.

WHAT MY ADDICTION HAS TAKEN FROM ME

As per the previous one, this is a powerful exercise, yet it is reversed. God wants YOU to recover the losses that were taken from you. YOU are deserving of having God replace what was taken from you! Again, you must be totally honest and have taken the time to identify all the losses! These losses can be your job, marriage, reputation, self-worth, etc.

God is in the HEALING business. HE is in the REPLACEMENT business; HE is in the RESTORING business; HE is in the TRANSFORMATION business. HE is in SETTING THE CAPTIVE FREE business! YOU are not to receive shame or guilt as you truly process this list by hand. It is only through honesty before the Lord. HE knows all anyway, so write it down before HIM and before YOU. Get this out in the LIGHT so it is not kept in darkness any longer!

P.S. I am proud of your honesty; make it 100% true and leave nothing hidden. I am excited about your eventual healing and being set free!

WHAT IF IN FIVE YEARS FROM NOW YOU ARE UNRECOVERED

(Not Healed, Not Transformed, Not Free from Captivity)

This is big, men. When your wits are all about you and when you can look at things all around you, and you STILL do not get your act together and write it out, again in handwriting, what will life look like in five years? If this addiction stays a part of your life, imagine the stress and grief for yourself and your loved one. Recall how fast the past year has flown by; blink and you are now at the age of _____. Blink several times more, and what will life look like for you in five years when you are the age of _____?

Write where you will live, how your wife will be in five years if things do not change, where your children will be, what friends are in your life, what your job career will look like, etc. Where will you be emotionally, spiritually, and physically? How much time and money will you be spending on your addiction? For once in your life, perhaps, be raw and honest about what this will look like — your life — if things do not change in five years.

Again, by handwriting only, get your notepad out and begin writing from your heart!

If you think for a moment that you cannot lose your marriage, children, or job, you are walking in a world of fantasy; what it may look like now can vaporize in a moment.

Be **authentic** and **honest** from the deepest part of yourself.

WHAT IF IN FIVE YEARS FROM NOW YOU ARE RECOVERED

(Healed, Transformed, and Free from Captivity)

This exercise is just the opposite of the above. Men, and this is not pie in the sky, hoping the above will your life. You have to be accurate for yourself only, not for your wife (if married), your children (if you have them), your parents, your siblings, your in-laws, etc.

It will take a lot for the above to happen five years from now, and it is not a world of fantasy. It can only occur with much hard work over months and perhaps years.

Again, in handwriting only, get your notepad out and begin writing from your heart:

My life in five years, ***being healed, transformed, and free from captivity***, will genuinely look like this because I was diligent, focused, worked hard, had counseling, went to group, developed connectivity and accountability, and cut out all negatives in my life and replaced them with positives. The words below are as real as it gets in the reality of what I will have:

CALL SOMEONE

Phone calls can be the very thing that may save you from acting out today or any day. The process's first step, the TWELVE STEPS, talks about the word "we." "We" means that you need someone else in your journey of healing.

"I," in the past, was the most significant focus in the addict's world. Previously, the sex addict did not have the resources to get help due to his powerlessness. In being powerless, sex addicts cannot fight sexual addiction alone. What the addict can do is involve others in the fight with him, which dissipates the energy that comes against his life to destroy it.

Again, sexual addiction cannot be dealt with alone. Let me repeat that SEXUAL ADDICTION CANNOT BE DEALT WITH ALONE. Even if it were not just me, none of the sexual addiction experts in the field have seen anyone who has experienced sexual addiction healing alone and maintained not only abstinence but a lifestyle of living in freedom.

A lifestyle of sobriety is a much greater goal than just staying abstinent. There are several ways to address it. This commandment/rule is about making phone calls. One way is to wait until you get into a crisis and then call someone to help you. This method does not work because if you do not have a relationship with anyone, you are putting up barriers that could isolate you.

When you are not alone, you are accountable. The way to make phone calls is to make one call in the morning to a man in the group and another call in the evening to another man in the group.

Tell that person you would like his permission to make that phone call to have accountability and connection. That way, you check in with someone, and eventually, the phone calls turn into conversations that develop in the journey of change and transformation.

Isolating allows very few relationships that are not sexual. Sex addicts need relationships. Part of re-socializing is making phone calls, feeling connected, and getting acceptance right at the beginning of the day and the end of each day.

That is why "groups" are so significant. This all builds strength each and every day. Like prayer, a phone is a tool you can use to help yourself get stronger, especially within the first ninety days. However, with that said, this must be a continuum during which you are going to need other people to help you more than ever before. The men you call will benefit just as much if not more, than you when you call them. Remember, this is genuinely a two-way street. This tool will help you in your sobriety TODAY!

It's another tool to be used on your journey of healing!

FORGIVENESS and GRIEVING ASSIGNMENT

FORGIVENESS SCRIPTURES:

- John 20:23
- Matthew 18:16–35
- Matthew 6:14–15

BLESSING SCRIPTURES:

- Romans 12:14–21
- 1 Peter 3:8–9

HEART SCRIPTURES:

- 1 Corinthians 4:4–5
- Psalm 139:23–24
- Romans 1:18
- Hebrews 3:13

- Matthew 15:8

- Proverbs 27:19

- Romans 8:5–8

- Psalm 51:6

- Daniel 2:22

- Psalm 7:9

- Jeremiah 17:5, 9:10

Find a private and secluded place to go through this assignment, as your mind needs to be focused and your heart ready to engage in the process. Have a prayer time to prepare for this special time with God and yourself. Invite the Lord to plow your heart and mind; invite Him to be with you as you go through the process. Just have a quiet time of prayer and fellowship before you begin. Your heart must be totally engaged in this process. This time cannot be considered an "assignment" or something "just to do." Forgiveness and grieving are two of the primary keys to healing the inner soul. Your life cannot move forward healthily until you walk through this.

Get in touch (embrace, remember, feel, visualize) with your hurts, pains, rejections, abandonment, molestation, verbal abuse, etc.

Step 1:

1. **WRITE DOWN** your most recent hurts and who did it to you, no matter how big or small.

2. **WRITE DOWN** how you reacted to that hurt, externally (outward behavior) and internally.

3. **SPEAK OUT:** Repent of your reactions (be specific) and receive God's forgiveness.

4. **SPEAK OUT:** Forgive the person and/or persons that offended you, and bless them in the name of Jesus Christ

of Nazareth. You may also have to forgive yourself.

Be Quiet Before the Lord

Step 2:

Repeat STEP 1, asking the Lord to reveal to you WHAT IS NEXT (Psalm 139:23–24), and keep doing this, step by step, until the time you come out of your mother's womb. Take time to experience every hurt, and work your way, day-by-day, week-by-week, month-by-month, and year-by-year. Embrace the moment and visualize yourself there at the moment of the hurt. Grieve those times, experience that grown man, that college-age man, that teenage boy, that adolescent boy, and that young boy. Embrace the moments and visualize yourself there. Grieve those times when the emotional and/or physical trauma was extended to you. Stay in the moment. You may have to be in those moments for a while. You must also forgive and grieve what you did not get from your family of origin, which you should have received in a well-adjusted and mature home. Some of this afflicted harm may have come from outside your family; they perhaps knew about it and/or you kept it a secret.

FORGIVENESS is putting everything in a "filing drawer," placing a lock on it, and never opening it up again. It gives to God and lets HIM throw it all into the sea of forgetfulness. When you can be in the presence of the one who hurt you, and hurt and pain do not come up, then you know that true forgiveness has occurred.

WHEN THE TIME IS _R I GH T_ , TAKE ALL THAT PAPER, PAGE AFTER PAGE OF THIS MAJOR WORK OF YOUR HEART, AND ROLL IT UP, TIE A STRING AROUND IT, AND GO TO A PARTY STORE. Get The APPROPRIATE NUMBER OF BALLOONS, AND GO TO AN OPEN FIELD, TIE the PAPER TO THE BALLOONS, "LET IT GO," AND WATCH IT DISAPPEAR up in THE SKY. It is a symbolic picture, but a REAL ONE, of "LETTING IT GO." This moment in

time will mean a lot to you, and you will remember it forever. It is hard work, but you did it, and God will do the rest of it by healing your heart. You cannot heal your heart, but HE can and WILL!

CLEANING HOUSE

This is not about getting a broom, dust rags, or furniture polish to clean your home; this is another type of CLEANING. Cleaning your house at the beginning of being set free will save you from the experience of keeping that ONE magazine, video, or open access to the internet that could be costly and cause you to relapse. You do not want that, do you? So be smart! Many sex addicts have had their first relapse with the "one thing" that they did not throw away!

To prevent this from happening, it is imperative that YOU and two strong accountability men whom you give permission to walk through every room, explore it to the depths they think necessary, and remember you gave them permission to do so. So, anger and/or saying, "You do not trust me!" is not allowed.

To clean the house further, how about getting rid of cable, not watching TV for six months, and installing filters on your computer and all tech devices? Also, be accountable for your responsibilities, and not just to men, but also to your wife and family.

Some say ninety days of sobriety from some of this material. I say sixth months, as this allows you to seek to embed new healthy neuropathway patterns. I would rather err on the side of caution, and one reason among many is your life. Also, your family is more important than any subscription of any kind, the internet, TV, etc.!

GET THE PICTURE, MEN — Cleaning Out!

Like I said, in the beginning of your healing, it is better to err on the side of caution than to be too cautious. This is also about BOUNDARIES; you can process them with your counselor and accountability men.

This exercise can be a great beginning for your transformation. Cleaning out is not a rush job, men. It is tedious and thorough, and you allow your men to turn and look into every nook and crevice — no questions asked IF YOU ARE SERIOUS. Most men don't get this thorough. The men who are diligent on this journey, step by step, walk into freedom. It is the men who are lazy who fall deeper into their addiction.

Make sure you search your car, workshop, and office during off hours. I never recommend that our wife ever participate in any of your exercises; that is, YOU and YOUR ACCOUNTABILITY MEN, ONLY! This way, OBJECTIVITY is uppermost, and don't you want that?

Men, this can be a NEW BEGINNING only if you choose to do so! Radical thinking! Radical is as radical is! General George S. Patton was radical; if we only had his fortitude in today's government! What a different world we would live in!

The day my accountability men and I cleaned my house, office, car, workshop, and fishing cabin was:

_____.

The MEN WHO HELPED ME WERE

_____ and _____.

WHO I SHOULD NOT SEE

Most people want to be liked by everybody. An addict, whether knowingly or unknowingly, surrounds himself many times with other addicts. This makes it challenging to decide who you should and shouldn't see during the early part of your healing. You may ask, "Do I have to give up all of my friends?" Thankfully, not all your friends have this addiction issue.

In giving up "some of your friends," you must set apart all negative relationships, including your closest friends and your family, if necessary. Negative relationships can be a trigger to you.

Do you want to lose your marriage and perhaps your life to please your family and friends? Radical is as radical is! This is the area that many addicts live in negativity, but not so with non-addictive relationships.

WHAT ARE YOU TRULY WILLING TO DO?

HERE ARE THE PEOPLE I KNOW I CANNOT BE AROUND:

1. _____
2. _____
3. _____
4. _____
5. _____

SAFE PEOPLE TO BE WITH ARE:

1. _____
2. _____
3. _____
4. _____
5. _____

I, _____, on this day of _____20___ commit myself to the boundaries of saying NO to negative friends and say yes to SAFE PEOPLE, and this will be enforced forever! The only way this can change is if the negativity of those above individuals seek the Lord and are healed and transformed by the Lord Jesus Christ!

WHAT MY ADDICTION HAS COST ME IN DOLLARS

To be real before yourself, God, and your spouse, the cost in financial terms has helped many addicts have their eyes opened and put all in perspective to the damage that sexual addiction has done in their lives.

The knowledge of financial losses from sex addiction has assisted some addicts in saying "no" to acting out. Many clients have done this exercise, which helped identify financial losses to their families. Many discover that the average costs over a lifetime caused by their sexual addiction were approximately $250,000 dollars (according to Dr. Doug Weiss, author of *Untangling the Web*).

In today's dollars, I think that number is low for many addicts. Many wish, as I imagine YOU wish, you had those monies in hand today. To list the cost of your addiction, you may want to consider several things:

Cost of actual pornographic material purchased $_____

Cost of Professional sex services $_____

Cost of any legal fees (including divorce) $_____

Divorce Losses $_____

Child $_____

Missed Opportunities (college, job promotions) $_____

Missed work hours $_____

Loss of job $_____

Guilt spending (to make yourself or your wife feel

better) $_____

Losses by trusting others that were untrustworthy $_____

Other:

_____ $_____

_____ $_____

_____ $_____

Total: **$_____**

TRAVEL TIPS

Increasingly so, in today's world, many men travel, and the addict must have guardrails in place. For some sex addicts, this is their prime acting-out time because they are unaccountable. Unaccountable time and money make for a dangerous combination for an addiction that wants to flare back up, even on the journey of healing.

Let's take an example. You are asked to go to New York on a certain day and stay there for four days. As an addict, you may have little thoughts that creep in and say, "I can go here," "I can do that," and little by little, that imagination takes hold and slips back and slips back forward, and so by the time you are in New York in your spare time, you are acting out and spending monies to do so. When did you begin to act out? Not when you did, but when you started having images in your mind and thinking, did you act out?

How do you prevent this?

1. You look ahead of time for groups that meet in that area so that you can go there and be accountable. You get them to sign an accountable paper to give to your accountability men when you get home.

2. I would say that you take AMMONIA CAPSULES along with you so that when you feel the aura taking place to act out, pop one under your nose so that it resets your thinking.

3. Make at least two or three daily phone calls to your accountability men. Make sure you have permission to call your men of accountability 24/7 if need be.

4. Make available ahead of time, and after your accountability men look at our credit charges and any extra monies taken from your bank account or investment account. They can actually see these afterward to make sure you have stayed together and not have the

opportunity to spend any money on sexual activities.

5. Take your Bible with you.

6. Take a journaling notebook with you.

7. Take a book that you are processing via homework from your counselor or your addiction group.

8. Plan your off time ahead and the quality type of activities you can do.

9. When lonely, go to a public area in a hotel, and men, you cannot go to a bar! In addition, men, no alcoholic drinks at all, period, zero, and one, as they pull down your defenses. In fact, you should incorporate this in your everyday life. This is a defensive strategy and being radical in every area of your life!

10. If out of town over the weekend, find a church and Bible study to go to. Perhaps you may even be invited out to lunch with some members afterward. If not, you have made a favorable decision to attend; CONGRATULATIONS!

GOODBYE LETTER

Saying goodbye to a dry and parched land to the positiveness of all that Christ has to offer!

This can be one of the most powerful exercises that you, the person with an addiction, do. Still, if you do it as an exercise, it will not work, as this is an exercise from within the depths of your heart. This is not a checkoff √; it will be just that, a check-off.

This is where you sit down in a tranquil place, and your heart is ready to say goodbye to your addiction from the depth of your being.

I would hope that by now, you can see that this journey of addiction has been disastrous, and you can no longer have this bad relationship with your addict! I would pray that the bright

LIGHT of CHRIST is being seen by you on this addiction. It has been so damaging to you, your family, and others. Are you willing to waste your soul to the evil one or surrender your soul for salvation to Jesus Christ of Nazareth, the Son of the living God?

In this goodbye, you also have the opportunity to say HELLO to HIM and walk the walk that HE wants you to walk, according to God's Word.

Address it as **"Dear My Sex Addiction:"** and only write by hand, and this is not a two-sentence document; it is a multiple-page, tearfully written letter of goodbye, and you finalized it with permanence. That is the only way you can say goodbye; otherwise, you are just playing a game.

CHAPTER 17
Walking in Freedom

Men, get this set in your mind, brain, thinking, etc. There are no such things as the following for your healing:

- Steps

- Stages

- No checkoff list

- Etc.

The same holds true for grief:

- Steps

- Stages

- No checkoff list

- Etc.

Only through a Process — A New Pathway, A New Journey — can you use the appropriate verbiage for yourself, but it will not be steps, stages, checkoff lists, etc.

Some pathways are different for each individual because YOU came from a unique background than I came from, and I came from a unique background than my close friend came from; that makes us UNIQUE and ties into what God says in Psalm 139 that we are fearfully and wonderfully made; we are genuinely different! Let's praise God for that! So, what you have to process will differ from what Billy Bob has to process, and what Billy Bob has to process will differ from what James has to do.

I know what I'm talking about:

- Betrayed in marriage/divorce

- Loss of marriage

- Loss of in-laws

- Loss of nieces and nephews

- Loss of a son by suicide

- Son caught up in alcohol

- Having a new marriage

- Having a new child

- Having new in-laws at a different stage in life

- Having new friends

- Having Christ as the true foundation of my life (and that is all a process)

If you buy a book with stages, steps, a checkoff list, etc., throw it in the fire and burn it.

Are you ready to begin the journey of a pathway that little travel because it is not an easy pathway?

First, have you come to the end of yourself? Are you sick and tired of being sick and tired? You cannot do this because your wife wants you to, your pastor wants you to, your parents want you to. Unless you are in this state of mind, you are playing games with yourself and others. Unless you can look within yourself as best as possible and see that you are miserable and that life cannot go on like this, change will not happen. Everyone has a unique creation; there is no other fingerprint like yours in this world, neither in the past nor in the future. You differ from others, as they are from you. So many factors come into play: your DNA, your family of origin, your experiences from childhood to the present, and more. Again, before you were formed in your mother's womb, God knew and created you. I want you to hear that. You were meant to be!

Do you want to be healed and changed, and are you ready to

do ALL THE WORK REQUIRED FOR CHANGE? This is a journey of PERSERVANCE, FOCUS, BEING INTENTIONAL, BEING VUNERABLE AND TRANSPARENT, HOLDING NOTHING BACK, ALL SECRETS HAVE TO COME OUT AND PLACED ON THE TABLE! Most men say they are but don't finish the race. They don't want to go on the less traveled road; they would instead choose a smooth one and avoid being challenged to the nth degree. **James 1:2–5 states the following:**

> *2 Count it all joy, my brothers, when you meet trials of various kinds, 3 for you know that the testing of your faith produces steadfastness. 4 And let steadfastness have its full effect, that you may be perfect and complete, lacking in nothing. 5 If any of you lacks wisdom, let him ask God, who gives generously to all without reproach, and it will be given him.*

There is no gain without pain!

Are you ready to go to counseling (competent), group, do homework, sit under a lamp to read God's Word, pray out loud to the Lord, surrender your life to the Lord, and read books on issues that are not just about sex addiction? If not, then you are not ready for change, you are just blowing smoke! You must be ready for change!

There is no such thing as a perfect pathway, no perfect counselor, no perfect group, no perfect church, but with that said, you can do a lot of work within these imperfect places with "people" in them.

If you are in rehab and/or have been, short-term rehab will not work, and in counseling and Group, there is no such thing as short-term counseling. Being in a group and counseling is a run that takes time and differs for each individual. And I am talking one to three years. Gulp! That's right! You spent twenty years in addiction and expect a change in six months, so forget it. I never wasted my time with men unwilling to do the work; I referred them out, and in groups, I could be tough and banned men from coming to the group, as they caused disruption for those who were serious about change.

Also, men, this is not about discussing your wife. However, you certainly hurt her; this is about YOU and working totally and entirely on YOU. Not your wife. So, get your eyes off her and get your eyeballs on yourself! Got it?

LET'S BEGIN THE JOURNEY. ARE YOU READY?

Let's go to **COUNSELING** first. Find a competent counselor skilled in the issues of sexual compulsivity; in addition, they know how to process your family of origin trauma of any kind. They know how to delve into your identity (how you view yourself), and your sexual compulsivity, and they require you to do homework extensively outside of the counseling room. If you do not become a student of the issues yourself, you will more than likely fall by the wayside in your addiction. Your pathway of healing will differ from another because you are that. It may be necessary to work on traumas. That is what a skilled counselor is about. The counselor will need time to uncover and understand different layers of your identity. There is no quick fix here; it is a process.

Previously in the book, we discussed your family of origin, growing up, finding out about patterns in your genogram, processing your relationship with the Lord, the trauma of any kind, how you have hurt your wife, and the material on the brain. It would help if you insisted your counselor peel this onion. Your presenting problem to the counselor will be your sexual acting out, but that is just the symptom, not necessarily the issue.

Be patient as you process the above. Out of these discoveries, your counselor will then have you process each area that is particular to YOU. A great counselor will not only seek to educate you but also require that you educate yourself in reading certain books, process workbooks, and the home they hand out for you. Healing cannot occur in a counseling room; it is what goes on outside the room. YOU are doing what is necessary to break free, as instructed.

The homework contained in this and other chapters is for you to process, which will help you gain understanding. If you use this book in a group, you can process it paragraph by paragraph and complete the questions at the end.

- Forgiveness and repentance will more than likely be part of the process. Forgiveness is often the key to opening the heart to receive other information because it releases those who have hurt you, intentionally or unknowingly.

- You must have **two strong accountability men** who volunteer to keep you on track, and you can call them 24/7 if need be. These men cannot have an addiction or other issues they are processing. You need men in your life who are of strong moral character, dependable, and can get into your face by permission from you to keep you on track because they care about YOU. This book describes accountability in a separate chapter.

- As stated, you must have an expert in **counseling on this issue of sexual compulsivity. Make sure you do your due diligence here and ask the counselor's questions. Don't waste your time on anyone who is not seasoned and steeped in experience on this issue!**

- You must have **ESCAPE PLANS,** and you must practice them. Examples are in a separate chapter in this book.

- You <u>absolutely</u> must have **BOUNDARIES** put into place for situations that you will not allow in your life and what you will not do or go to, such as people, places, or things in an unhealthy environment. Some boundaries may be family members, and they don't have to understand (usually they do not). Still, it is about protecting you and your family; you are not about feeling guilt or shame about setting those boundaries.

- Men, you must be **INTENTIONAL** in this journey with a focus and target to attain.

- Men, you must have **EXCAVATION** take place in your life, with the old being dealt with and the NEW of Jesus Christ filling you up in HIS TRUTHS, which are in the Bible. This can be a painful process, but it is required in your healing journey, setting the captive free, and transformation.

- **You must be part of a GROUP!** You must attend at a minimum once a week. You are not to go to a group that goes in a circle and declares their addiction. Flee from that type of group.

You are to be in a Christ-centered, biblically-based group. In this group, you must educate yourself on the issues. An influential leader who is free from addiction possesses a strong biblical relationship with the Lord and is well-informed about sexual compulsivity. There must be a prayer to begin this group and at the end. Confidentiality must be maintained so that nothing leaves the room. Transparency and vulnerability should be present among all the men and the group leader.

Rushing through the material just to check it off for that night is not possible. If you don't finish the material, you start the following week because the discussions and sharing can be so robust that you don't want to rush through things. If this is the case in any group, leave it and find one that is not a checkoff box — many churches have groups like this, and it is a rush through. If it takes a year to process a book, workbook, etc., with excellent material, so be it. You should desire quality in the material you process. Quality is of the essence and of the highest order! And being INTENTIONAL is ALL THAT YOU DO! God will reward your efforts in time! Guaranteed!

It is necessary to develop the community. Over time, men in the community begin to trust others to open up and healing takes place. This is brother helping brother with keen leadership and directing all. If it is a six-week or eight-week group, don't waste your time with it because this issue is deep in the many facets of the addiction, which takes time to process.

- As men come and go and books are processed, the group must maintain continuity with few breaks. The leader's sharing processes God's Word. People with addiction come and go, but many stay in developing connectivity; that is why CONTINUAL is a must.

- As stated, this issue is complex. Dr. Patrick Carnes, the expert who certified me as a CSAT (ASAT) by IITAP, developed thirty steps to work through, and there are many things to process in each of those steps. He is the expert on this issue and knows that short-term programs do not work. Men, they do not. Short-term programs can be a start, but what do you do when they end? You guessed it — you're searching again.

- Battle Lines from May 2004 to June 30, 2019, was continual with few breaks. What messed up our program was when the church suddenly changed our meeting rooms, and we would drop from seventy men to fourteen men and start all over again. Men do not like change, and the church does not understand that dynamic. And it was hard for this leader to relight it and exhausting to seek to get it going again in the same manner. I could never get it back to where it once was. This also discourages volunteers who seek to help besides the people with an addiction themselves.

- Whether in counseling or in groups, you are to identify yourself by "Hi, my name is xxx, and I have an issue with sexual compulsivity." Or "Hi, my name is xxx, and I am a son of the King of Kings, my Lord and Savior Jesus

Christ, and I have an issue with sex addiction." AA, SA, etc., identify you by your addiction. If you keep telling yourself that you are a sex addict, then this is who you believe you are! **YOUR ISSUE DOES NOT IDENTIFY YOU.** I would never allow a man to identify himself in counseling and/or group by his issue!

ACCOUNTABILITY — MEN, YOU MUST HAVE ACCOUNTABILITY WITH ANOTHER MAN, AND TWO ACCOUNTABILITY MENTORS ARE MY RECOMMENDATION. There is no getting around the fact that this is a must! No excuses to you, men; there is NO OTHER WAY, so do not try to get around this if you want healing!

- These men cannot make your choices for you, but they can help you have a winning mindset. Your accountability mentors can help you develop and fix your mindset to accomplish the goals of being set free. Allow them to have permission to confront and challenge you in moving from negative thinking to positive thinking and accomplishments. If they have been where you are in the past and have become victors, then you cannot con them, as they know from whence they came. The confrontation may seem too personal, but it is because they are for you and want to see you on a journey of being set free.

- Having an accountability man in your corner, especially two of them, and giving them permission to confront you at any time will force you to be consistent. This is not a marriage; it is for you to reach the goals set before you.

- If you are unclear about your goal, your accountability men can help clarify that. Most people fail their goals because the target is broad; here, with addiction, you need a narrow bullseye! Do you want to be better? Would you like to experience healing? Do you want to be set free? Do you want to be transformed? That's why you have a man in your life to help you accomplish this goal of having your issue of sex addiction, something you can look into your rearview mirror as a thing of the past later on.

Setting specific goals is where you separate the professionals from the amateurs. Your secret to success is giving permission to two men to keep you accountable, as you cannot do this alone.

Proverbs 29:18 states, "Where there is no vision, the people *perish*: but he that keepeth the law, happy is he." The word "perish" has been highlighted by this author.

A great accountability partner (two men in this case) will seek to help you reach your goals, but they cannot do it for you. Without a plan, you will perish. Your situation will differ from another man's; thus, you need specific things to do that are particular to you.

As General Patton said, HE HAD A PLAN OF ATTACK, and you MUST HAVE A PLAN OF ATTACK!

Accountability men will keep you going, even when you do not want to. They may be harsh, but it is for your benefit.

Of course, at any time, you can say goodbye to them. But you will say hello to a deeper embeddedness of your addiction if you say goodbye to your accountability partners. You have to decide if you are going to be this man: 1 Corinthians 9:24–27:

> *24 Do you not know that in a race, all the runners run, but only one receives the prize? So run that you may obtain it. 25 Every athlete exercises self-control in all things. They do it to receive a perishable wreath, but we are imperishable. 26 So I do not run aimlessly; I do not box as one beating the air. 27 But I discipline my body and keep it under control, lest after preaching to others I myself should be disqualified.*

You have to beat your body to win the prize. No pain, no gain.

Great accountability men will help you keep going, even if you want to quit. You give them permission before you start and make a commitment that they can get in your face to confront and challenge you to achieve your goals and not quit.

Your accountability mentors want you to take control of your life, and they will help you build that into your life through their challenging encouragement and keeping you focused. They desire you to be free from your addiction, to help create your IDENTITY in CHRIST, and for you to love and like yourself. They expect your personal development to be on this journey and beyond after you say goodbye to them.

Another area of accountability is the different software programs that have porn blockers and, within them, are weekly reports to your accountability men. Suppose you slip up and start falling back on old behavioral patterns. In that case, the software will send an alert test or email to your accountability partners, who will be able to call you and prevent you from unwanted actions. The system of accountability can also have screen time on tech devices, which makes for additional accountability to the person with an addiction and has a positive psychological effect on the process. Removing these bad habits will bring countless benefits, including more time with friends and family, better focus and productivity, and better overall mood and energy.

There are many choices, and some of the few choices are COVENANT EYES, BARK-BEST PARENTAL CONTROL SOFTWARE, ACCOUNTABLE2YOU, and X3WATCH. Do your own due diligence on these or others but do it with your accountability men as well.

Indeed, there are ways around most technology. However, if someone is serious about breaking free from being out of control of their online sexual activities, then porn-blocking software and accountability will help.

Network content filtering is critical to my recommended approach in establishing an effective porn-blocking system. I am not a computer tech man, but as I understand it, you can set up your router to block devices connected to your network from accessing specified keywords, internet domains, or a combination of both. You can also set blocking to be continuous or set up a blocking schedule.

Controlling internet access and content in this digital age is crucial to safety and productivity. The best router models serve as gatekeepers of internet access and offer a comprehensive solution: the ability to block websites by adjusting router settings. Whether it's for parental controls, reducing distractions, or enhancing network security, understanding how to manage content at the router level is essential for any connected device.

Blocking sites through your router involves modifying network rules to restrict access to specific websites and/or content categories.

This process, known as content filtering, is a crucial aspect of network management. It allows network administrators or parents to set restrictions and time limits for internet usage.

Accessing the router settings through a browser allows you to input the IP address or URL of the sites to be blocked.

This method ensures that all devices connected to the network, including mobile devices, gaming consoles, and even smart TVs, adhere to the set rules.

You have many ways to protect your electronic devices and bring about accountability; your due diligence and accountability, men, are essential in your healing journey to find the right one for YOU. Be smart and not lax in this.

YOUR GROWTH is your accountability and men's greatest desire for you! And you know what? You are now a WINNER because you have surrendered your life to the Lord and a WINNER in breaking this addiction.

I use terminology as **"serious as a heart attack,"** and that is the **MINDSET** you want your accountability men to have WITH YOU!

You can also find accountability men via online platforms,

websites, or blogs. I do not favor this because you do not have the eyeball or physical presence of accountability, man. Let's say you have two strong accountability men; one you can physically meet for breakfast on Saturday morning to catch up, and the following week, you meet with the second accountability man. Your best bet on accountability is a face-to-face, physical presence, so find those two men. You can do it.

These two men must stay the course with you, and later, they can CELEBRATE with you your victory as an overcomer who has been healed, set free, and transformed.

Your journey will be challenging. You will travel a less-traveled road, and it will have twists and turns, but as you, at times, shift into 4-wheel drive, you will overcome. Your journey will be challenging because ninety-nine percent of men have been addicted since they were little boys — teenagers — and early college, firmly establishing patterns.

Make a lifestyle change if you want to walk into freedom. Suppose you're going to walk into freedom. In that case, you MUST change your lifestyle by cutting out all negativity, like a surgeon's knife. As previously stated, that might include family, close friends, etc.

Over time, with PERSISTENCE AND DEDICATION, you can move towards healing. Still, you are the determining factor, and you cannot compromise any more extended lifestyle choices.

When I brought up **EXCAVATION**, that means with a therapist in counseling. You will choose to process those things that perhaps you do not know yet and some you do know that must come out of your life. Let's make somewhat a list of those things:

- Jealousy

- Lust

- Anger

- Manipulation (having the upper hand)

- Wanting to always be in control

- Wanting always to be right

- Lying

- Unforgiveness

- Unrepentant

- Inability to say, "Please forgive me. I was wrong when I did that to you..."

- Bitterness

- Low self-esteem

- And on and on

The above is a must; your inner being must be conscious of the old and newness put back in. And the only truth is that without Christ, you cannot get rid of any negativity. If you move things out, it is only through mind over matter, and guess what? That is not healing, and those issues will come back more so because you refused to surrender your life to HIM, and have HIM, in the process, cleanse you!

There is not enough room to share about each man's inner issues, which are varied and many, some more painful than others. Whatever those are, whatever you are in denial about, you must have a counselor to process with you and to find possible issues that have never been dealt with. That is part of being set free. Acting out sexually is the SYMPTOM, and usually, there are root causes, such as the above or which are mentioned in the Trauma section of this book, to work through. Do not let PRIDE keep you from doing this work.

Guys, you must be **INTENTIONAL** (planning, expecting, arranging, focusing, etc.). Without being intentional in your approach (planning, expecting, arranging, focusing, etc.), you will be lackadaisical and ultimately slaughtered. You will not have healing or freedom from captivity. It's like putting an old 1950 Ford motor into a 2024 Mercedes Benz 350 GLE instead of the standard motor. Guess what? It won't work and last!

Your journey is not only the addiction but anything that has caused you issues in your life to be dealt with. A competent counselor can help unearth these things for you.

It is like standing by a swimming pool, looking at it, and enjoying it, and it is quite another to jump all in. This journey of healing and change is about jumping all in.

Once again, repeat and develop new habits and activities. Replace the negative with the positive. You are rebuilding much of your brain, putting in new, taking out old, not just porn and sexually addictive behaviors, but all the negatives. You are practicing SELF-CARE each moment of the day because you're walking into NEW DAYS. You are taking off the old way the old and putting ON the new!

You KNOW your triggers and temptations, and you are deciding to identify them and seek to avoid them, taking proactive steps to do so.

You are developing and will develop a strong support community around you. Guess what? YOU DESERVE GOOD!

I want to share what you do with a stimulus. If you entertain it in the least, the chemicals ignite in your thoughts, and you have milliseconds to escape. You know you only have a millisecond because the chemicals produced by the neuropathways will capture you. Visually, I hope this makes sense in its rough form.

What is your game plan to stop and escape? There are suggestions for escape throughout this book. Your accountability men are there for you, but you have to call them! Escape. You must plan ahead, or you will get caught up in the thoughts and chemicals. An "AURA" takes over when you are doing what you said you would not do. YOU MUST KNOW YOU WILL BE TESTED, AND YOU MUST HAVE A PLAN OF ESCAPE. You reinforce the neuropathways every time you act out, and the chemicals demand a higher high.

The below is simplified, yet telling. Process it. You must have a game plan. You must know your triggers. You must know how to escape. You must fight against what draws you, and every time you do not act out, those chemicals settle down, and you are relaxed. You won a victory. Keep choosing to win! And in your winning, you build new NEUROPATHWAYS. Little by little, you are building a new road...eventually, it will be Interstate 10!

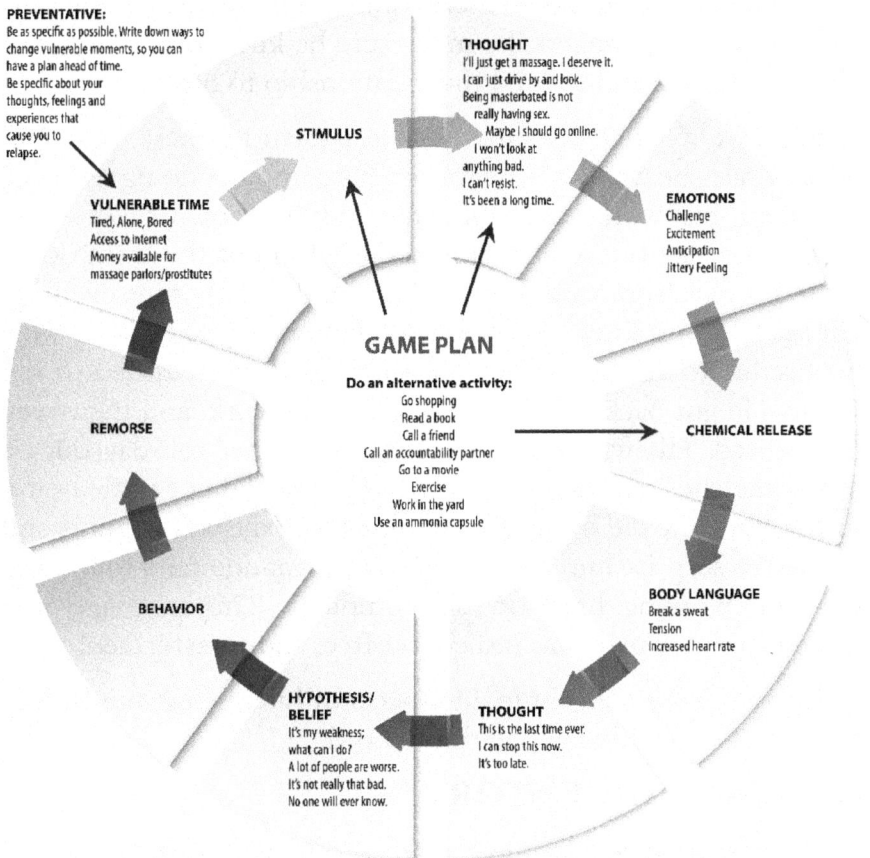

PREVENTATIVE:
Be as specific as possible. Write down ways to change vulnerable moments, so you can have a plan ahead of time. Be specific about your thoughts, feelings and experiences that cause you to relapse.

STIMULUS

THOUGHT
I'll just get a massage. I deserve it. I can just drive by and look. Being masterbated is not really having sex. Maybe I should go online. I won't look at anything bad. I can't resist. It's been a long time.

VULNERABLE TIME
Tired, Alone, Bored
Access to internet
Money available for massage parlors/prostitutes

EMOTIONS
Challenge
Excitement
Anticipation
Jittery Feeling

GAME PLAN
Do an alternative activity:
Go shopping
Read a book
Call a friend
Call an accountability partner
Go to a movie
Exercise
Work in the yard
Use an ammonia capsule

CHEMICAL RELEASE

REMORSE

BODY LANGUAGE
Break a sweat
Tension
Increased heart rate

BEHAVIOR

HYPOTHESIS/ BELIEF
It's my weakness; what can I do? A lot of people are worse. It's not really that bad. No one will ever know.

THOUGHT
This is the last time ever. I can stop this now. It's too late.

THE GAME PLAN TO STOP THE SEQUENCE

Men, as you know, this all happens within minutes — sometimes seconds — you do not have much time to stop acting out in your addiction and reinforcing it in your brain.

ACTING OUT

Right up to this point, you have time to escape before the chemicals and neuropathways take over.

TRUE STORY:

This applies to the above GAME PLAN. I had a gentleman in Battle Lines who was addicted to porn. In his profession, he was a medical researcher. He had been coming to the Group for some time and put in place some escape plans and practiced them out, and knowing his triggers, he made sure he knew how to escape. He was married and wanted that relationship to heal.

His wife went on a four-day out-of-town business trip. One night, while she was away, he was on his computer doing research regarding his work, and suddenly, out of nowhere, he was triggered to act out. He instantaneously ran out the front door, went onto his front yard, and sat down in the cool of the evening. He sat there until the chemicals in his brain settled down, with no residue to act out. When all was settled, he returned to his home. He got back on his computer to do work, and there was he focused. His wife had a cancellation of her last day out of town, and she came home one day early. She did not come home to test him. She did not call to let him know she was coming; she wanted to surprise him. She entered the front door and found her husband working hard on his computer. This marriage was healed, and this man was healed, set free, and transformed!

This man was diligent in all aspects of his healing, but his #1 focus was his relationship with the Lord.

OPPOSITE TRUE STORY

We had amid our Group a man who would horribly "binge" on his addiction to porn and masturbation for days at a time. He would literally be sick of his addiction. This went on month after month. We had men in the Group reach out to him, seek to challenge him, etc., to no avail. His big culprit was a big-screen TV.

So, I decided I would do something that would possibly bring him to the table to seek true healing. I went to Office Depot and bought raffle tickets. That night at group, I tore them in half and placed one half on the chairs the men would sit on and the other half in a hat. We started in prayer, introduced the new men, and went over the guidelines with the latest men. Before we started our lesson, I told them we would have a drawing tonight. I shook the hat, went to the middle of the room, and drew out a ticket.

I read the number off and said, "Who won?"

A doctor in the group said, "I did."

I told him to come to the middle of the room and announced, "He won a big screen TV." Then I asked the man with the binging addiction to come forward and offer his personal big screen TV — the one he binged on — to the ticket holder.

The man with the binging issues could not and would not give up his big flat-screen TV. He would not let it go. It revealed to all unless you are literally sick and tired of your addiction, you will stay in that addiction. This man loved his addiction more than seeking to be free, although he was sick of himself at times for his binging.

Freedom requires a price, a discipline, a desire to truly change and go all out to do so, and then some stay in the lack of discipline and, deep inside, enjoy their addiction more than the price of freedom, no matter the cost to do so. The addiction causes entrenchment, being in a deep ditch, a power stronghold that the chemicals demand more and more. The neuropathways become more substantial and broader, being wired day after day in the effect of the addiction.

CHAPTER 18
Your Story

To be transformed by the Word of God, we must read it. But as you know, writing transforms us as well. By now, writing is likely second nature to you, and it's a wonderful, cathartic habit to utilize often in the years ahead.

What I want you to get in touch with, now and later, is what your story is and what your story will be. I want you to get in touch with every aspect of your life and share with yourself, the Lord, your wife, and your family about what your life is expanding to and what your future looks like.

Don't just write things out; get honest about your yesterday, today, and tomorrow life. I want you to dig deep within yourself and write it down slowly while getting in touch with your emotions, feelings, inner self, and the Lord.

You are valued; write what you have learned about yourself and the things you have processed, eliminating the negatives and replacing the positives, including friends. Please write down your new activities and why you enjoy them.

Bring forth your relationship with the Lord and personalize your experience with HIM in written form.

Share about your newfound freedom, friend, wife, and blossoming relationship.

Write about your journey with your counselor and individual and couple counseling and share your experience with the group.

Share what you have learned about YOU that you never knew before. Is this good? Bring it forth to share with others. You deserve God's best!

Write to other men about what they should do on this journey of healing and freedom. Speak truth to them from your perspective and set a time to share it with your group!

Just write!

You have a bright and blessed future ahead of you. You'll continually grow in faith for the rest of your life, just as you'll journal, read the Word of God, and stand firm in your recovery for the rest of your life. Now go, serve God, serve your family, and walk boldly and confidently by faith.

Always remember Philippians 4:13:

> *I can do all things through Christ who gives me strength.*

AUTHOR'S BIO

Benno Bauer Jr. grew up in Kerrville, a small town in Texas and graduated from Texas Lutheran University with a degree in accounting. He became an apartment developer in Houston with more than 4,000 apartment units and some high-end homes.

When God called him into ministry, Benno became a staff pastor/counselor at one of the biggest churches in America under Dr. Ed Young — Second Baptist Church in Houston. He also became a Certified Sexual Addiction Therapist (CSAT — ASAT) through the International Institute for Trauma & Addiction Professionals (IITAP) under Dr. Patrick Carnes, the premier expert on the issues of sexual compulsivity/addiction, after recognizing how pervasive and devastating sex addiction had become to men in the Houston area and beyond. This was an opportunity to begin an incredible and much-needed ministry. He is also a Certified Anger Resolution Therapist (CART).

An incredible 28,432 men took part in his Battle Lines group from May 2004 to July 1, 2019, and Benno counseled over 19,000 sessions of approximately 30,000-plus people (men and couples). It has been his honor to help sex-addicted souls take back their lives, restore marriages, mend families, and deeply connect with God.

Benno's personal interests have to do with God's green earth. "I find relaxation and blessings in the great outdoors, such as authentic cattle drives, hunting, fishing, river rafting, etc. Adventures in the wild include places like the Yukon, Alaska, British Columbia, Mexico, several states, and Texas," he notes.

He also loves photography and has created many tabletop photo albums for his family. He loves music of all genres, from classical to Oldie Goldies of the Fifties and Sixties, and frequently tunes into his favorite artist, Willie Nelson, with a cigar while relaxing on his patio!

Benno, an avid reader, enjoys many books, from the Bible and biographies to history, fiction, and non-fiction. His greatest hope is that those in the clutches of sex addiction find help and healing through this book.

"I have experienced life in the utmost of pain and the highest of joys; there is not much I have not experienced via physical or experiential pain," Benno adds. "I am blessed to be married to Jan for thirty-six years and have two living children (an adult daughter and an adult son)."

RECOMMENDED BOOKS

This list is not all-inclusive, nor is it in any particular order. You may have anger issues, you may have jealousy issues, you may have experienced deep trauma in your life, you may have faced abandonment in your life, etc. I have read 600-plus books on the brain, trauma, and sex addiction, and hundreds of books on Christian living, the Bible, etc. With that said, you and your counselor can process what is appropriate for you.

- *Help Her Heal* by Carol Juergensen Sheets

- *Torn Asunder* by Dave Carder

- *Worthy of Her Trust* by Stephen Arterburn and Jason B. Martinku

- *Safe People* by Dr. Henry Cloud & Dr. John Townsend

- *The Body Keeps Score* by Bessel Van Der Kolk, MD

- *The Brain That Changes Itself* by Norman Dodge MD

- *The Developing Mind* by Dan Siegel, PhD

- *At The Altar of Sexual Idolatry* by Steve Gallagher

- *Changing Course* by Dr. Claudia Black

- *Changes That Heal* by Dr. Henry Cloud

- *Childhood Disrupted* by Donna Nakazawa

- *Caring Enough to Forgive* by David Augsburger

- *How To Help Your Spouse Heal From Your Affair* by Linda MacDonald

- *The Healing Path* by Dr. Dan Allender

- *The Work of Repentance* by Steve Gallaher

- *Tired of Trying to Measure UP* by Jeff VanVonderen

- *Disciplines of a Godly Man* by Robert Hughes

- *Mindsight* by Dan Siegel, PhD

- *Betrayal Bond* by Dr. Patrick Carnes

- *Conquering Pornography* by Dennis Fredericks

- *Cybersex Exposed* by Jennifer Schneider, L.P.C

- *Cybersex Unhooked* by David Delmonico, PhD

- *Facing The Shadows* by Dr. Patrick Carnes

- *Family Secrets* by John Bradshaw

- *Faithful & True Workbook* by Dr. Mark Laaser

- *Healing The Shame That Binds You* by John Bradshaw

- *Homecoming: Reclaiming and Championing Your Inner Child* by John Bradshaw

- *Reclaiming Virtue: How We Can Develop the Moral Intelligence to Do the Right Thing at the Right Time for the Right Reason* by John Bradshaw

- *Shadows of the Cross* by Craig Cashwell, Pennie Johnson, and Dr. Patrick Carnes

- *Don't Call It Love* by Dr. Patrick Carnes

- *Healing Wounds of Sexual Addiction* by Dr. Mark Laaser

- *In The Shadows of The Net* by Dr. Patrick Carnes

- *Out of The Shadows* by Dr. Patrick Carnes

- *Porn Nation* by Michael Leahy

- *Pure Desire* by Ted Roberts

- *Rebuilding Trust* by Jennifer Schneider, L.P.C. & Burt Schneider

- *The Drug of The New Millennium* by Mark Kastleman
- *The Storm of Addiction* by Connie A. Lofgreen, M.S.W. CSAT
- *Unwanted* by Jay Stringer
- *Untangling the Web* by Dr. Doug Weiss
- *Wired For Intimacy: How Pornography Hijacks the Male Brain* by William M. Struthers
- *Your Brain on Porn* by Gary Wilson
- *The Neuroscience of Human Relationships* by Louis Cozolino
- *Inside / Out* by Larry Crabb
- *Sexual Detox* by Tim Challis
- *The Meaning of* Marriage by Tim Keller
- *What Did You Expect* by Paul David Tripp
- *How Should We Then Live* by Frances Schaeffer
- *The Power of* Integrity by John MacArthur
- *War of Words* by Paul David Tripp
- *Run to Win* by Tim Challis
- *Spiritual Leadership* by J. Oswald Sanders
- *The Treasure Principle* by Randy Alcorn
- *Dangerous Calling* by Paul David Tripp
- *Christian Disciplines* by Oswald Chambers

www.ingramcontent.com/pod-product-compliance
Lightning Source LLC
Chambersburg PA
CBHW060038100426
42742CB00014B/2635